DATE DUE

NO1.9'98			
JY 1 '99			
JY22'99			

SPORTS AND FITNESS EQUIPMENT DESIGN

Ellen F. Kreighbaum, PhD
Montana State University, Bozeman, MT

Mark A. Smith, MS
Independent Ergonomics Consultant

Editors

Human Kinetics

Library of Congress Cataloging-in-Publication Data

Sports and fitness equipment design / [edited by] Ellen F. Kreighbaum,
    Mark A. Smith.
        p.   cm.
      Includes bibliographical references (p.) and index.
      ISBN 0-87322-695-X (case)
        1. Sports--Equipment and supplies--Design and construction.
    2. Human mechanics.   3. Physical fitness--Equipment and supplies-
    -Design and construction.   I. Kreighbaum, Ellen F.   II. Smith, Mark
    A., 1961-
      GV745.S68   1995
      796'.028--dc20   95-33993
                                                                       CIP

ISBN: 0-87322-695-X

Developmental Editors: Peggy Rupert and Christine Drews; **Assistant Editors**: Anna Curry and John Wentworth; **Copyeditor**: Peggy Darragh; **Proofreader**: Myla Smith; **Indexer**: Norman Duren, Jr.; **Typesetter**: Yvonne Winsor; **Text Designer**: Stuart Cartwright; **Layout Artists**: Tara Welsch and Yvonne Winsor; **Photo Editor**: Boyd Lafoon; **Cover Designer**: Jack Davis; **Illustrators**: Nicole Barbuto, Paul To, and Gretchen Walters; **Printer**: Braun-Brumfield

Printed in the United States of America   10   9   8   7   6   5   4   3   2   1

Human Kinetics
P.O. Box 5076, Champaign, IL 61825-5076
1-800-747-4457

Canada: Human Kinetics, Box 24040, Windsor, ON N8Y 4Y9
1-800-465-7301 (in Canada only)

Europe: Human Kinetics, P.O. Box IW14, Leeds LS16 6TR, United Kingdom
(44) 1132 781708

Australia: Human Kinetics, 2 Ingrid Street, Clapham 5062, South Australia
(08) 371 3755

New Zealand: Human Kinetics, P.O. Box 105-231, Auckland 1
(09) 523 3462

Contents

Preface

A comprehensive study of sports and fitness equipment serves many people. The rapid development of new designs and new equipment, crafted with space-age materials, requires knowledge that is both broad and deep. Designers, materials and mechanical engineers, marketing specialists, health promotion professionals, retailers, and users all need accurate information. The effectiveness of each piece of equipment depends on design, composition, materials, and use and on its appropriate match to the skill level and strength of the user. The marketability of equipment is determined by its popularity, which is only partially influenced by how effective it is.

Pieces of equipment have been made and used for centuries to enhance performance and to protect participants in sport events. But only during the second half of the 20th century has sports and fitness equipment become a specialized field of manufacturing. Two events stimulated sporting goods manufacturers to expand their research and development. First, the U.S. space exploration program resulted in a plethora of new synthetic materials, designed for light weight and unsurpassed strength. Because sport performance is affected by the weight of the equipment that a performer must manipulate and by its strength and force absorption, sporting goods manufacturers were quick to incorporate these new materials into their products.

The second event to stimulate design development was the fitness boom that began in the 1970s, which was characterized by an increase in earnings and leisure time for many people. People were also becoming more aware of health issues and disease prevention, and into the 1980s *wellness, holistic health*, and *exercise* became buzzwords and phrases. Not only was sports and fitness equipment being purchased in quantity by schools and professional teams, but people began demanding better products for their own activities. As running became a popular leisure pursuit and an approach to preventing cardiovascular disease, the market for running shoes became one of the first to explode. With more and more miles being put on their footwear, runners demanded greater protection from overuse injuries, and manufacturers invested thousands of dollars in fitness research and development. Serious fitness activities expanded to include swimming, cycling, rowing, weight lifting, tennis, racquetball, cross-country and downhill skiing, hiking, and mountain climbing.

As new activities became popular, participants needed instruction. Health clubs, fitness centers, and corporate wellness programs began springing up in what became one of the fastest growing businesses in the country. Universities created specialized curricula to educate professionals in sport management, exercise science, movement science, fitness leadership, and exercise physiology. The American College of Sports Medicine developed a certification program for fitness instructors, and private organizations like the International Dance Exercise Association offered certification to would-be exercise leaders. Fitness is now big business in both the public and private sectors. And although instructors in the fitness realm are now being well prepared through various educational programs, little has been done to help them sort through all the sports and fitness equipment available and to advise laypeople on how to make equipment choices.

Sports and Fitness Equipment Design is offered to professionals and students in the exercise and health fields, as well as to equipment designers, engineers, retailers, and consumers. Whether one is employed as a physical educator, an exercise/fitness leader, or a corporate wellness director, choosing and advising others in choosing sports and fitness equipment is an important aspect of the job. Students, clients, and employees need information in order to select appropriate equipment for workouts and recreational activities. Engineers and designers are hired by sporting goods manufacturers to create new and effective equipment designs, retailers must have appropriate information to convince customers to buy new products, and consumers need knowledge to make wise equipment choices.

The content and format of *Sports and Fitness Equipment Design* are based on a course on the subject that has been offered at Montana State University since 1978. It has grown to become a required course for all physical education-related options other than public school teaching, and many students in that option choose it as an elective. The course addresses foot-ground interfaces (footwear), striking implements, and personal fitness equipment, with each unit introduced by a discussion of the relevant kinesiological and biomechanical aspects. This introduction familiarizes students with body positions and movements as they relate to equipment use and helps students understand some of the technical marketing language used in selling equipment. Chapters 1, 6, and 11 of *Sports and Fitness Equipment Design* focus on these biomechanical concepts.

Specific information used in the three units of the course is also included in this text:

Foot-Ground Interfaces

- Running and court shoes
- Trail and hiking boots
- Cross-country ski boots and bindings
- Downhill ski boots, bindings, and skis

Striking Implements

- Tennis rackets
- Racquetball racquets

- Golf clubs
- Baseball and softball bats

Personal Fitness Equipment

- Bicycles
- Aerobic exercise equipment
- Resistance training equipment
- Watercraft

As is explained in the introduction, the course (and this text) presents perspectives for each piece of equipment. In the course, the instructor addresses biomechanical aspects. Local retailers then are invited to display various brands of equipment and to highlight design innovations. Finally, the perspective of the user is addressed. Coaches and athletes are good resources and often give guest lectures; they frequently help separate marketing hype from real-world equipment use. Coaches and athletes also demonstrate the importance of individual differences in choosing equipment. What is touted as best may not be the best for everyone. Broken equipment accumulated by the instructor is used to demonstrate design features and shortcomings, and students are supplied with supplemental reading materials, such as sporting magazines (e.g., *Runner's World, Outside Ski*) and brochures from retailers and manufacturers.

Although *Sports and Fitness Equipment Design* provides an introduction to sports and fitness equipment from the standpoints of the designer and manufacturer, the retailer, and the user, this text is not for students only. Designers should find helpful the discussion on equipment parts, presented in a manner that allows new designs to be developed without sacrificing the necessary mechanical components. Engineers will be able to apply biomechanical aspects of dynamics to sports and fitness equipment design and manufacturing. Retailers will learn more about the equipment-user interface so they can serve individual customers knowledgeably. And the consumer will be equipped to choose appropriate, safe, and effective equipment.

It is important for equipment professionals and users to be aware of how quickly the materials and construction of sports and fitness equipment change. While this book was being prepared, many new materials and designs became available. But by knowing the basics of how sports and fitness equipment is made and used, you'll be equipped to evaluate the quality and effectiveness of future innovations.

Introduction: Perspectives on Sports and Fitness Equipment Design

Ellen F. Kreighbaum, PhD
Montana State University, Bozeman

Sports equipment may be addressed from the perspectives of three groups: designer, retailer, and user. Each group has its own perspective on sports equipment manufacture, sales, and use.

▶ The Designer

The designer's perspective incorporates three design elements: biomechanics, anthropometrics, and aesthetics. Biomechanics includes the mechanics of materials used in the equipment, the mechanical properties of the equipment, and the biomechanics of equipment use, including the physical characteristics of the user. Space-age materials have been replacing traditional materials such as wood, metal, canvas, and leather. Now equipment is filled with such things as Kevlar, ceramic fibers, ethyl vinyl acetate, Gore-Tex, Cambrelle, boron fiber, and titanium. The new materials make possible improvements that otherwise could not be made in the mechanical properties of the equipment, providing such things as strength, lightness, cushion, and "breathability."

A second aspect of design incorporates anthropometrics, the study of sizes, shapes, weights, and proportions of the human body and its segments. The use of anthropometric parameters by the designer of sports equipment helps to establish the variety of sizes, shapes, and proportions needed to fit different parts of the human body.

Today, as the manufacturers become cognizant of the variability in body shapes, sizes, and proportions, we see equipment designed specifically for females. In the recent past, equipment and wearing apparel has been manufactured for women on the principle that the female form was merely a smaller version of the male form. However, with sports equipment purchases increasing, manufacturers can afford to create varying sizes and shapes to accommodate all people without sacrificing profits.

The manufacture of running shoes is a good example. Prior to the mid-1980s, shoe manufacturers could not justify building a running shoe for women on a different last (the wooden model around which the shoe materials are shaped). As women began to spend more and more on athletic apparel, manufacturers decided they could afford to build equipment specifically for women. Thus, Brooks came out with the first pair of running shoes built on a woman's last. These shoes fit women better because the heels are smaller relative to the forefoot. Similarly, the ski industry began producing skis for women that were not merely scale-down versions of men's skis—rather, they had different flex and torsional characteristics than men's skis.

Finally, a third design aspect, aesthetics, is probably the most important for the continued sales of an item, but least important for its practical use. People buy popular colors, trendy logos and designs, and new innovations; they lean to what's new and popular: the "sizzle" in the current year's equipment. Although appearance influences popularity, encouraging users to buy new equipment for aesthetic reasons, technical features may remain the same as the preceding year's equipment.

▶ The Retailer

A second perspective on sports equipment is presented by the retailer, who has two considerations: business management and merchandise marketing. A retailer must stock inventories containing a number of sizes, brands, and models, keep a record of sales, and display merchandise to encourage sales and create the greatest profit. Manufacturers and retailers can create new markets by selling the idea of a need for specialized equipment for each new event. For example, new footwear has been designed specifically for aerobics, walking, and cross-training.

New sales are created using attractive and colorful designs and by companies who provide free equipment to important and frequently seen athletes sponsoring various items. Media testimonials about the equipment by famous people and slick gimmicks that sound like grandiose innovations are additional marketing strategies. Be aware of sales techniques that convince you to select products that may look good but may be inappropriate or unsuitable for your body type and ability.

Each individual is unique, and not until his or her uniqueness becomes a dominant part of the gross sales of specialized sports equipment will equipment be made to fit that person. Fortunately, due to the large numbers of sales in all types of sports equipment, manufacturers can diversify their products and still make a profit.

Endorsements and Equipment

In the November 1988 issues of *Sports, Inc.*, two headlines read "Endorsements Add Up For Joyner-Kersee" and "$1-Mil Runner," referring to Florence

Griffith Joyner's endorsement income, which surpassed $1 million in deals with manufacturers of items as diverse as toys, running shoes, and audio products. Famous people sell products, but you needn't be nationally famous to be on the endorsement roll. One buyer's magazine suggested that top members of a club be solicited and offered a 20 percent reduction in equipment costs without telling anyone else in the club. These top players use the equipment; others see them using it and identify with them, thinking that they could be as successful if they bought the same equipment. These people were probably skilled players anyway, apart from the use of new equipment. Testimonials of respected and admired users boost sales of good and bad sports equipment. Remember, what's good for one person may not be good for another.

Marketing and Equipment

Marketing is the mainstay of retail sales success. Marketing strategies include promoting new, innovative designs, using trendy colors and buzzwords, organizing the current inventory to capture buyers' attention, and unloading outdated and slow-moving merchandise with special-purchase sales. There are two ways to sell more sports equipment: attract new users, and convince people that they need more than one (racket, set of clubs, type of aerobic workout equipment, or pair of athletic shoes).

High-tech buzzwords fill advertisements. Vibration free, ceramic, boron, graphite micro-mid, asteroceramic, energy wave, flexlite, motion control, vibrasorb, stabilized flight, hydroflow, anatomical cradle, and adjustable flex are but a few of the concepts and space-age materials that entice the buyer. At the same time, sales personnel are courting juniors, mining seniors, and dazzling everyone else. It's hard not to be swept into the market.

With all of the information from trade magazines, manufacturing representatives, sales representatives, and trade show presentations, the retailer has a difficult time discerning solid information from hype. This book will provide the retailer with knowledge to identify and cut through the information that is bombarding us. In the following sections, basic scientific information is presented that can be applied to a variety of equipment types and brands. Because the markets are changing so rapidly, solid foundational principles must be understood to evaluate new equipment developments and designs.

▶ The User

Finally, one must consider the equipment from the user's perspective. Aesthetic appeal largely influences the consumer to buy a product to begin with. If the consumer is uncomfortable using the equipment once purchased, additional purchases will not be made from that retailer and in turn from that manufacturer. Each user has a unique body build, strength, and ability. Furthermore, the use of equipment takes place in different environments from dry to wet, rocky to smooth, in cold and warm temperatures, or at high or low altitudes. Each piece of equipment should be designed and purchased with a specific environment in mind.

Equipment must be comfortable to use, aid in successful performance, and be affordable as well as fit the user's size, shape, strength, and ability. Unfortunately, the popularity of the brand, model, or color may supersede the important characteristics of fit and suitability. You must be wary of the gimmicks, gizmos, and "sizzle" behind the sales pitch. We are captivated by the glitz; if it isn't there, the best designed equipment is no longer sold and used and is ultimately discontinued by the manufacturer.

The production of sports equipment begins with the designer and manufacturer who must understand the biomechanics of an item's use, the variations in body types, the breadth of users' individual skill levels, and their different strength and fitness levels. These design considerations influence the effectiveness of the equipment and ultimately its successful sales.

The retailer knowledgeable of the biomechanical principles that go into the equipment design and manufacture can translate those principles into understandable concepts for the consumer. Not all manufactured goods are based on sound principles, and the retailer must be able to cut through the misinformation and help consumers select appropriate equipment for their use.

▶ Summary

The future sports practitioner and user should be able to sort through the glitzy, high-tech terminology and promotional hype. An understanding of the way the body works, an appreciation of the quality of materials used in making sports equipment, and a knowledge of mechanical concepts related to the use of that equipment will lead to constructive advice to clientele and informed choices for users of all abilities. The following chapters will start you on your way to making quality assessments.

PART I

Foot-Ground Interfaces

CHAPTER 1

Biomechanical Considerations for Foot-Ground Interfaces

Ellen F. Kreighbaum, PhD
Montana State University, Bozeman

Foot-ground interfaces are materials and equipment placed between the foot and the ground surface. Frequently the interface is a street shoe with a leather sole and a leather upper, but the special demands of sports require foot-ground interfaces that provide specific biomechanical charactcristics to hclp athletes perform more effectively and safely.

This introductory chapter presents the basic biomechanical principles important to the design of the shoe; it also addresses the important structural characteristics of the lower extremity and foot that influence the fitting of footwear (no two feet are exactly the same, even if they are the same size). In the chapters that follow in Part I, authors will discuss the design and materials of footwear used in running and jogging, hiking and climbing, and cross-country and downhill skiing, both historically and in present day. The anatomical and mechanical determinants should be fully understood by the designer, the manufacturer, the retailer, and the user.

▶ Mechanical Aspects of Foot-Ground Interfaces

Any discussion of footwear for either the athlete or the recreational user should be based on the mechanical factors inherent in movement as well as the human form and function. A key ingredient in interfacing with the ground is friction.

Friction is the force that is generated between two contacting surfaces, which resists their sliding past one another.

Types of Friction

There are three types of friction—static friction, sliding friction, and rolling friction. **Static friction** develops between the footwear and the ground up until slipping occurs. The force of static friction builds between two surfaces while the horizontal component of force increases: Thus, in human locomotion, this friction force between the footwear and the surface increases as the body continues to increase the push against the surface.

static friction—A force generated when two surfaces in contact tend to slide past one another without any present motion.

Sliding friction is present between two surfaces when they are in contact and are sliding past each other. Sliding friction force is less than static friction; static friction builds to the point of slippage, at which point the friction force is greatly reduced.

sliding friction—A force generated when two surfaces in contact slide past one another.

For most activities, performance is enhanced if slipping does not occur; running, hiking, and climbing as well as sports activities that are based on locomotion (tennis, racquetball, track and field events, etc.) depend on high friction force. However, in some activities, including skiing and ice skating, sliding on a surface is critical, and high static friction deters effective performance.

rolling friction—A resistive force generated when a wheel is rolled along a surface.

Rolling friction is generated during the rolling of a wheel along a surface. Although rolling friction has the least force of all of the types of friction, it must be taken into consideration during such activities as inline skating, roller skating, cycling, harness racing, and auto racing.

Characteristics of Friction

Whether increased or decreased friction is desirable depends, of course, on the type and the purpose of the equipment one is using. By understanding what properties increase and what properties decrease friction forces, users and equipment specialists can make informed choices.

Friction force generally depends on two characteristics: the component of force pressing the foot and the ground surface together, called the normal force, and the coefficient of friction. The **normal force** depends on the weight of the body and the angle of the surface against which the force is applied (or the angle at which the force is applied to a horizontal surface). The normal force is illustrated in Figure 1.1.

normal force—The force component of a body that is perpendicular to a surface upon which it rests.

The normal force is always perpendicular to the surface against which it is applied. If you are standing on level ground, the normal force equals your body weight. If, however, you are standing on a sloped surface, because the body's weight is always directed downward vertically, only a component part of your weight will be directed perpendicular to the surface: The greater the angle of the slope, the lesser the normal force being applied to the supporting surface. The greater the normal force is, the greater will be the static friction force that can be built up before slipping occurs. So people who weigh less create less friction force against a horizontal surface, and likewise surfaces of greater and greater angles create proportionally less friction force given that all other conditions are equal.

coefficient of friction—A ratio of the maximum static friction between two surfaces and the normal force exerted between the two surfaces.

The second component of friction force, the **coefficient of friction,** depends on the characteristics of the two surfaces pressing together. We know that some surfaces are "stickier" than others. Wet surfaces are more slippery than dry surfaces, smoother surfaces are more slippery than rough surfaces, and leather on wood is more slippery than rubber on wood. The type of sole material and the type of surface material are both important determinants of frictional characteristics.

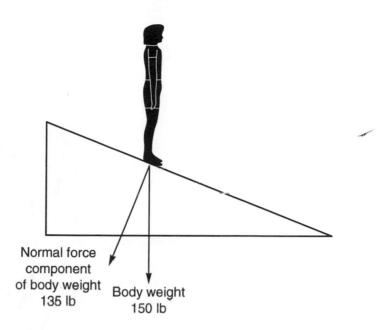

▶ Figure 1.1 The weight of the body against a surface creates normal force.

Normal force
component
of body weight
135 lb

Body weight
150 lb

The actual contact area is one characteristic that influences the amount of friction and is different from the area of a person's footprint in a given shoe. Thus, a larger shoe does not provide greater frictional capabilities than a smaller shoe, just as a larger automobile tire does not provide greater friction than a smaller tire. Imagine a coaching shoe with deep spaces between ribs or nubs on the bottom. When you stand in that shoe, the nubs do not squish down eliminating the spaces. The material in the outsole of the shoe lining the spaces between the nubs does not contact the ground. The actual contact area excludes the material not in contact with the ground and is less than the area inside the perimeter of the shoe.

The relationship between friction force (F_{fr}), normal force (N), and coefficient of friction (μ) is expressed by the equation

$$F_{fr} = \mu N.$$

That is, the force of friction may be determined by multiplying the normal force by the coefficient of friction. The coefficient of friction may be determined for a given surface and a given shoe by testing the angle at which the shoe begins to slide on a surface. The easiest method for calculation uses a wooden plank: Place the shoe on one end of the plank and begin to slowly lift that end of the plank. At some point, the shoe will begin to slip. Note the angle of the plank at that point. Using a table of trigonometric functions, find the tangent of the angle where slipping begins. That tangent function is the coefficient of friction of that shoe on that surface. Of course, friction force is greater with a body in the shoe because of the greater normal force, but the coefficient of friction is independent of the normal force, so this method is usable. (For an interesting experiment, try testing several types of outsoles on the same wooden surface).

▶ Anatomical Aspects of Foot-Ground Interfaces

Discussion of footwear for either the athlete or the recreational user should be based on the human form and function as well as the mechanical factors inherent in human movement. Comparing the anatomical structure of different bodies, you

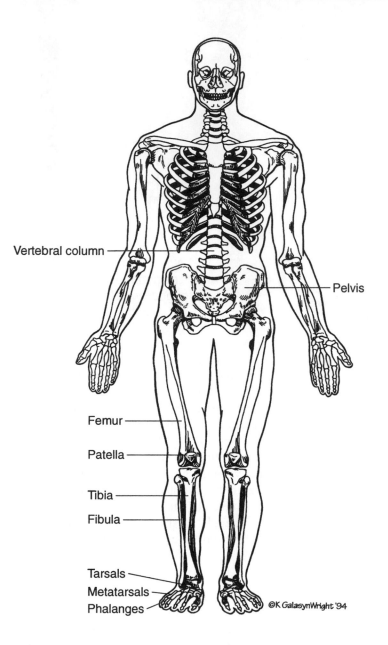

Vertebral column

Pelvis

Femur

Patella

Tibia

Fibula

Tarsals

Metatarsals

Phalanges

©K GalasynWright '94

▶ **Figure 1.2a** Major bones of the body.

find many of the same characteristics, but also there are many differences between people and between a person's left and right foot. Although most similarities are obvious, the differences often elude the casual observer. To make the evaluation more complicated, one must consider the atypical mover such as those found in Special Olympics, in Masters' meets, or in age-group competitions.

Some of the similarities and differences in the human form, specifically in the lower extremity, will be identified in this chapter. In addition one must be aware of biomechanical interactions between the body segments that also influence the selection of appropriate types or brands of footwear.

Anatomy of the Lower Extremity

The important skeletal components of the human body related to foot-ground interfaces consist of the vertebral column, the pelvis, and the two lower extremities

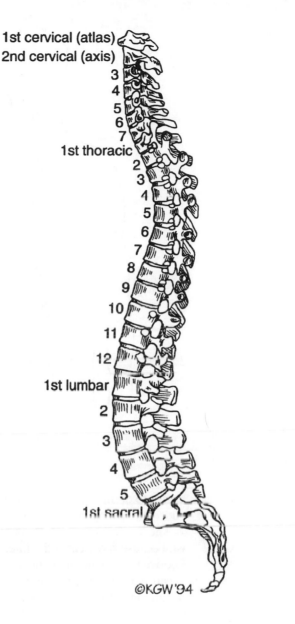

1st cervical (atlas)
2nd cervical (axis)
3
4
5
6
7
1st thoracic
2
3
4
5
6
7
8
9
10
11
12
1st lumbar
2
3
4
5
1st sacral

©KGW '94

▶ **Figure 1.2b** The vertebral column.

consisting of thigh, leg, and foot bones. The major bones of these areas are shown in Figure 1.2a.

For our purposes we will consider specific parts of the vertebral column, which consists of 25 separate bones classified into four areas: the cervical or neck, the thoracic or upper back, the lumbar or lower back, and the sacrum, which serves as a bridge between the vertebral column and the pelvis. These sections consist of 7 cervical vertebrae, 12 thoracic vertebrae, 5 lumbar vertebrae, and the sacrum. These sections of the vertebral column are shown in Figure 1.2b.

Each section of the vertebral column has its own particular characteristics, but for this discussion it is necessary only to know that movement or displacement of the column is made possible by the small movements between any two contiguous vertebral bones. Many small movements, when occurring simultaneously, provide a larger movement or displacement. These displacements are an important component in locomotion (walking, running, or jumping), they are a

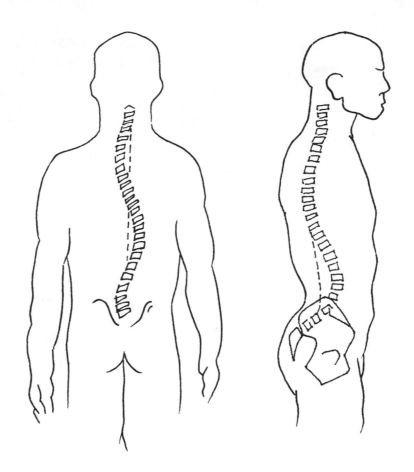

▶ **Figure 1.3** Two misalignments of the spine: (a) scoliosis and (b) lordosis.

buffer to damp the vibrations and to absorb the forces with which the body must contend, or they compensate for the displacement or movement of another part.

The last function, compensatory movement, is important to the footwear specialist, because footwear is the interface between the human structure and the ground. Footwear can help maintain an already existing ideal alignment of the body parts; it can help correct, or compensate for, misaligned body parts; or it can cause a misalignment of body parts if inappropriate. Inappropriate footwear can create or exacerbate two misalignments of the vertebral column—scoliosis, a lateral curvature (Figure 1.3a), or lordosis, an exaggerated lumbar curve (Figure 1.3b). For example, scoliosis may be caused by uncorrected, unequal leg lengths; lordosis may be caused by excessive heel height in footwear.

Lower Extremity Misalignments

The ideal alignment of the pelvis and lower extremities is characterized by the principles of architecture. That is, vertical alignment provides the best structure to minimize excessive torques; ideal alignment of the lower extremity and the foot is shown in Figure 1.4.

Lateral Deviations

varus—An alignment in which a body segment runs inward or medially from its proximal to its distal ends.

There are two general types of deviations from the ideal alignment. In the first, one or more of the various segments deviate laterally inward or outward. In the second, a segment is rotated or twisted inward or outward relative to the next adjacent segment. The first lateral deviation of a segment, **varus,** is a condition in which the segment tends excessively inward from its top end

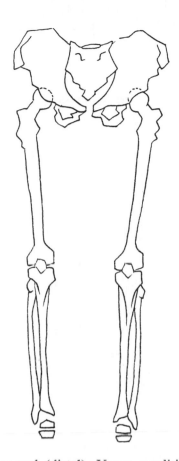

▶ **Figure 1.4** Ideal alignment in the lower body.

(proximal) to its bottom end (distal). Varus conditions of the femur, tibia, rearfoot, and forefoot are shown in Figure 1.5.

Varus conditions cause excessive strain on the lateral, or on the medial tissues surrounding the joints. As indicated in the diagram, a varus condition will put added stress on the lateral side of the proximal joint and the medial side of the distal joint. For example, a varus condition in the tibia will put undue stress on the lateral side of the knee and the medial side of the ankle as the foot rotates to interface with the horizontal ground. In the case of the forefoot, the medial metatarsal heads one and two are elevated more than the lateral metatarsal heads four and five. Thus, the forefoot is aligned so that the first metatarsal head is higher and the fifth metatarsal head is lower.

A person with a varus condition should wear a shoe or boot that either compensates for the misalignment (filling) or corrects the misalignment (correcting). Opinions on whether to fill or correct differ with the specialist and with the type of athletic footwear used.

valgus—An alignment in which a body segment runs outward or laterally from its proximal to its distal ends.

The second lateral deviation, a **valgus** condition, is defined as the deviation of a segment outward from its top (proximal) end to its bottom (distal) end. Figure 1.6 illustrates femur, tibia, rearfoot, and forefoot valgus.

Valgus conditions produce undue stresses on the joints just opposite to those produced by varus conditions. That is, femoral valgus puts excessive stress on the lateral side of the knee; tibial valgus puts excessive stress on the medial side of the knee and the lateral ankle joint. In the forefoot a valgus condition is seen when the first and second metatarsal heads are lower than the fourth and fifth heads. Again, footwear can either attempt to correct this condition or it can compensate for it by filling the space produced between the plantar surface of the foot and the ground.

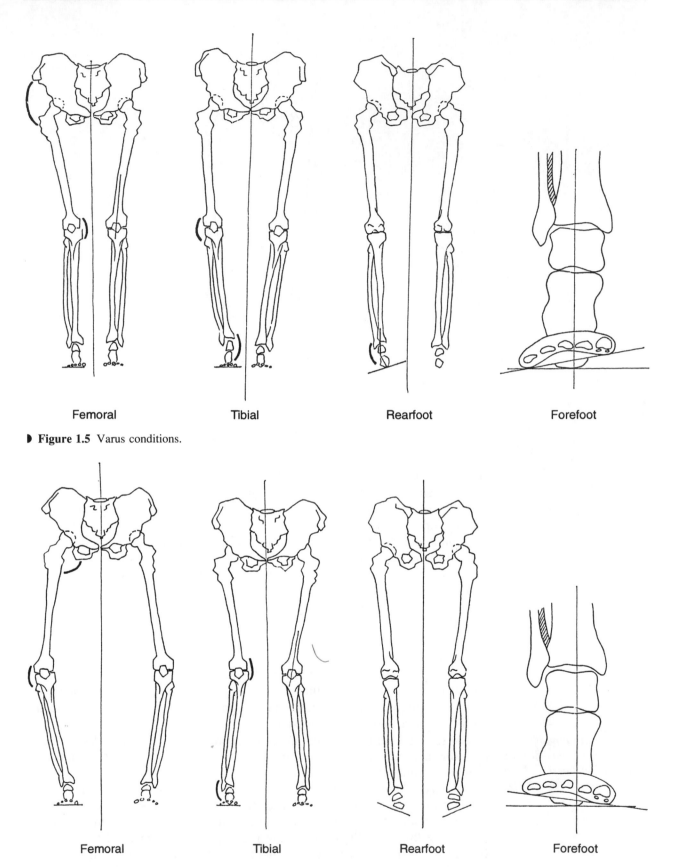

Femoral   Tibial   Rearfoot   Forefoot

▶ **Figure 1.5** Varus conditions.

Femoral   Tibial   Rearfoot   Forefoot

▶ **Figure 1.6** Valgus conditions.
Figures 1.4-1.6 drawn from figures in Kreighbaum and Bartels, *Biomechanics: A Qualitative Approach for Studying Human Movement*, Boston: Allyn-Bacon, 1995.

Torsional Deviations

torsion—A force that causes a part of the body to be twisted around its longitudinal axis.

femoral torsion—An alignment in which the femur is rotated medially around its longitudinal axis and relative to the tibia.

tibial torsion—An alignment in which the tibia is rotated laterally around its longitudinal axis and relative to the femur.

The second major type of lower extremity deviation is torsional misalignment. **Torsion** is a twisting of one segment around its long axis so that the segment is not facing forward, but rather, is rotated inward or outward; thus its front surface is not directed straight forward.

Femoral torsion is an inward twisting of the femur on the tibia. It is commonly seen in females and is related to a knee problem called chondromalacia. Footwear does not affect femoral torsion to any great extent. **Tibial torsion** is the outward rotation of the tibia relative to the femur. Tibial torsion is more commonly seen in males and has been associated with an imbalance in strength between the medial and lateral hamstring muscles. Although seemingly the same misalignment, looking at the knee joint we see that tibial torsion results in a toe-out foot position, whereas femoral torsion does not. This toe-out position during weight bearing encourages an eversion of the subtalar joint and a consequential pronation of the foot. Footwear cannot correct tibial torsion, but footwear can accommodate or compensate for the misalignment.

Foot Structure

The foot itself has been called a "mobile adapter" to the terrain on which it rests. It is made up of numerous bones among which varied movements take place. The foot bones are the tarsals, metatarsals, and phalanges and are illustrated in Figure 1.7.

Several aspects of foot structure are important in choosing footwear. One aspect, arch height, is described as high, neutral, or low. Foot impressions of each arch height are shown in Figure 1.8. Another aspect of the foot structure

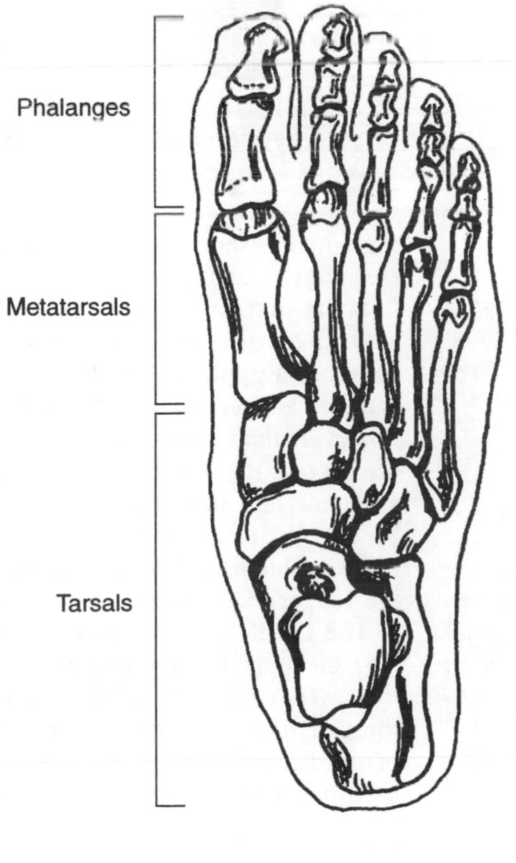

Phalanges

Metatarsals

Tarsals

▶ **Figure 1.7** Anatomy of the foot.

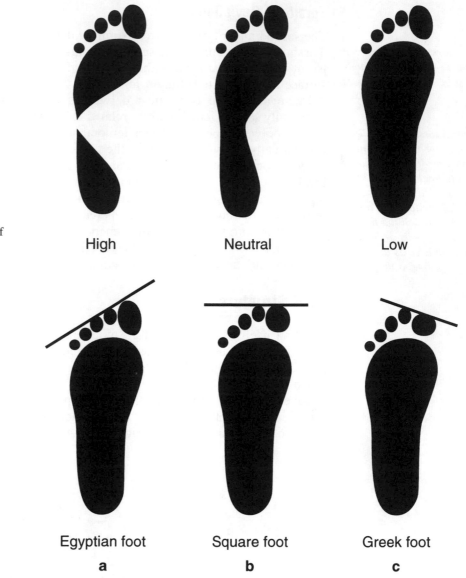

Figure 1.8 Three types of foot arches.

High   Neutral   Low

Egyptian foot   Square foot   Greek foot

a   b   c

Figure 1.9 Three toe configurations.

square foot—A toe struc-ture in which the first and second toes extend forward an equal distance when a person is standing.

Egyptian foot—A type of foot structure in which the ends of the toes form a di-agonal line, the first toe be-ing the longest and each toe being slightly shorter.

Greek foot—A type of foot structure in which the end of the second toe extends farther forward than the first toe when a person is standing.

that impacts shoe selection is toe length, of which there are three configurations (see Figure 1.9).

If the first and second toes are the same length, the foot is called a **square foot**. If the first toe is longer than the second and remaining toes, the foot is called an **Egyptian foot**. If the first toe is shorter than the second toe, the foot is called a **Greek foot**. Most footwear will accommodate the first two structures; however, the Greek foot can present some problems in selecting footwear. If the second toe is considerably longer than the others, one may have to buy a shoe one-half size larger so that the long toe is not impacted by the shoe end. Frequently, the second toe lengths are not the same on both feet, which becomes more problematic because the shorter foot must be placed in a longer shoe, or the longer toed foot in a shoe too short for it.

The Greek foot also may be created not by a longer second toe but by the first metatarsal being shorter than normal. When you bear weight in walking then, you tend to ''fall off'' the end of the short first metatarsal, or you shift the weight more to the center of the foot (i.e., to the head of the second and/ or third metatarsal). The short first metatarsal may also be hypermobile; that is, it has a greater range of motion up and down than normal.

Morton's neuroma—A condition created by a hypermobile first or second metatarsal that results in nerve irritation between the metatarsals.

This hypermobility can irritate nerves that run between the metatarsals resulting in an inflammation of those nerves, a condition called *Morton's syndrome* or **Morton's neuroma**. Shoes can be adapted to decrease the hypermobility of the first metatarsal by placing a metatarsal pad under the head of the bone. Moreover, hypermobility can encourage overpronation in the otherwise normal runner. If the person walks with a toeout gait or pronates due to another factor, the stress on the first metatarsal head is increased.

Understanding these aspects of foot structure and the implications of each is necessary for designing and selecting footwear. But in order to make the best decisions, this knowledge of anatomy must be balanced with knowledge of the biomechanical requirements of particular sports.

▶ Applications of Biomechanical Parameters to Foot-Ground Interfaces

Different shoe designs reflect requirements and characteristics unique to a particular sport and individual body anthropometrics. We finish this chapter with a brief description of footwear design considerations for running, court play, hiking, and cross-country skiing.

Running and Court Shoes

Running or jogging generally involves forward linear movement on a level surface. Shoes designed for this activity must be custom fit to the user's individual alignment. Some shoes are designed for high arches, some for a pronator, some for a supinator. The toebox height must be considered for those with "high toes." The mechanical aspects of design include the patterning of the sole, the materials used in the outsole, the frequency of use, and the number of miles run each week. (See chapter 2 for further discussion.)

Hiking Boots

The user's individual anatomical characteristics and the mechanical aspects of boot design must correspond in the appropriate boot. The type of terrain over which you will hike, the slopes, the surface characteristics, and so on are factors in selection. There are boots designed to accommodate all different environments, but one does not want to overbuy or underbuy in terms of boot capabilities. Weight of the boot is an important consideration. Its use may dictate the need for a steel or fiberglass shank for extra support; the choice of a more flexible alternative may be appropriate depending on its intended use. The biomechanics of foot support for various hiking and climbing activities will be addressed in chapter 3.

Cross-Country Ski Boots and Bindings

There are two types of cross-country skiing: track skiing and skate skiing. The biomechanical characteristics of boots used in each type are quite different. The boot must fit the user's anatomical characteristics besides being suitable for either track skiing or skate skiing. Most recreational skiers track ski, which is, for the most part, a linear activity. You do not have to be particularly concerned about either cornering and the torsional stress that cornering places on the boot-binding interface or about the transfer of force between your leg through the boot binding to the ski. However, if you are a skate skier, you place more sideways force on the boot-binding–ski complex. You would select very different boots for these two activities. Chapter 4 addresses these differences.

Downhill Ski Boots, Bindings, and Skis

To analyze the transfer of force through the boot binding to the ski and the snow-covered surface you must know the anatomical alignment of the lower extremity and understand friction and the transfer of force. A lower extremity showing a tibial varus requires a differently designed boot than a lower extremity with a tibial valgus. Friction components are important to analyze the edging characteristics of the boot and binding, ski and snow interface. Chapter 4 provides information to analyze unique situations for appropriate boot selection.

▶ A Look Ahead

Now that you have learned about the mechanical and anatomical aspects of selecting the proper footwear, we proceed in the following chapters to present more specific information on the history of specific sports equipment, the materials and design of footwear, and how manufacturers have addressed individual differences in designing their footwear to accommodate users' various functional deviations of the lower extremities.

Consumables are continually changing in materials, design, colors, and popularity. Therefore, we intend to provide you with basic principles for evaluating future equipment innovations.

CHAPTER 2

Running and Court Shoes

Thomas E. Johnson
Athletes Foot, Bozeman, Montana

The athletic shoe, or "sneaker," as we called it only 15 years ago, is now largely extinct. We have been flooded with new terminology arising from the manufacture of high-tech sports equipment such as EVA, pronation, supination, and Energy Return, to name a few. After reading this chapter you will have a good basic understanding of the construction of a shoe, design and materials terminology, as well as how shoes differ from one another.

▶ Running Shoes

The running shoe has been the driving force in the footwear boom beginning in the mid-1970s. Running as a sport became one of the most efficient methods of getting in shape. This incentive prompted major manufacturers to invest money, devoting research and development to the industry. From this surge consumers benefit by improvement in the athletic shoe. Footwear today dramatically enhances comfort and performance for the modern athlete, regardless of his or her ability, or level of play.

The footwear market as a whole can be very confusing. Fast-paced marketing and innovative updates make a complete understanding of the models available very difficult. As the market changes, new models and technologies make yesterday's styles obsolete. After learning the basic structure of a shoe and understanding the function of the design, you will be able to look at any shoe regardless of manufacturer, style, size, and so on and be able to recognize and evaluate each of its features. You can then judge quality and determine the type of foot and sport for which the shoe was designed.

Shoe Structure

What makes a running shoe different from many other types of footwear? The biggest factor to consider in running shoe design is a shoe's ability to help absorb and disperse shock. At a normal jogging pace the average runner will expose the skeletal frame with about three to five times the normal body weight. Exposing the body to that type of constant force over time will result in injury to the lower extremities as well as muscle fatigue and poor performance. Also, the running shoe is devised primarily for forward motion. The way in which a running shoe is built does not accommodate lateral movement, such as basketball, racquetball, or other activities that demand side-to-side motion. These sports require a court shoe (discussed further in this chapter). Figure 2.1 illustrates the anatomy of a typical running shoe.

Outsoles

The two primary functions of the outsole are traction and durability. Traction varies with the needs of the individual runner. The most common surface is pavement or concrete, which doesn't require much traction from the shoe. Wet pavement decreases some of the surface traction.

Durability, particularly of the outsole, is one of the biggest wear factors of a running shoe. Most running takes place on pavement or concrete, which may be the most common surface, but it is also one of the hardest and most abrasive. Carbon rubber, used for most outsoles, is the type of rubber used in the manufacture of automobile tires. In fact, some shoe manufacturers use Goodyear Indy 500 rubber or other brand name rubber in their outsoles for maximum durability.

A second type of rubber used in outsoles is blown rubber, which, as its name implies, is injected with air to make the rubber more porous. The injected air also gives it a lighter and spongier quality. One problem with blown rubber is that it has less durability than carbon rubber. You can tell the difference between the two rubbers by comparing thickness. Blown rubber injected with air is much thicker, whereas the more durable carbon rubber is quite thin.

A feature of the blown-rubber outsole is a heel area with a carbon rubber insert to give more wear at the strike zone. Up until now, outsole wear and

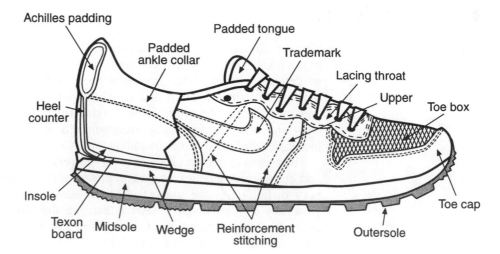

▶ **Figure 2.1** Anatomy of a running shoe, including its outsole, midsole, and upper.

traction were the only functional characteristics considered in design. Shoes today are designed with a definite cushion system to the outsole. Each manufacturer's cushioned outsole is slightly different but with the same idea in mind: an outsole that is not totally flat but rather concave, creating a rebounding action (see Figure 2.2). On impact the weight of the foot is suspended in the center and is supported on the perimeter, which causes the system to act like a trampoline. Some research shows a 10 percent increase in shock absorption. Secondly, with a suspended center, the perimeter tends to force the weight distribution over the center of the shoe for added stability.

Outsole patterns will vary, depending on what that manufacturer is trying to achieve. For example, an off-road shoe may have rubber nubs for traction; a racing shoe will use very thin, smooth rubber for a light, flexible feel.

Midsoles

The midsole is the workhorse of a running shoe. Originally it consisted of nothing more than a leather midsole and outersole that was updated to some basic rubber compounds until the first expanded or open-cell foams were used. The most common foam used, ethyl vinyl acetate, or EVA, was chosen by manufacturers because of its light weight, cost-effectiveness, and ease to mold and shape, as well as being an efficient shock absorber. In its infancy the most widely used form of EVA was a single density sheet cut to size with no modifications. As the market advanced and runners' needs changed, it was common practice to use different densities of EVA measured in *durometers*, a measure of hardness on a scale of 1 to 100 that measures the firmness of a midsole material. Low numbers indicate material that is softer than that expressed by higher numbers. The biggest advantage of EVA dual or tri densities is that a midsole can be made with firmer densities of EVA where the foot needs extra support, and a shoe can be fine-tuned to fit the individual runner's needs. Softer EVA gives cushioning; foot support is given with firmer EVA.

The modern cushioning system was not perfected overnight. As the running market expanded, so did the number of injuries, which most manufacturers interpreted as a sign of inadequate cushioning systems, or as a lack of shock absorption. At this point most shoe designers started incorporating softer midsoles, hoping to aid the runner and reduce the number of injuries. Much to

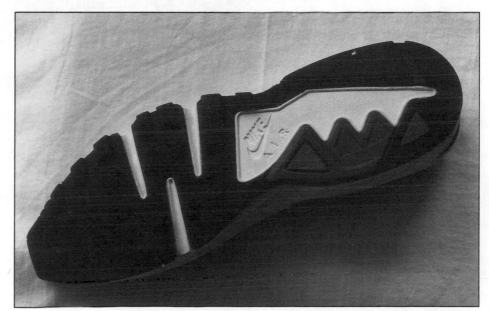

▶ **Figure 2.2** The sole profile of a running shoe is carved out in the center for a two-function feature.

their dismay, the number of injuries increased. The injuries were not all caused by shock or shock-related factors, but rather by the inability of the shoes to control excessive foot motion. The softer shoe design sacrificed the foundation stability—a factor as critical as shock absorption. This fact alone segregated shoe models into two basic categories: stability shoes and cushion shoes. In the cushion shoes a softer midsole was used for the runner who had no major foot motion and whose primary concern was cushion. This softer shoe, however, would not do for the runner who had a very mobile foot or a flat foot and who needed the extra motion control. The initial design to control this excessive foot motion used a duel-density EVA midsole (see Figure 2.3). The shoe had a firmer density EVA along the medial side (inside) to prevent the shoe from rolling inward causing excessive pronation.

The single biggest problem with EVA foam is the open-cell structure. EVA has the property to absorb and disperse shock, but it also has the disadvantage of compressing. This causes a problem over time, because the shoe becomes less efficient the more you run. Research varies on how much and how fast the EVA compresses, but some say as much as 20 percent in the first 50 miles. To solve the compression problem, traditional EVA was precompressed. This had a twofold effect, first making the EVA denser—which in turn provided more support—and secondly, it compressed at a slower rate.

Some companies also were experimenting with other materials to use as a substitute for, or to enhance EVA. Nike, Inc., one of the first companies to remedy the compression problem, incorporated the idea of putting air units sealed in polyurethane (PU) into the midsole of the shoe (see Figure 2.4). The air units varied in size, depending on the price of the shoe, the amount of stability desired, and the amount of cushion needed (see Figure 2.4). The biggest

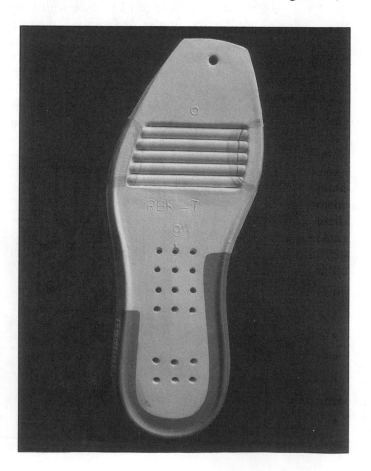

▶ **Figure 2.3** The EVA sole is for the runner with a mobile foot.

advantage of the air unit was that, regardless of total miles run in the shoe, the cushioning did not change. The shoes had as much shock absorption after 1,000 miles of running as they did the day they were purchased. The Nike innovation soon prompted other companies to design their own types of midsole in answer to the compression problem.

In 1991 Saucony introduced the GRID (Ground Reaction Inertia Device), a composite with Hytrel filaments molded in an interlocking configuration like string on a tennis racquet, designed to work with the midsole to reduce shock and enhance stability. The strings are graded based on the athlete's foot size and weight to maximize performance. The GRID system works in unison with the Dome Torsional Rigidity Bar or TRB. The Dome TRB is made of thermoplastic urethane built in a concave sphere to offer more stability and cushioning. Also featured in the Saucony line is the Ionic cushioning system, a midsole made from resilite polyurethane (Saucony's exclusive polyurethane compound) and molded triangular pillars to give extended life in cushioning and stability.

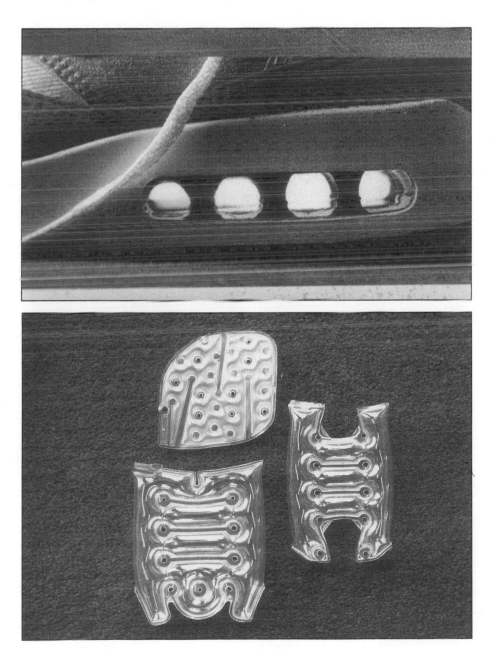

▶ **Figure 2.4** A profile of Nike's air units (top) and their different sizes (bottom).

Asics Tiger introduced gel packets in the core of their EVA midsole (see Figure 2.5). These are small packets filled with a semifluid silicone-based gel which helps to disperse vertical impact into a horizontal plane to absorb shock.

In mid-1988 Reebok introduced ERS (Energy Return System; see Figure 2.6), which consisted of Hytrel tubes located in the midsole of the shoe, encapsulated in polyurethane. The model price depended on whether the tubes were located in the heel, or in both the heel and forefoot. PU provides the shock absorption; ERS tubes supply energy return. On impact the force of the body preloads the tubes in a spring-like fashion. As advertized, the preload of the energy tubes releases energy to aid the runner who can run with less energy and run faster.

Upon further examination the industry agreed that the ERS system bolsters the longevity and cushioning effects of the midsole, but there are more questions still unanswered, such as: Does energy return work in footwear? Beginning in 1991 ERS tubes were made of Hytrel foam rather than nylon. This gave a softer ride than the original Hytrel tubes. A second system was introduced by Reebok using Hexalite and Evalite. Hexalite is a three-dimensional honeycomb-like plastic structure that helps disperse shock. Evalite is a foam similar in chemical makeup to compression-molded EVA; it is soft and light, but has the resiliency of PU. The Hexalite is encapsulated into Elvalite, and its use in the heel only or both forefoot and heel will determine price structure.

Converse introduced the Wave in 1988. The Wave material (a small portion of the midsole) is an EVA-type compound that is lighter with better shock-absorbing characteristics than EVA. Converse made the same claims as Reebok, saying the Wave had energy-return properties. Both companies have shifted their claims for now. Converse also introduced another new technology in early 1990. REACT, as it was called, is an encapsulated unit under the heel that is filled with a liquid-gas combination. This unit gives additional shock absorption because it does not break down. Another unit is placed around the ankle to give superior fit.

Etonic, using midsole technology available since the late 1970s, designed a system called the Dynamic Reaction Plate (DRP). Originally made of a fiberglass plate, it was sandwiched between the EVA in the midsole and helped

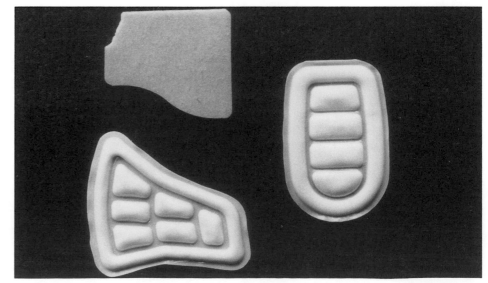

▶ **Figure 2.5** A sampling of the gel packets that are used in midsoles to dissipate shock.

▶ **Figure 2.6** A shoe with an Energy Return System that uses Hexalite.

disperse the shock of running. As time and technology advanced, Etonic changed the fiberglass to a composite of carbon and fiberglass fibers called TL-61. Carbon fibers run across the plate for stability, and fiberglass fibers run its length for flexibility. The plates are formed in a variety of shapes to accommodate shoe design (either cushion or stability). In late 1990 to early 1991 Etonic introduced a second phase of the DRP. The new system, StableAir, consisted of independent air cells, which unlike Nike's pressurized cells are filled with unpressurized, ambient air. The air cells are used in conjunction with the DRP plates to give a stable yet cushioned ride. Again, the amount of air cells and their location determine the shoe's cushioning and stability features as well as price.

New Balance introduced the ENCAP and C-Cap midsole technology. ENCAP is an outer shell of PU with an inner core of EVA, a combination that gives the cushioning properties of EVA with the stability and longevity of PU. C-Cap is a similar system except that the inner core of EVA is surrounded by precompressed EVA which gives it similar properties to ENCAP at a lower shoe price. In addition to the ENCAP, New Balance added ABZORB, a highly shock absorbent compound sealed in ENCAP to create ENCAP II and designed to enhance the cushioning and longevity of the midsole.

Avia introduced the ARC technology for their midsole system which is a Hytrel plate formed in a concave fashion with protruding fingers. Sealed in PU, the stability models have shorter, wider fingers; the cushioned models have longer, thinner ones. This technology enhances the cantilever outsole design in that you get a rebound effect from the concave shape of the sole and ARC unit.

Brooks uses what they call Hydroflow, a sealed chamber filled with silicone fluid. The unit is divided into two separate chambers. The pressure of the heel strike during the running motion will force the silicone fluid from the rear chamber into the forward one. As the running gait is completed the fluid flows back into the rear chamber ready for the next heel strike. Up until now these hydro units were only in the shoe heels, due to their thickness, because locating them in the forefoot would decrease the shoe's flexibility. By redesigning the size of the Hydroflow unit they are now placing them in the forefoot.

New in the 1991 season was the introduction of a plate system similar to Etonic's, the Brooks Propulsion Plate. The main difference in the Brooks plate is that it runs the entire length of the sole. In theory the plate takes the downward energy of heel strike and moves it forward to the forefoot for the toe-off phase then releases, providing propulsion into the next stride. The Hydroflow unit is also used in unison with the plate for cushioning.

Adidas took a slightly different approach. Rather than market only a cushion system, they contrived a whole new concept in midsole design. Adidas cut a groove across the midsole helping the forefoot to act independently from the rearfoot—in theory allowing the foot to act anatomically correctly. To compensate for excessive twisting action in the foot, Adidas incorporated a Kevlar bar lengthwise into the midsole. This controls the torsional twist of the foot by keeping it stable in the shoe. Adidas claims this system reduces muscle and tendon strain, reducing injury. For cushioning, Adidas used a new midsole compound called Purolite, very similar to EVA without the compression problems. Also there is a hole cut in the heel of the midsole and filled with foam beads called Softcell, another cushion-aid device incorporated into the torsion system. Adidas is still currently using the Web, a mesh or webbing wrapped around the midsole in its entirety. As the shock takes place at the heel, it is then dispersed down the mesh to spread the energy of the shock over the entire shoe.

Turntec is a rather small and young company but by no means a newcomer. Jerry Turner has been in the athletic shoe industry for years and has been instrumental in creating some of the technology used today. Turntec footwear uses a product called ZO2, which gives extra protection to the runner. ZO2, a silicone pad built into the sock liner of the shoe, is located inside the shoe next to the heel for closer contact with the foot and more efficient shock absorption. In addition to ZO2 pads, Turntec has launched a new technology dubbed ART (Anatomical Rebound Technology), which also parallels Etonics' Dynamic Reaction Plate. A Hytrel trampoline (plate) located in the heel of the midsole helps absorb heel impact. Turner has also incorporated a concave anatomical heel for the foot to rest down into for a more natural fit. This concept utilizes the natural fat located under the calcaneus bone in the heel for cushioning.

In 1994 Nike introduced another innovation to enhance cushioning and stability called the Air Max^2. The system consists of three chambers: The lateral and medial chambers have a pressure of 25 psi for stability, and the center changer has a 5 psi for cushioning.

Uppers

The upper is the part of the shoe that holds the shoe together and also secures it on your foot. Early designs used leather, but more recently a nylon and leather combination was introduced that is still the standard today. Most of the suede or leather trims are being replaced with synthetics as well. Nike originally introduced a synthetic material called flight suede, which has the advantage of moisture resistance. A leather product, unless treated, will absorb moisture, making the shoe heavier, as well as drying out the leather.

The main objective of the upper is to offer foot support and keep the shoe centered on the foot. The heel counter is a rigid or semirigid piece at the heel of the shoe that keeps the heel of the foot centered over the rear of the shoe. It can be made from various materials, and these affect shoe price. In the lower priced models, it is made of a paper product, but the cardboard softens as the shoe is worn, or as it gets wet. The other material commonly used in heel counters is thermal plastic, a compound that costs more, but one will keep its integrity longer, giving more support to the foot on a more consistent basis. The heel counter is usually covered with one or two layers of suede leather or some type of synthetic trim. For greater stability, manufacturers add a heel stabilizer unit, a horseshoe-shaped piece of a ridged plastic or PU that is added to the base of the heel counter for additional motion control.

In 1991 Nike revolutionized the upper fit by introducing the dynamic foot sleeve. This innovation incorporated a lycra sleeve into the upper of the shoe to give it a glove-like fit. Other companies now use this fit system to enhance their shoes' overall comfort. A newer version of this sleeve-fit system incorporated mesh panels with the lycra sleeves to reduce heat buildup.

The most basic portion of the shoe is the lacing throat (see Figure 2.7). Besides keeping the shoe on your foot, the lace may be the key to comfort. Blood is supplied to the foot across the instep. Lacing the shoe too tight restricts the flow of blood, causing the foot to "fall asleep," or to go numb. For this problem the staggered lacing throat was introduced. Having a zigzag appearance, its biggest advantage is that the lace can accommodate different foot shapes. A motivating factor for manufacturers, incorporating the staggered lacing system means that one shoe style will fit a broader spectrum of feet.

The logo design on most quality athletic footwear is usually more than just a stripe or check telling you what brand it is. Most companies try to incorporate support into the logo design on the footwear, making it dual purpose. Made out of a nonstretch material, it is sewn into the lace throat and glued under the midsole. When you lace the shoe tight, it will pull the logo design up next to

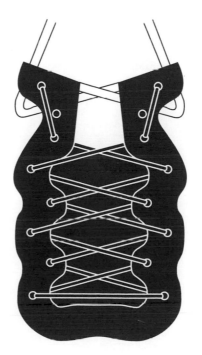

▶ **Figure 2.7** The staggered lacing throat allows runners a customized fit.

the foot for additional support. For a safety feature, piping or trim is added made of a Scotch Lite reflective material to reflect light when running in the dark. Reebok in late 1989 introduced an upper technology that revived sales in a sagging market. The company expanded the concept in spring and fall of 1990, and for fall of 1991 made nine shoe categories with this new system called the Pump. The concept behind the Pump is to give the user a custom fit in the upper with use of an air bag system. The bag unit has a built-in pump device allowing the wearer to pump the bag unit up to give the foot a personalized fit, thus accommodating different foot shapes. The bag units will vary in size and shape depending on the shoe price and the fit system being offered for the type of sport. For example, the fit system in a basketball shoe highlights the ankle support of the shoe compared to the running series offering more arch support. A more recent version of this fit system utilizes the instaflate system, which uses a CO_2 cartridge for faster inflation.

Lasts

A *last* is the wooden or metal device that is shaped like a foot around which the shoe is built (see Figure 2.8). The last will dictate the size as well as the overall shape of a particular style. Not only will the last mandate the overall characteristics of a model, but it also forms the basic foundation for the foot. Earlier in this chapter we were talking about features in a shoe that would give support to different types of feet. The last is a major contributor to that overall support, being the foundation on which the foot will stand. All the features in the upper will be of little value without a supportive shoe base.

Shoes come in three last shapes or configurations, as well as three different kinds of lasts. The first shape, a straight last, is straight (Figure 2.9a) and gives more support on the medial (inside) side of the shoe. As the foot pronates, rolling over to the inside, there is a base under the foot to offer support. On the other hand, for the underpronated foot there is the curved last, the second type (Figure 2.9c). As the name implies, the last will have a C-shaped curve, most having about a 14-degree curve. The curved last offers little support and succumbs to the lack of support on the medial side. The curved last is ideal for the foot that has a neutral gate, or the foot that wants to roll to the lateral (outside) side. A runner who pronates in a curved-last shoe will usually have problems. As the foot rolls inward, there is a lack of support under the medial side due to the "C" shape of the last. The third shape, a modified last (Figure 2.9b), is a combination of the other two. This shoe has a slight inward curve

▶ **Figure 2.8** A wooden last.

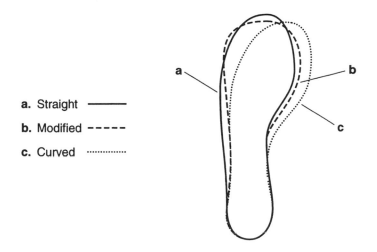

a. Straight ———

b. Modified - - - - -

c. Curved ⋯⋯⋯⋯

▶ **Figure 2.9** The type of last used depends on where the runner's foot needs support.

(7 degrees) to accommodate the shape of most feet and also affords good inside stability.

The construction or design of the shoe, also called lasting, contributes to support features on the shoe interior. There are three types of construction lasting: board lasting, slip lasting and combination lasting (Figure 2.10). The first type, board lasting, is a shoe with a full-length Texon fiber board, running from heel to toe. Texon is a thin, rigid, high-density cardboard that offers the advantage of torsional stability to the shoe, stabilizing the foot during a torquing or twisting action in its longitudinal axis and supporting the overpronating foot. For the off-road runner, this last minimizes the feel of stubble in the forefoot of the shoe as the foot comes in contact with rocks, branches, and other obstacles. One disadvantage to the full board last is that it stiffens the forefoot of the shoe, restricting the flexibility of the shoe's forefoot. For this reason very few companies still use this last in running shoes. Slip lasting may be compared to a moccasin since it uses no Texon or fiberboard in its construction. The slip last has very little torsional support and thus is not a good lasting for the pronator. Its big advantage is greater comfort due to fewer foot restrictions. This type of lasting is also great for racing shoes or rigid feet with a high arch.

Choosing the Correct Running Shoe

A runner needs to look at all shoe features before buying. First consider your foot type, then determine the features required. One fairly easy way to determine your foot type is to take the "wet test." Wet your foot and stand flat-footed on a dry surface. The imprint that you leave will give you a good idea if your foot is mobile, rigid, or neutral. If the print is very broad through the arch area, you have a very mobile foot, and chances are you will need a stability shoe for pronation. On the other hand, if your foot leaves no print at all between the ball of the foot and heel, then you have a very rigid foot and need a shoe with very little support and extra cushion (i.e., a shoe that is slip lasted on a curved last) (Figure 2.11). If you are somewhere in the middle, you will have no special needs and will probably have good luck with most shoes.

Finding a shoe to accommodate every foot may seem impossible. However, if you know the materials and can recognize the basic features of shoe construction, and if you know what foot type you are trying to accommodate, then you should be able to match those features with any runner's needs.

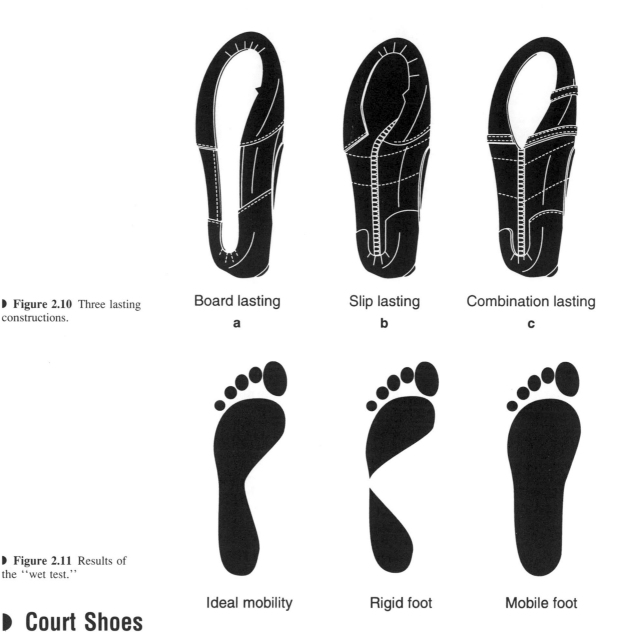

▶ **Figure 2.10** Three lasting constructions.

Board lasting
a

Slip lasting
b

Combination lasting
c

▶ **Figure 2.11** Results of the "wet test."

Ideal mobility

Rigid foot

Mobile foot

▶ Court Shoes

A court shoe is defined as an athletic shoe designed for lateral stability and traction in addition to forward motion. The biggest difference between a court shoe and a running shoe is in the basic types of motion that each accommodates. A runner is moving forward in a straight or curved path. The typical court motion is lateral as well as forward and includes sudden starting and stopping. The requirements of the court shoe compared to the running shoe change greatly with this in mind. An athlete using lateral motion creates greater stress on the outside of the shoe. As the body goes in motion to the right, the play may suddenly change direction to the left. The athlete must make a foot plant and abruptly change direction to the left to follow the action of the game. In doing this, the body's momentum is established in one direction; then suddenly it must change to the opposite direction, which requires a force that stresses the outside edge of the shoe.

If the athlete is using an ordinary running shoe, two things usually happen: The running shoe, typically too high in the heel area, will place the foot too high off the ground. This in turn will cause the foot to roll off the outside edge of the shoe. This tendency to roll not only affects the person's ability to change direction easily, but it may also cause the foot to roll off the outside edge and sprain the lateral ankle. Secondly, the running shoe does not have the side stability to handle the outward pressure, and sooner or later the upper will tear loose from the midsole.

To accommodate this side-to-side pressure, the manufacturers lowered the whole shoe platform closer to the ground to maintain a lower center of gravity. This helps keep the foot upright and stable. Court shoes also have what is called a *shell sole* (Figure 2.12). Newer and lighter court shoes are using 1/2- to 3/4-inch shells that have less sidewall rubber but still maintain forefoot support. To attach the upper to the shell sole, it is not only glued but also sewn to the sidewall for extra toughness that prevents the sides from giving out. On the contrary, the running-style upper is only glued to its midsole.

Outsoles

The outsole design or tread pattern on court shoes is also quite different from other styles of footwear (Figure 2.13). Understandably, traction is a major factor in any court sport. The *herring bone* is probably the most common tread pattern for court shoes because it is fairly efficient in providing traction in all four directions. A modified version of the herring bone design adds a pattern of circles on the ball of the foot. Because there is no edge or side to a circle, it will enhance stopping ability in all directions. Also, putting a circle under the ball of the foot facilitates a pivot or rotation without undue stress on the knee.

Some outsoles have an outrigger—the outsole is flared at the lateral forefoot area to give a broader base for added support. With this broader base you are less apt to fall off the outside edge of the shoe platform.

Outsole design for traction is somewhat complicated. Too little traction is obviously a problem; on the other hand, too much friction while performing a pivot with the foot fixed transfers rotational stress to the knee. The outsole must combine features for the proper blend of traction and slide.

One last feature of importance in the outsole is the compounds used. For the typical indoor shoe a softer rubber is used to increase traction with the floor. Most indoor floors are typically wood, and a softer sole will have better traction. On the other hand, an outdoor court, such as an asphalt tennis court, is very abrasive. In this case a harder compound is used in the outsole and in the toe area to prevent rapid wear. For outdoor court play polyurethane, with an even greater abrasion

▶ **Figure 2.12** A shell sole is built up on the sides to create a pocket for the foot.

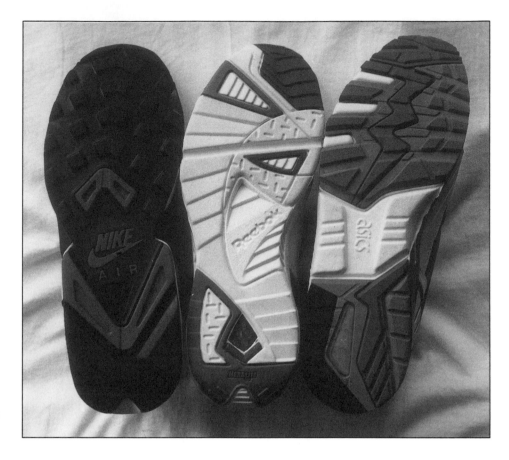

▶ **Figure 2.13** Three kinds of outsoles.

factor than most rubbers, is put in the outsole of tennis shoes. Many shoe manufacturers have gone to private companies and have had special compounds made to use in their outsoles. There are many different names, but they all have the same purpose in mind—good traction with a longer life span.

Midsoles

Running shoes are still the driving force in the research and development of technical features. In a typical vertical jump, the body is subjected to stresses up to eight times the body's weight. The development of the running shoe made technology available to the court shoe market. As mentioned before, EVA was the major cushion material used in running shoes. EVA material is being used in most court styles as well as Air, Gel, ERS, Energy Wave, and other systems. These cushion systems have been introduced to midsoles to enhance athletes' endeavors as well as reduce their injuries. Introducing these new systems also acts as an extension of running technology, which helps in marketing the shoes.

Uppers

The court shoe upper is similar to a running model, but is primarily made of leather for extra stability and durability. A new addition to the court-style upper is the forefoot strap, which is typically made of an extra piece of leather or soft piece of polyurethane to prevent the outside forefoot from over stretching at the little toe. Stretching is caused by the increased pressure of the lateral motion. To compensate, the heel cups are extended up higher in the back, creating a deeper heel pocket helps to stabilize the foot. The introduction of polyurethane foot frames has also helped in stabilizing the base of the foot and is used widely in most footwear categories. It has an anatomical shape that accommodates the natural foot shape. By dropping the foot down into the shoe frame, you maintain a lower center of gravity.

Uppers are found in three basic styles: lowtops, midtops, and hightops. A low top is the old standby that is somewhat lighter than the other two but gives fairly good overall stability. The midtop design has a deeper heel pocket that in turn creates greater heel security. It does not help ankle stability, however, because the upper ends at the ankle joint axis. In order to gain ankle support, the upper must extend past the ankle itself as in the high top.

▶ The Cross Trainer

A new type of shoe evolved in the late 1980s: the *cross trainer*, which originated as a result of the more versatile athlete doing more than one activity. These fitness buffs do not do any one sport to the exclusion of the others, but enjoyed a variety of sports. Rather than buying a running shoe for a limited amount of running and a basketball shoe for one or two games a month, the versatile athletes could buy a cross trainer for all activities.

The cross trainer, spawned by Nike (Figure 2.14), was accepted very quickly. It consists of a court shoe in the forefoot by the way of support straps, partial shell sole in the midfoot, and a court shoe outsole. In the rear foot it is more of a running shoe with a slight heel rise to allow for cushion, but it is low enough to accommodate lateral movement. The cross trainer makes an excellent shoe for those who participate in a wide variety of sports; it is unsuitable, however, for sport specificity. The manufacturing of cross trainers coincided with the market's "fitness revolution." Athletes in general were stretching their horizons in a multisport direction spurred by the increasing popularity of triathlons as well as the variety available in athletics.

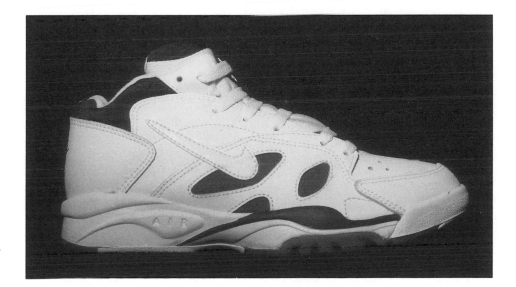

▶ **Figure 2.14** Cross-training shoes carry exercisers through any sport.

▶ Summary

The athletic shoe revolution may seem rather fast-paced and at points somewhat expensive. However, as a whole, the serious athlete, the recreational enthusiast, or those who merely want to stay in fashion have all benefited. Overall features have improved to give us more performance than ever before. This has been done with enhanced fit and lighter shoe weight, but also with uncompromised comfort.

One key feature that cannot be overlooked is overall fit. Features like air bags, gel packets, and lycra-sleeved units are used in vain if your performance footwear does not fit properly. So the old adage "If the shoe fits wear it," is now truer than ever. This is one area in which athletic shoe companies have seen big opportunities to expand their market shares. Midsole technology has slowed down, and fit now is the new frontier.

CHAPTER 3

Hiking and Climbing Boots

Mark A. Smith, MS

Boots used for hiking go back as many years as boots themselves. American recreational climbers first used slightly modified boots made for loggers around the turn of the century. These boots were entirely leather, except for metal lace fittings and the hobnails pounded into the leather sole. This basic "work boot" was 8 to 10 inches high, and the user relied on socks or straw for warmth and cushioning.

World War II signaled the end of the logger's boot for American recreational wildlanders. The Mountain Troops of the Second World War brought from the Alps a European climbing boot called the "Eigerboot" (Manning, 1986). This European design was the boot that Dr. Frankenstein fitted to his brainchild, and the direct predecessor of the modern hiking boot. It was a complex construction of thick leather slabs reinforced with steel, and was padded, hinged at the ankle to permit walking, lined for warmth, and heavily soled with rubber lugs.

As the popularity of backcountry recreation grew so did the hiking boot industry. Manufacturers began to develop lighter and less expensive boots that were well suited for mountain trails and meadows. Environmental concerns grew as well, and the unforgiving heavy lug sole was viewed with contempt as it tore up the fragile countryside. This, coupled with the elusive search for the featherweight boot, led a running shoe manufacturer, New Balance, nearly a decade ago to merge running shoe technology with the needs of the hiker. These new, so called trail boots or "ultra lights" (Komito, 1989) entered the hiking boot line offering the light weight of nylon (with leather reinforcement) and more flexible, softer soles, all at a lower price.

At the other end of the hiking boot spectrum, expedition or mountaineering boots seem to be gravitating toward the rigidity, durability, waterproofability, and cold resistance of plastic (Woodward, 1985). Lately these boots have been accepted by many expedition mountain climbers, yet traditional leather boots are still the mainstay for most serious hikers (Manning, 1986). Presently, the hiking boot industry is dynamic, and it appears to be striving to meet the needs of every type of outdoor recreational hiker.

This chapter is organized into sections that describe anatomy and construction and types of hiking boots (classified according to use in order of durability). Types of hiking boots discussed are trail, hiking, climbing and mountaineering, expedition, and technical rock climbing (not actually part of this category). Anatomy and construction will be discussed first because the type of hiking boot depends on what the boots are made of and how they are constructed.

▶ Anatomy and Construction

All boots are composed of three parts: the upper, the middle (insole and midsole); and the lower (outsole). This section discusses the three types of upper material (leather, leather-synthetic, and plastic), the components of the boot (anatomy), and boot construction.

Types of Upper Materials

upper—The topmost portion of the boot, which is attached to the midsole and outsole.

The **upper** can generally be described as the portion of the exterior boot that exists above the sole. It can be made of leather, a combination of leather and synthetic fabric (e.g., nylon), or plastic. No material, however, has yet been found that matches leather's combination of flexibility, breathability, waterproofability, durability, and comfort (Manning, 1986). Nonetheless, plastic and the leather-synthetic combination boots are often chosen, depending on the hiker's needs and the environment in which the boots will be used.

Leather

Leather goes through a lengthy and complex process before it is ready for use on boots. It has to be cleaned, treated (tanned), and cut to a usable thickness. Tanning is accomplished by one of three methods: chrome tanning, vegetal tanning, or combination tanning, which combines the first two processes (*Hiking Boot Repair,* 1979; Manning, 1986).

Chrome tanning is the most commonly used technique in America and Europe (*Hiking Boot Repair,* 1979; Manning, 1986). The process involves placing cleaned hides in a rotating drum and running them through a solution of chromium salts. Coming out of the tanning solution the leather looks dry and has a hard finish. The pores of the leather are then waxed or silicon filled for some degree of water repellency and stiffness. Depending on the type of leather, it is treated with oil to make it softer.

Vegetal tanning uses an oil-like vegetable material derived from plants and woods called *bark tannin* (*Hiking Boot Repair,* 1979; Manning, 1986). This process is favored by some manufacturers because it gives a soft, supple finish that has a wet, oily look.

Hide straight from the animal is too thick for even the heaviest boots, so it has to be split into sheets of varying thickness. The highest grade leather, originally the outer protective layer of the cow, is called *full-grain* or *top-grain* leather. Full-grain leather is used for the upper in all-leather hiking boots because it is stiffer, more waterproof, and more abrasion resistant than any other layer. It may, however, be reversed (called *rough-out*) when sewn to the boot, leaving the water-repellent side next to the foot. The reversal results in a rough outer leather exposed to the elements. Some boot makers believe that this preserves the leather's water repellency because the water-repellent side will never be exposed to the abrasive elements of the exterior world (Manning, 1986).

Other layers taken from the hide are called *splits* (Manning, 1986). Splits are traditionally used for insoles and midsoles in leather boots. When used for an upper, split leather is called *suede,* which is a poor choice for wet trails because it is not waterproof. But it performs well on dry, hot paths because it is lightweight and very breathable. For this reason synthetic-leather boot makers frequently use split leather for the leather-reinforced portion of the boot.

Leather Synthetic

The application of running shoe technology was the catalyst for leather-synthetic development of uppers and midsoles in hiking boots. The quest for the lighter, more flexible, and more breathable boot was answered by incorporating nylon fabrics to the upper (Chase, 1985a; Komito, 1989; Manning, 1986). These types of boots may weigh up to 34 ounces less than their all-leather counterparts. Reduced weight translates into less leg fatigue and a shorter time to break in the boot (Manning, 1986). Because nylon breathes more effectively than leather, leather-synthetic boots also prevent sweaty feet. However, what leather-synthetic boots offer in breathability they tend to lose in waterproofness (Manning, 1986). They also won't stand up to abuse as well as all-leather boots, because a mix of fabrics requires more seams, which compromises the structural integrity of the boot; nylon is also less durable than leather.

Nylons used include ballistic nylon, nylon pack cloth, DuroMesh™ nylon, and the most popular, Cordura™ (Manning, 1986). These fabrics may be coated with a water-repellent substance. At areas of heavy wear, leather is sewn (rather than or in addition to gluing) to increase boot life. Full-grain or a split leather is used depending on the intended use of the boot.

Plastic

Hiking boot makers borrowed yet another technological advance from another sport, skiing. It all started when Bob Lange in the early 1960s decided to give up making hula hoops in favor of developing plastic ski boots. Lange's polyurethane breakthrough gave skiers not only stiffness, lightness, and durability, but also warmth and waterproofness (Woodward, 1985).

By the early 1970s many Alpine ski boot companies were experimenting with plastic mountaineering boots. It wasn't until an Italian boot manufacturer, San Marco, perfected the technique of injection molding the uppers and cementing the soles that plastic boots found favor with mountaineers (Woodward, 1985). For cold-weather technical climbers the benefits were obvious. Plastic boots were exceptionally durable, warm (especially with the prescribed inner boot), waterproof, stiff (for cramponing), and light. On the other hand, drawbacks were lack of breathability and insufficient flex at the ankle (Manning, 1986; Woodward, 1985).

Components of the Upper

The boot shown in Figure 3.1 represents a composite of parts for all boots. Discussed in this section are the various components found in all types of

collar (or scree collar)—The uppermost part of the boot, usually around the ankle area; its purpose is to protect the ankle and Achilles tendon from trail hazards.
heel—The raised portion of the outsole that supports the heel bone.
toe—The foremost portion of the boot.
tongue—The flap of material that fits into the lacing system of the boot.
closure—Any part of the tongue and lacing system that keeps trail debris and water out of the boot.

boots. The major parts of the upper where these components exist are the **collar, heel, toe, tongue** and **closure,** and the lacing system.

The Upper in General

The upper provides all the support for the foot except for the sole (Manning, 1986). Two schools of thought exist as to how best to build an upper (Manning, 1986). One school holds that a single piece of leather should be used, thus keeping seams—lines of potential weakness and leakage—to a minimum. The other school defends sectional construction; that is, making the upper from two or more pieces of leather believing that the upper can more easily be made to conform to the contour of the foot; and that smaller pieces of leather can be used, or leather can be combined with other fabrics for a less expensive and lighter weight boot. Whatever the case, all-leather boot makers typically opt for single-piece construction, whereas leather-synthetic manufacturers are forced to use sectional patterns.

Boots with stitching on the upper use three varieties: single, double, and triple stitching (Manning, 1986). Double stitching, the most popular, has two lines of stitching at every point, thus reducing the chance that all stitches will be cut at once. Triple stitching adds yet another layer of protection.

The interior lining may be complete or partial. Linings are either a softer, supple leather like pigskin or calfskin, or some type of fabric (usually Cambrelle, a soft, rugged nylon that feels like tightly woven wool). In the better boots the lining lets the foot glide in and out of the boot and minimizes chafing, hot spots, and blisters.

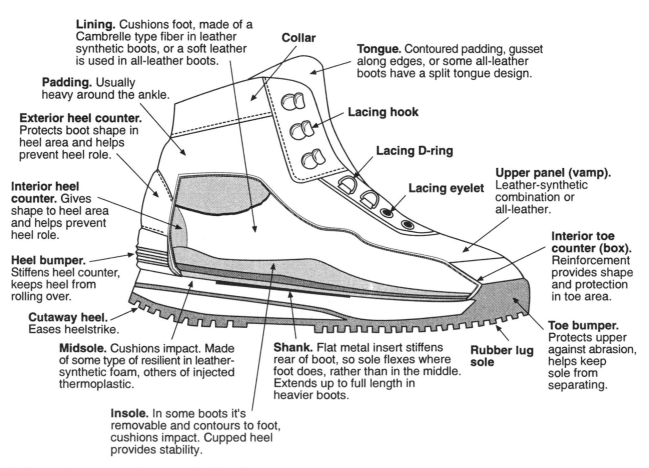

Lining. Cushions foot, made of a Cambrelle type fiber in leather synthetic boots, or a soft leather is used in all-leather boots.

Collar

Tongue. Contoured padding, gusset along edges, or some all-leather boots have a split tongue design.

Padding. Usually heavy around the ankle.

Exterior heel counter. Protects boot shape in heel area and helps prevent heel role.

Lacing hook

Interior heel counter. Gives shape to heel area and helps prevent heel role.

Lacing D-ring

Lacing eyelet

Upper panel (vamp). Leather-synthetic combination or all-leather.

Heel bumper. Stiffens heel counter, keeps heel from rolling over.

Interior toe counter (box). Reinforcement provides shape and protection in toe area.

Cutaway heel. Eases heelstrike.

Midsole. Cushions impact. Made of some type of resilient in leather-synthetic foam, others of injected thermoplastic.

Shank. Flat metal insert stiffens rear of boot, so sole flexes where foot does, rather than in the middle. Extends up to full length in heavier boots.

Rubber lug sole

Toe bumper. Protects upper against abrasion, helps keep sole from separating.

Insole. In some boots it's removable and contours to foot, cushions impact. Cupped heel provides stability.

▶ **Figure 3.1** Anatomy of a composite hiking boot.

Most boots have padding at least around the ankle. The padding material is typically made of foam, rubber, or felt and inserted between the outer wall and the liner. Insulated boots are designed for extreme cold and should be avoided for ordinary hiking purposes.

The Collar

Most hiking boot collars fall in the ranges of 5-1/2 to 7-1/2 inches high, though cuts as low as 4-1/2 inches can be found in walking and trail shoes (*Hiking Boot Repair,* 1979; Manning, 1986). The *collar,* commonly called the *scree collar,* has two functions. First, and most important, the collar is designed to support and protect the ankle from misstepping and trail hazards. The second function is comfort while hiking, primarily in the Achilles tendon area. Some collars include a roll of foam padding around this area. Still other collars are cut lower around the tendon area and are padded to reduce irritation.

The Back of the Upper (Heel)

interior heel counter—Forms a cup around the heel to help anchor the foot in the boot and prevent heel roll; it is usually a stiff leather sewn into the upper.

exterior heel counter A stiff patch of material applied to the outside of the boot primarily for protection of the boot itself.

heel bumper—A stiff exterior device placed between the upper and midsole or outsole to prevent the heel from rolling over the edge of the sole.

toe counter—A stiff material placed in the toe portion of the boot upper to protect the toes from rocks; also called a toe guard, hard toe, or box toe.

An **interior heel counter,** found on all but the lightest boots (*Hiking Boot Repair,* 1979; Manning, 1986; Perlman, 1988a), is a concave piece of leather, rigid fiber, thermoplastic, or molded nylon inserted inside the upper (interior heel counter) or outside the upper (exterior heel counter).

The **exterior heel counter** performs more of a protective function for the boot itself. The interior heel counter cups the heel and helps anchor the foot to the boot sole. Its purpose is to minimize ankle roll (twisting) and vertical motion during heel lift. Running shoe researchers have found that lateral stability of the foot is best ensured by a stiff heel counter.

A heel cup or **heel bumper** is an exterior device that stiffens the heel counter and helps to further prevent the heel from rolling over. Also originally designed for running shoes, the heel bumper is placed on some leather-synthetic boots to guard against abrasion.

The Toe

Rock-toe encounters are so frequent that nearly all modern all-leather hiking and climbing boots have hard toe sections called **toe counters** (or toe guards, hard toe, or box toe) (*Hiking Boot Repair,* 1979; Manning, 1986; Perlman, 1988a). Some leather-synthetic boots have hard toe counters as well. Toe counters range from being slightly stiffened by a piece of plastic inside the toe area to complete forefoot protection by leather, leatherboard, or molded nylon.

Many softer, more flexible boots leave out the toe counter for comfort. But such boots will almost always have a *toe bumper,* which is actually part of the sole glued to the upper. The toe bumper is designed to protect the upper against abrasion and help keep the sole from separating.

Tongue and Closure

There are three concerns for the boot designer for the tongue and closure area (Manning, 1986). The tongue and closure is designed to prevent water from coming in through the gap around the lacing area, allowing easy entry and exit into and out of the boot, and to ensure comfort while walking. There are two basic tongue designs in modern hiking boots: the *gusseted tongue* and the *split*

▶ **Figure 3.2** Heavy-duty leather expedition boots with split tongue design (left) and gusseted tongue design (right).

tongue (*Hiking Boot Repair,* 1979; Manning, 1986). Both are illustrated in Figure 3.2.

gusseted tongue—
Sometimes called the bellowed tongue, it uses extra material attached to both the upper and the tongue that folds in when the boot is laced up to keep trail debris and water out of the boot.

The primary feature of the **gusseted tongue,** sometimes called the bellowed tongue, is that it prevents water from seeping into the boot. This type of tongue is attached (sewn) to the front of the boot with folds of fabric or leather giving it a bellowed appearance. When opened, the gusseted tongue allows the foot to easily enter and exit the boot. Folded, this tongue style forms a neat, comfortable watertight barrier. Some variations of this style use two tongues: a soft inner tongue designed purely for comfort and an outer gusseted tongue for waterproofing. Gusseted tongues are mostly found in lighter, all-leather hiking boots and leather-synthetic boots.

split tongue—Overlapping
flaps of material or leather that fold over the tongue to prevent trail debris or water from entering the boot; usually found in heavy-duty boots.

The simple **split tongue** has halves of the upper drawn together over an inner tongue by laces. Like the gusseted tongue, it can keep water from entering the boot, though not as well. Most split tongue designs are more sophisticated, having two tongues, a soft inner tongue, and an outer tongue split down the middle in which both halves overlap. This split portion is actually part of the upper. Used primarily in heavy hiking boots, the more elaborate split tongues open very wide, permitting easy foot entry when the boot is either wet or frozen.

There are some designs that incorporate both tongue styles. Whatever the case, if the boot is designed for more than light walking it should be large, long, well padded, and contoured to snugly and comfortably fit the foot while laced.

Lacing

Boot lacing systems can include eyelets, D-rings (also called swivel eyelets), hooks, or a combination of them all (Manning, 1986). Only a few boots have all eyelet lacing. Eyelets are formed by grommets set directly into the upper, and they have the advantage of being very durable; but they are quite tedious to lace, especially if the boot collar is high.

More common are boots that either have eyelets or D-rings partway up; then hooks are employed for quicker lacing and unlacing. D-rings are attached to a clip that is riveted to the upper. Similarly, hooks are a single piece of metal riveted to the upper. Utilization of both the D-ring and the hooks combines easy lacing with maximum water repellency. (Note that using eyelets would be difficult and cumbersome, if not impossible, for split-tongue designs.)

As for laces, nylon is almost exclusively used in modern hiking boots. Formerly leather was used, but with a tendency to stretch when wet it loosened easily and frequently broke. Nylon has greater durability and far less elasticity under all conditions when tightened.

Components of the Sole

All elements of the upper combined—the collar, the heel counter, and the toe counter—are designed to protect the upper part of the foot from dirt, water, and trail hazards that may cause ankle twisting. The function of the sole—insole, midsole, and outsole—is to protect and cushion the sole of the foot from hard trails and sharp objects and to provide traction (Chase, 1985a; Manning, 1986).

The recent running shoe advances in technology are having their most profound impact on insole and midsole design. This is especially true for leather-synthetic types of boots.

Insole

insole—The inside bottom portion of the boot that bears the weight of the foot.

The **insole** is what the foot rests on when inside the boot. It is contoured to the foot for support and provides some cushion for impact. All-leather type boots usually have soft and sometimes padded leather that functions as the insole. Some leather boots may also have a Cambrelle (nylon), sweat-resistant liner layered over the leather.

The lighter, leather-synthetic boots will frequently have a removable insole that is disposable once it has either worn out or lost its cushioning effect. Removable insoles can be dried out overnight if they get wet, or can even be replaced with a spare pair—both advantageous features. Removable insoles are typically formed with some type of polyurethane foam covered by a layer of tightly woven cotton or Cambrelle. Foam insoles can more effectively be shaped to the contour of the foot than all-leather insoles. Such contouring forms a cup around the heel for stability and a snug fit.

Recently, some boot makers have been concentrating on more sophisticated padding in the insole at certain high-impact points. Spenco Gel has shown up in the heel and the ball of the foot in more elaborate boots (Chase, 1985b).

Midsole

midsole—The portion of the boot between the insole and the outsole used to stiffen the boot and absorb shock; it is usually made from layered leather in more rugged boots and from an EVA foam in lighter hiking boots.

As hiking boots have evolved, the **midsole** has become the foundation of the modern boot (Chase, 1985a). Offering stiffness and cushion to the foot, the midsole is the portion of the boot to which other boot parts are attached. It is in the development of the midsole that running shoe technology has had the greatest impact. Breakthroughs have come in the form of lighter boots and greater comfort to the foot.

The design of most hiking boots has changed, becoming more like the lighter, stronger, and more flexible running shoes since most of the weight came out of the sole (Chase, 1985a). Instead of the traditional stiff and heavy solid high-carbon rubber, layered leather, or wood that some heavier boots still use, boot makers are using materials like **EVA** (ethyl vinyl acetate) for the insole (Chase, 1985a; Manning, 1986). EVA was the first of the new foamy plastics used that could compress and spring back into shape. Newer expanded rubber composition has been used by other boot makers to avoid the permanent compression of EVA after prolonged use (i.e., EVA will squash down underfoot and stay squashed).

EVA—An abbreviation for ethyl vinyl acetate, a foamy material used in the mid-soles of lighter weight hiking boots because of its flexibility, resiliency, and light weight.

heel wedge—A stiff foam or leather wedge placed in the midsole to absorb shock.

At the heel of the midsole there may exist a stiffer, more dense plastic foam called a **heel wedge** to further absorb heel shock (Chase, 1985a; Manning, 1986). Some boots also have forefoot wedges. Today there are many variations on the theme of lightweight midsole construction, but all try to accomplish the same goal: a lighter, more durable, and more flexible boot.

shank—A metal plate or some other stiff material placed in the rear of a boot so that the outsole of the boot flexes where the foot does.

Most heavy boots and some of the lighter, leather-synthetic boots have a **shank** (Manning, 1986), the purpose of which is to stiffen the rear of the boot so that the sole flexes where the foot does. Placed in the middle of the boot between the heel and the ball of the foot, the shank also provides support to the arch, protects the instep, and holds the foot straight (Manning, 1986). The shank can span the shoe length in heavier boots. There are a variety of shank materials, including tempered spring steel, plastic, reconstituted leather, laminated wood, and stiffened nylon.

Outsole

lug sole—Another name for the patterned bottom of the outsole.

outsole—The bottom-most part of the boot that is made of a hard, durable rubber and that comes in contact with the trail.

The original **lug sole (outsole)** was invented by an Italian, Vito Bramani, in 1935 (*Hiking Boot Repair,* 1979; Manning, 1986; Schnee, personal communication October 11, 1989). Vibram lug soles are synthetic rubber designed with deep cleats to provide superior gripping power. Today, there are dozens of rubber compounds and lug designs for hiking boots; only a few are illustrated in Figure 3.3. The materials range from very hard and durable high-carbon neoprene rubber to soft gum rubber. The harder soles, resistant to cuts and abrasions, are very long wearing and are used in heavier duty boots.

Softer soled boots were developed with environmental concerns in mind because they don't tear up the terrain like high-carbon rubber. Rock climbing boots use the softest form of rubber to grip the rock and conform to a variety of shapes that are needed in crevasses.

Lug patterns vary in geometrical pattern, pattern design, and lug depth. The geometrical design name is the style of the pattern itself. The illustrations in Figure 3.3 show several examples of lug geometry. More demanding terrain requires a more aggressive geometry for gripping power, much like an off-road vehicle has much stronger looking tread than typical passenger car tire tread. Rock climbing

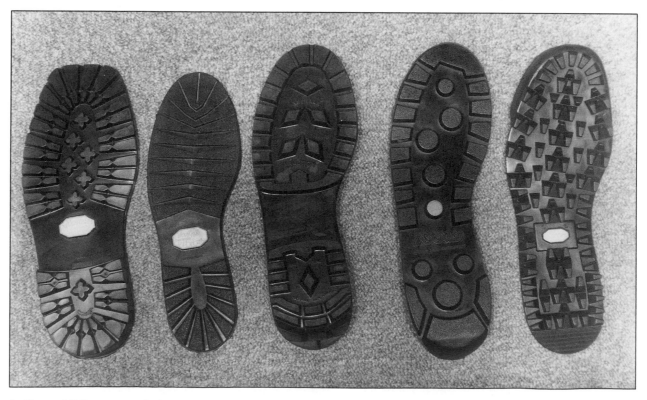

▶ **Figure 3.3** Lug pattern designs.

boots have subtle geometry, if any at all, because rock climbers need to have as much surface area of the soft gummy sole on the rocks as possible.

Density of the pattern refers to how closely and frequently the pattern is duplicated on the sole. For example, rib patterns can be very close together making many ribs, or generously spaced apart creating only a few ribs. As you can see, density is closely related to geometry. Basically, high-density patterns are used on gentler terrain; low-density patterns are found on boots used in more demanding conditions.

Lug depths range from shallow to deep. A shallow lug has less traction than a deep lug on every sort of surface except rock faces. However, shallow lugs are less disruptive to delicate landscape. Some lug designers are incorporating a beveled pattern (Komito, 1989) that opens at an increasingly greater angle toward the bottom to better shed trail debris, keeping the lug free of encumbering mud and soil.

Some lug designs use a cut-away heel or beveled heel rather than the conventional squared-off design (Manning, 1986; Perlman, 1988a). A cut-away heel is said to offer greater comfort and a quicker stride, because the shape of the sole is contoured for more natural foot placement thus easing heel strike.

In general, relaxed geometry, high-density, low-depth lug patterns are used for gentler terrain and rock climbing. Conversely, aggressive geometry, relatively lower density, and high lug depth are found in heavier boots that are used for more difficult, rocky terrain.

Boot Construction

last—A form around which a boot is built that determines the size and fit of the boot.

Various processes are utilized in joining the sole to the upper. Boots are manufactured according to a predetermined foot model called the **last** (*Hiking Boot Repair,* 1979; Perlman, 1988a). This form determines the shape, shoe size, and fit of the boot. Lasts are made to conform to specific measurements for length, girth at the ball, waist, instep and heel, heel height, and tread and toe spring.

Typically, uppers are attached to the soles by a cementing (adhesive) process and/or with one of several stitching methods. The method employed is a major contributor to boot strength, durability, and flexibility. There are five basic methods in boot construction: vulcanizing, cementing, Littleway construction, the Goodyear welt, and the Norwegian welt (*Hiking Boot Repair,* 1979; Manning, 1986). Each method has its own distinct advantages.

Vulcanizing and Cementing

vulcanizing—A process of outsole manufacturing where the outsole is bonded by heat and pressure to the midsole; it is considered the weakest form of boot construction.

cementing—The process of bonding the midsole to the upper.

Vulcanizing, the weakest form of construction, is a process where a preformed rubber outsole is bonded by heat and pressure to the upper (Manning, 1986). However, this process is the most inexpensive, and it can be found in some of the lighter boots and rock climbing boots.

Cementing, shown in Figure 3.4, is becoming a very popular process with the proliferation of lighter, leather-synthetic boots (*Hiking Boot Repair,* 1979; Manning, 1986). With the development of more sophisticated adhesives the outsole can be glued or cemented directly to the midsole or upper. Coupling the vulcanizing and cementing techniques is called *injection molding.* In this process, molten neoprene rubber (the outsole) is applied under pressure to the midsole; as it dries the outsole is formed.

Littleway Construction

Although **Littleway construction** (Figure 3.5) uses a stitching process, the term usually is not included because ordinarily the term "welting" is reserved

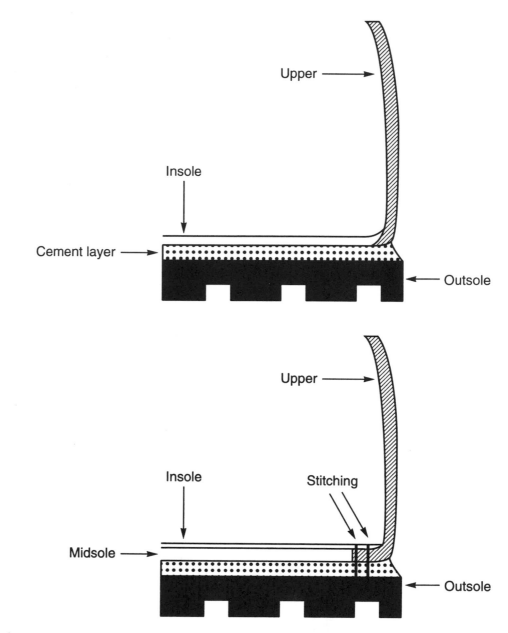

▶ Figure 3.4 Cemented construction.

▶ Figure 3.5 Littleway construction.

Littleway construction—A boot construction technique used in trail and hiking boots to attach the upper to the outsole by means of folding the upper material under the insole and sewing it directly to the midsole, where the outsole is then glued.

for outside-stitched or welted boots (*Hiking Boot Repair*, 1979; Manning, 1986). Welting is the process of stitching the components of the boots together (*Hiking Boot Repair*, 1979; Manning, 1986). A welt is the narrow piece of leather stitched to the top edged surface of the outsole located outside of the upper.

Nevertheless, Littleway construction does utilize stitches—the inside-stitching method. In this method the upper is folded under and sandwiched between the insole and midsole, the outsole is glued (or sometimes vulcanized) to the bottom of the midsole, and the layers are fastened together by a double row of lockstitching. The stitches pass through all but the outsole and are concealed within the boot, thus protected from moisture and abrasion from the outside world.

Littleway construction enables the sole to be trimmed very closely and nearly flush with the upper. This is a desirable feature, because it allows the force of the hiker's weight to be converted directly underfoot. Other advantages of Littleway-constructed boots are that they tend to be lighter, more waterproof than outside-stitched boots, and they are less expensive to build and repair.

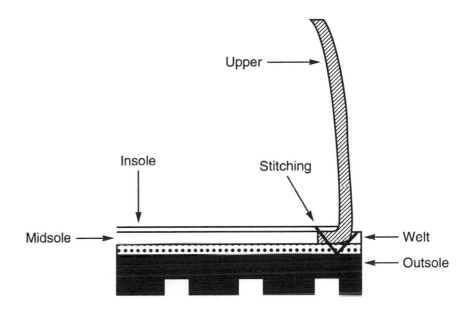

▶ Figure 3.6 Goodyear welt construction.

The better trail shoes, most hiking boots, and a few climbing boots are constructed this way.

Goodyear Welt

Goodyear welt—A boot construction process that singly stitches a welt around the periphery of the boots to fasten the upper to the outsole; it is typically used in more rugged boot types.

As its name implies, the **Goodyear welt** incorporates a welt in the boot's construction (*Hiking Boot Repair*, 1979; Manning, 1986) (see Figure 3.6). In this form of boot construction the welt and the insole are the unique features. The upper is placed and secured between a rib on the insole and the welt; there the upper is sewn. The welt goes around the entire perimeter of the boot and is sewn vertically to the midsole layers. A Goodyear-welted boot can be recognized by the single line of stitching on the welt.

The Goodyear welt dates back many centuries, but gained wide popularity about 100 years ago with the invention of the Goodyear stitching machine (*Hiking Boot Repair*, 1979). This meant the boot could be sewn by machine rather than the much slower hand process. Today, most men's street shoes are made with this process as well as many American brand name boots.

The Goodyear welt is typically used in heavier hiking boots and tends to be somewhat stiff and heavy. Accordingly, such characteristics provide the necessary protection and support on more demanding, rough terrain.

Norwegian Welt

Norwegian welt—The most heavy-duty boot construction, used in mountaineering and expedition boots, which uses two rows of stitches through a welt to secure the upper to the outsole.

The **Norwegian welt** (refer to Figure 3.7), sometimes called the European welt, is the most durable form of boot construction (*Hiking Boot Repair*, 1979; Manning, 1986). Thus, boots constructed with the Norwegian welt process can typically be found on heavy-duty hiking and mountaineering boots. This welt features two rows of stitching: one row angling inward, almost horizontal, securing the insole to the upper; the second sewn vertically, joining the midsole to the outward-turned upper. Norwegian-welted boots can be identified by two or more rows of stitches on the welt.

An advantage of the Norwegian welt besides durability is that with this type of construction the last can remain in the boot until construction is completed. This allows for more consistent construction without distortion of the boot,

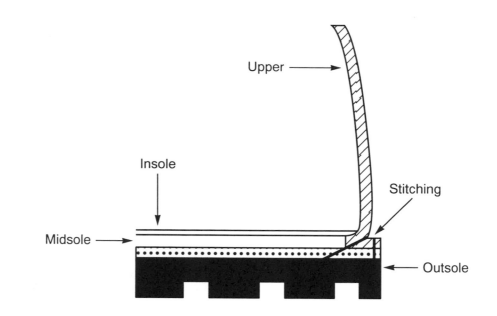

▶ **Figure 3.7** Norwegian welt construction.

thereby ensuring a good fit. However, disadvantages are higher manufacturing costs and the vulnerability of the outside stitching to leakage and wear.

▶ Types of Hiking and Climbing Boots

There are four general types of hiking and climbing boots: trail shoes and boots, which can be classified into inexpensive and expensive categories; hiking boots (leather-synthetic and traditional all-leather varieties); climbing and mountaineering boots; and expedition boots (*Hiking Boot Repair,* 1979; Manning, 1986). Technical rock climbing boots will also be discussed as they are highly evolved and specialized climbing boots.

Trail Boots

trail boots—The lightest member of the hiking boot family, which is usually made from a leather-synthetic combination.

Sometimes called "trail shoes" because of their light weight and light-duty use, **trail boots** are usually fashioned from nylon and split, or suede leather uppers and flexible soles (Figure 3.8). Trail boots are intended for gentle terrain with light loads (if any at all) (Manning, 1986; Schnee, personal communication, October 11, 1989). They offer little support and protection from the harsher outdoor elements.

The more inexpensive trail boots are limited to day hikes at best (Manning, 1986; Schnee, personal communication, October 11, 1989). Trail boots in this category resemble heavy-soled shoes or walking shoes. Scaled down in all aspects, some models may be found with elementary toe and heel counters. Midsoles are sparse and the outsole is typically a shallow, low-impact lug.

More expensive trail boots begin to resemble boots more than shoes; yet they are still classified as shoes by traditionalists because of the low-cut collar, lack of traditional boot-like looks, and their relatively short life expectancy. The typically used Cordura nylon uppers are reinforced with split leather; the ankle is supported by a stiff heel counter; and the midsoles are more substantive, with some sort of compression-resistant foam like EVA. Trail shoes, both expensive and inexpensive, often employ simple eyelet lacing systems. Outsoles are harder and stiffer, even though the lug design is typically shallow and relatively less aggressive.

▶ **Figure 3.8** Trail boots and shoes.

Construction of this boot class is done cheaply, usually by vulcanizing, cementing, injection molding and/or inside stitching. Because these boots are not made for durability, repair is often impossible and not worth the money or effort.

Hiking Boots

hiking boots—A general class of outdoor footwear for walking on trails; also a more specific type of boot that is typically light weight and made of a synthetic-leather combination or from just leather. These boots can be used for a variety of hiking ranging from day hikes to longer excursions like backpacking trips.

Hiking boots come in two basic categories: leather-synthetic combinations and all leather (*Hiking Boot Repair,* 1979; Manning, 1986; Schnee, personal communication, October 11, 1989). Boots in this category earn their name by offering adequate support and protection on rougher terrain.

Leather Synthetic

Leather-synthetic hiking boots, shown in Figure 3.9, have experienced the greatest growth of any hiking boot in recent years (Komito, 1989). Some forward-looking hikers believe the future market will render the ultimate lightweight hiking boot (Komito, 1989; Manning, 1986). With contemporary nylon panels like Cordura substituting for heavier leather, sophisticated foam midsoles, and thinner lug soles, these boots are pounds lighter than their forerunners of only a few years back.

Uppers are constructed of nylon combined with top-grain leather or suede. The collar is padded and extends over the ankle. Tongues are usually padded and gusseted; the heels have counters and heel bumpers. Similarly, the toes are at least stiff, if not possessing counters, and toe bumpers are usually present. The insoles and midsoles are well padded with EVA foam. Frequently, steel shanks can be found between the insole and midsole. There is a great variety of lug designs in this boot type, ranging in all three dimensions (geometry, density, and depth). Construction is usually a combination of Littleway and cementing.

▶ **Figure 3.9** Synthetic leather hiking boots.

All-Leather

All-leather boots are the standard in hiking (*Hiking Boot Repair,* 1979; Manning, 1986; Perlman, 1988a). Examples of all-leather hiking boots are illustrated in Figure 3.10. They weigh more and are more expensive but possess greater durability than their leather-synthetic relatives. All-leather boots are dimensionally similar to the leather-synthetics; however, they are somewhat structurally different. The uppers are made from one piece of top-grain leather. Toe counters are nearly always included, and heel counters are stiff and sturdy. High-compression foam, or layered leather midsoles are usually not visible, because the outsole appears to be all one piece connected to the upper. Within the midsole is a strong shank possibly extending up to three quarters of the boot length. A variety of lug patterns also exist, usually heavy-duty combinations. Norwegian and Goodyear construction can be found in a few models; however, the inside stitching that Littleway employs is the standard.

Climbing and Mountaineering Boots

climbing/mountaineering boots—Heavy-duty boots with layered leather midsoles, aggressive outsole geometry, and Norwegian welt construction; used for rugged hiking conditions including snow and ice.

Climbing or Mountaineering boots are specialty boots for use on mixed ice, snow, and rock (*Hiking Boot Repair,* 1979; Manning, 1986) (see Figure 3.11) and are designed for climbing, not hiking. They can weigh up to 6 pounds per pair. Heavier duty in every way than ordinary all-leather hikers, they usually have greater ankle support and full shanks of fiberglass or steel. The result is a rigid sole that can be used with *crampons* (spiked metal platforms attached to the soles for climbing in snow and ice) (see Figure 3.12).

The uppers are heavy, highly water-repellent leather with reinforced toe and heel counters. Tongues are well padded and frequently of the split variety. The lacing system has D-rings on the lower portion and speed hooks nearer the top of the boot. Midsoles are layered leather. The outsole

▶ **Figure 3.10** All-leather hiking boots.

▶ **Figure 3.11** Climbing/
mountaineering boots.

lugs are hard (high carbon) and incorporate aggressive geometry and high depth. Construction is top quality, typically using the Norwegian welt method.

Expedition Boots

expedition boots—
Sophisticated boots de-
signed for extended winter
and high-altitude climbing;
each has an insulated in-
ner boot and a plastic
outer boot.

Expedition boots are also highly specialized boots used for winter and high-altitude climbing (Manning, 1986; Woodward, 1985). These boots can be found in either very heavy-duty leather or plastic. Leather expedition boots are an upscale copy of the mountaineering boot with the addition of one or two inner boots for insulation. Plastic boots seem to be the future in expedition footwear, however. Ski boot technology triggered the application of plastic in expedition boots. Most models feature injection-molded plastic uppers. The ankle is hinged

▶ **Figure 3.12** Plastic expedition boots. The boot on the right has crampons affixed to it.

and padded for greater freedom of movement. Inner boots are found in all models and can be replaced with insulated versions for extreme conditions.

Lug soles in both the leather and plastic versions are built with a slight roll to aid walking—the soles are too stiff to flex. All expedition boots are crampon compatible. Outsoles on plastic boots appear to be a part of the upper; some are stitched, other manufacturers use an unstitched technique called *microwelting*. Leather boots are almost exclusively Norwegian welt construction.

Technical Rock Climbing Boots (Rock Shoes)

technical rock climbing boots—Also called rock shoes, they are light, flexible, leather boots with sticky gum-rubber soles designed for rock climbing.

Technical climbing rock shoes, sometimes called *Kletterschuhes,* are footwear uniquely suited for technical rock climbing on nearly vertical rock faces (*Hiking Boot Repair,* 1979; Perlman, 1988b) (refer to Figure 3.13). They are not intended nor are they appropriate for hiking.

Rock shoes are designed to provide a "second skin" feel on the rock. The upper consists of either canvas or split leather. Some manufacturers bond or stitch canvas to the leather to prevent excessive stretching. Soft, sticky gum-rubber soles give exceptional gripping power. The sole pattern is either smooth or shallow. Toe and heel designs are critical considerations for serious rock climbers. The toe should be narrow (measured from sole to top), with the rubber sole overlapping the top of the toe. Such a toe design allows the climber to jam the foot into narrow cracks. The heel should be snug and stable. A stable heel transfers maximum power and control to the toe. Lacing is exclusively eyelet because this method offers the snuggest fit. Depending on rock conditions and characteristics and the type of climbing techniques required (e.g., jamming, edging, liebacking, smearing, stemming, or chimneying), more serious climbers will select shoes that are specially made for certain types of climbing conditions. All rock shoes use Littleway construction with the outsole sometimes vulcanized or glued to the upper.

A recent introduction to the rock climbing footwear market is climbing slippers (Moser, 1989) (see Figure 3.14). The greatest difference between rock shoes and climbing slippers is found in appearance and construction, much like the difference between ordinary street shoes and typical house slippers. Designed to be ultra light, completely flexible, with greater sensitivity, climbing slippers are made from a fraction of the materials used for

▶ **Figure 3.13** Technical rock climbing shoes.

▶ **Figure 3.14** Rock slippers.

rock shoes. They are made with elastic around the low-cut uppers, resembling Aqua Socks by Nike. Some models have light midsoles to enhance stiffness.

Rock slippers are a compromise between the support of rock shoes and the sensitivity of bare feet. Their real advantage is offering improved smearing and edging technique because of increased foot sensitivity. However, drawbacks are obvious, especially when the climber doesn't want to feel all the rock. For example, jamming your feet into a crack can be quite painful with little upper protection; neither do slippers provide much heel protection.

Summary and Trends

In light of the inclusive running shoe technology, more sophisticated and exotic materials, and more effective manufacturing techniques, the hiking boot industry is evolving dramatically. The search for the ultimate boot lies in maximizing support, durability, water repellency, breathability, flexibility, and comfort, while minimizing weight, break-in time, and environmental impact of the soles.

Leather hiking boots are moving toward thinner leathers with lighter, more forgiving outsoles; sophisticated synthetic midsoles, cushioned foam footbeds; quick-drying, Cambrelle-type linings; and beveled heels. Leather-synthetic boot manufacturers are progressing in the same direction but are searching for an effective water-repellent component. Some manufacturers feel that a one-piece Gore-Tex bootie incorporated into the boot is an effective water repellent. Gore-Tex, a breathable, yet water-repellent membrane, was used in sporting jackets (Manning, 1986).

Whether Gore-Tex is effective or not is apparently up to the user. There are two sides to the Gore-Tex issue. Some hikers feel that, based on their experience, the material is virtually worthless and simply a sales gimmick (Manning, 1986). Still other hikers swear by the footwear attributes claimed by Gore-Tex (Schnee, personal communication, October 11, 1989).

In mountaineering and expedition boots you will continue to see the proliferation of plastic uppers. In fact, some boot makers are offering plastic designs in the light hiking category. However, the jury is still out as to how the market will accept them.

As you have seen, hiking boots come in many varieties. Each kind has its own unique purpose and qualities. When shopping for hiking boots, keep the attributes you are seeking in mind so as not to buy too much or too little boot. Also, select carefully, because today's boot makers are learning more about the shoemaking and design technology that can be applied to the outdoor hiking boot industry.

References

Chase, J. (1985a, May). Heart and sole. *Backpacker*, p. 27.

Chase, J. (1985b, September). Footnotes. *Backpacker*, pp. 28-29.

Hiking boot repair. (1979). Shoe Service Institute of America.

Komito, S. (1989, October). The ultralight boot test. *Backpacker*, p. 57.

Manning, H. (1986). *Backpacking, one step at a time*. New York: Vintage Books.

Moser, S. (1989, September). Climbing slippers. *Outside*, p. 85.

Perlman, E. (1988a, May). Boot camp. *Backpacker*, pp. 35-37.

Perlman, E. (1988b, July). Rock climbing. *Backpacker*, pp. 74-75.

Woodward, B. (1985, January). The warmest winter boots. *Backpacker*, pp. 67-69.

I would like to thank Harvey Manning, author of *One Step at a Time*, and REI Equipment Company for their permission to use illustrations and material from their text.

CHAPTER 4

Cross-Country Ski Boots and Bindings

Barbara Brewster
Snow Country *Magazine and* Big Sky *Journal, Belgrade, Montana*

The extraordinarily creative period in cross-country ski boot and binding systems since 1976 bears all the trappings of a renaissance. Innovations have resulted in products that both perform better and are easier to use.

The fundamental criteria for ski boots and bindings have not changed since ancient Lapps sought a winning combination to transport them to reindeer herds. That was and is for today's skiers a warm, dry, comfortable boot that, when interfaced with a durable binding, flexes for stride yet wields maximum control over a ski's direction on uphill, downhill, and flat terrain. The most dramatic changes are seen in the constructions and materials used to achieve that end.

In this chapter we trace the evolution of major boot and binding constructions to the skating and classic techniques and touring and telemarking categories that define systems today. Also we dissect their functional elements and highlight their unique properties, while probing theories and compromises that have elevated boot and binding systems to unheralded heights of performance, comfort, and skiing control.

▶ Anatomy of Ski Boot and Binding Systems

All cross-country ski boots are constructed with a heel, shank, sole, insole, heel counter, upper, toe box, tongue, and instep closure system. They are shoes,

I thank Salomon and Rottefella for permission to reproduce illustrations from their sales literature.

▶ **Figure 4.1** Nordic ski boot and binding system.

first and foremost, and they must provide as many creature comforts as possible. What distinguishes them most from hiking or running footwear is the boot sole that is designed to mate with a binding and ultimately steer a ski (Figure 4.1).

What differentiates types of cross-country ski boots from each other is their projected end use, which dictates appropriate design, constructions, and materials. Advancements like firm, machine grooming or track-setting of cross-country trails, the advent of ski skating techniques, and the telemark turn revival, which now includes running slalom gates on lift-served pistes and backcountry touring, have created the need for greater product specificity. At the same time, the diverse ability and income of skiers necessitates a broader boot selection that is anatomically and economically attuned to the distinct requisites of each skiing genre and skier profile.

No one book can address the needs of everyone; there are always trade-offs with any choice. The optimum lightweight boot won't be the stiffest, warmest, and driest. The desirable rigidity found in a skating boot sole construction won't accommodate the forward foot flex essential for diagonal stride (classic technique) and telemarking. Some boots are thoroughbreds that are bred to run. Others are workhorses built to withstand the rigors of a more rugged lifestyle.

Binding design also demands compromises. A 75-millimeter backcountry binding with boron steel bail, stainless steel rivets, and an aircraft aluminum body wins the torque stress test hands down. But it's not aerodynamic or user-friendly like the newer recreational system of polyacetate resin (such as the trademark Delrin) that provides easy step-in and exit, nor does it provide the snappy ski return revered by skaters.

Binding constructions differ, but their ultimate purpose is the same: Bindings are the link between ski boots and skis and the transmitters of physical impulses (for turning, accelerating, and braking) from the skier onto the snow. Each is comprised of an aluminum alloy or Delrin toepiece and attachment device that, in combination, position and secure the boot. Each is affixed to the ski with three screws (an exception being a two-screw Salomon racing binding—introduced and discontinued in 1987). Traditional binding toepieces secure the protruding sole of the boot with a bail or pins and rely on boot soles to flex for stride. Newer concepts incorporate flexing regulators within the binding housing.

A heel plate affixed to the ski helps prevent the boot heel from wandering off the side of the ski. Some heel plates have ridges that fit into slots in the boot sole. Others have spikes that penetrate into a soft heel pad. All styles improve lateral control of the ski. Recent systems have a Delrin or plastic steering ridge plate extending under the ball of the foot or from the toe tip through the heel. The ridge attaches to the binding toepiece and mates with a channel (or channels) in the boot sole. The result is better directional control and precise boot realignment in stride situations when the boot heel is elevated above the ski.

The cable is also part of today's binding repertoire. It is a loop that surrounds the boot and draws it into the toepiece. Tension and release are regulated by a throw mechanism attached to the ski ahead of the toepiece, or by an adjustable lever on the cable itself. Its use is limited, primarily, to mountain skiing.

▶ The Evolution of Systems

Before moving into today's systems, let's look at the innovations from which they evolved. Patents of 1889 and 1894 depict bindings with an instep strap that attached to the ski and a leather heel cable similar to today's snowshoe harness. These bindings indiscriminately accepted all forms and sizes of outdoor footwear and were popular into the 20th century. In the broad sense, the Rottefella (translation from Norwegian is "rat trap") bail binding patented in 1928 is the patriarch of cross-country boot and binding systems. However, most people consider its successor, the 75-millimeter Nordic Norm, to be the oldest system; it is the oldest still produced today (see Figure 4.2).

The Nordic Norm refined the old rat trap and standardized boot sole widths and side angles, the pin system, and the binding wings to achieve a more precise union of these interfacing components. This concept retained the heel lift capacity of the instep strap and provided more ski control by strengthening lateral stability. This system used three widths: 71 millimeters for children, 79 millimeters for

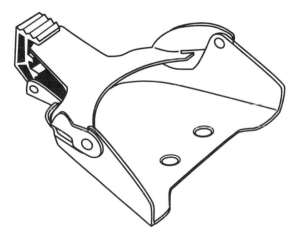

▶ **Figure 4.2** A 75-milimeter binding.

large boots and some mountaineering models, and the predominant 75 millimeters for all aspects of cross-country skiing. (Width is measured laterally across the outer two binding pins or sole holes.) This system was de rigueur for recreational touring, backcountry, telemarking, and even international-level racing up to 1976, when the Adidas Norm 38 system was officially introduced at the Winter Olympic Games in Seefeld, Austria.

Considerable technical juggling went on over the years; the collective inventive mind is never idle. However, no concept emerged beyond the drawing board or brief test interlude to challenge the preeminence of the 75-millimeter system between 1928 and 1976. Two designs of this venerable norm gained favor. The earlier one survives today for general touring and three-pin telemark skiing. In fact, as recently as 1986 it still accounted for 60 percent of cross-country ski boot sales. Its **binding chassis** consists of a metal bail (generally, aircraft aluminum) that clamps down onto the forward extension of the boot sole and three upright steel pins that enter corresponding holes under the toe protrusion of the boot sole.

binding chassis—The basic structural components of a binding.

A second version, the Kloa (translated "claw" from Norwegian), enjoyed relatively brief popularity, primarily among racers. It was used by members of the 1972 U.S. Olympic Cross-Country and Nordic-Combined Ski Teams (among others) competing in Sapporo, Japan, and it faded soon after. The Kloa secured the boot with a two-prong metal claw that dropped down into holes drilled through the top of the boot sole to the left and right of the toe box. A successor, the Bergans, enclosed the claw in a molded plastic housing, but it too disappeared into skiing's archives in 1976 with the advent of Norm 38.

▶ New Materials and Constructions Increase Skiing Efficiency

Adidas Norm 38 captivated racers and incorporated aerospace materials into constructions and new designs in ways that redefined cross-country ski boot and binding systems. The renaissance had begun. Essentially, Adidas replaced the welted leather and molded rubber soles of its predecessors with a stronger, stiffer, more torsionally rigid nylon polyamid called Hytrel. The inherent properties of this material unleashed countless new design opportunities. Adidas carved a longitudinal channel out of the boot heel and mated it with a raised heel wedge nailed to the ski for lateral stability. This improved the foot's ability to steer the ski. By elongating the sole toe, the flex point was shifted 15 millimeters forward of its 75-millimeter system location to provide freer forward flex in the diagonal stride. The sole toe extension was narrowed down to 38 millimeters, about half the width of its predecessors, which reduced friction against the sidewalls of machine-set tracks and enhanced speed.

Hytrel also made it possible to reduce sole thickness to 7 millimeters (about 1/4 inch) from the traditional 12 millimeters, a feature that lowered overall profile and lightened the load. The lightweight boot for racing in particular was enhanced by the use of nylon instead of leather for boot upper material. Foam insulating layers were positioned within the textile sandwich, a construction that is popular today (see Figure 4.3).

Norm 38-millimeter binding developed by Geze eliminated three pins in favor of a steel pin inserted horizontally through a corresponding side hole in the toepiece of the boot. It was succeeded by a clamp design that was later housed in plastic. Both designs ended left and right ski designations neither is seen in systems today.

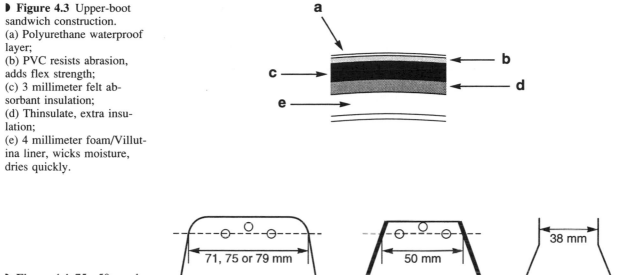

Figure 4.3 Upper-boot sandwich construction.
(a) Polyurethane waterproof layer;
(b) PVC resists abrasion, adds flex strength;
(c) 3 millimeter felt absorbant insulation;
(d) Thinsulate, extra insulation;
(e) 4 millimeter foam/Villutina liner, wicks moisture, dries quickly.

Figure 4.4 75-, 50-, and 38-millimeter bindings.

▶ Warmer Sole Compositions for Touring

As technology advanced it also began shifting geographically to Middle Europe. Norway, birthplace of the Nordic Norm, rebounded with two concepts from Witco, parent of Rottefella. The company essentially shrank the 75-millimeter dimension to 50 millimeters, retained the three-pin interface, plunked the emerging Racing Norm 50 on a 7-millimeter Hytrel racing sole and, in 1979, launched a Touring Norm 50 counterpart for recreational skiers (Figure 4.4 shows 75-, 50-, and 38-millimeter bindings.) The latter incorporated a 12-millimeter touring sole of polyurethane or molded thermoplastic rubber (TPR), which was warmer than Hytrel and was less slippery to walk on, but not as stiff as is desirable for racing. This type of construction survives in recreational boots today, but Norm 50 faded soon after the introduction of the Salomon Nordic System (SNS) in 1980 and 1981 in Europe and the United States, respectively.

▶ Flex Devices Alter Sole-Binding Constructions

Salomon, a French alpine boot and binding manufacturer, redefined the parameters of cross-country ski boot and binding construction when it launched its first Nordic product. Salomon Nordic System (SNS) incorporated the flex-regulating plate into the binding, thus shifting the forward flex function from the toe protrusion of the boot sole where it had previously resided. That move became a springboard for future systems constructions.

In effect, the company lopped off the projecting toe of the boot sole and created a separate flex plate. It could then offer its customers soft, medium, and stiff interchangeable polyamid flex plates that when inserted into the binding provided different degrees of resistance to regulate heel lift, and in the case of skating, to quicken the return of the ski to the boot after each stride. Next, Salomon designed a compatible sole groove and binding ridge plate for under the ball of the foot, which extended lateral control over a greater range of skiing movement than the Norm 38 heel ridge. Sole and binding plate were now in contact when the foot was flexed in stride, as well as when the foot was flat on the ski in glide. Salomon also added softer composition rubber antiskid inserts for walking and a D-ring for boot-to-binding interface.

Other systems like Dynafit LIN and Artex-Landsem ALS enjoyed brief interludes of modest popularity, and three made noteworthy evolutionary contributions between 1980 and 1989. Look Contact, for example, wove the technological advancements of the 1980s into the expired Swiss Long Step patent of the early 1970s and emerged with a fixed-axis flex system that is unique from the SNS flex plate design. Later systems adopted this mechanical hinge concept and devised proprietary, interchangeable flex regulators that compress as the heel is lifted. These snap the ski back after each stroke or stride, a feature that swells in importance in the ski recovery mode of skating.

In 1985, the Rossignol Nordic Concept (RNC) used the ski itself as the central ridge with which the sole groove mated. That same year the Alpina Control system also proffered a very wide, deeper sole channel, but mated it with a distinct binding ridge tacked onto the ski. Interestingly, this concept evolved in the Salomon SNS Profil that premiered four years later.

▶ Upper Materials and Insulations

Leather, synthetic leather, and textiles are used most frequently in cross-country ski boot uppers, often in combination. Nylon and polyester are favored for racing uppers because they are light weight. Leather or synthetic reinforcements add tensile strength and abrasion resistance in stress areas much like running shoes. Models designed for classic technique are low cut at the ankle for uninhibited forward flex for stride. Skating models are above-ankle cut for added stability and support, and several have Hytrel exoskeletal hinged cuffs and lateral stabilizers. Leather recreational models often have synthetic collars and tongues. Almost all touring boots are higher cut for warmth and added stability.

Tanned cowhide, the most widely used leather in boots, varies in quality and is split into layers because it is too thick for boot construction. The top or full grain (the hide's outer surface layer) stretches least, is most rugged, and is most water resistant. It is favored for backcountry touring and telemarking in 2.5- to 3-millimeter thicknesses. The term **Anfibio** in relation to full grain means that the leather has been oil treated. All other layers are called **split leather**. These are coated with polyurethane (PU) to improve their inferior natural water repellency and reduce the tendency of the leather to stretch. Thicknesses vary from 1.2 millimeters for light touring boots to 2.5 millimeters for general backcountry models that need to be more rugged.

Anfibio—Full grain leather that has been treated with oil for water resistance.

split leather—Inferior layers of leather found below the top grain.

Thinsulate seems to be the single most widely used insulating material. Other choices are wool, felts, and synthetic fleeces (like the popular trademarked Velutina). Hefty norpine boots, designed for mountain touring and telemarking, are upholstered with Evapor polyethylene foam insulation and Cambrelle, Tesivel, or other nonabrasive, foot-conforming linings. All are higher cut, and some have removable inner boots. The most specialized of telemark competition models reach midcalf and feature thermoplastic, hinged canting cuffs and ratcheted, spring-loaded buckles (see Figure 4.5).

Synthetic leathers are of multilayer sandwich construction. Some are as thick as 7 millimeters. The outer layer is a waterproof, extruded polyurethane backed with a strength enhancer like polyvinyl chloride (PVC). This layer is backed with an absorbent synthetic felt that traps moisture wicked away from the foot by a quick-drying fleece and foam liner. Some sandwiches also have a layer of Thinsulate Thermal insulation, 3M's polyester and polyolefin microfiber. Almost all light touring boots have synthetic or PU-coated split leather uppers.

▶ **Figure 4.5** Telemark competition boots.

Textile uppers, found almost exclusively in classic and skate racing boots, are also sandwich construction. A representative layering features double foam between a surface sheet of Gore-Tex or Sympatex with an inner tier of quick-drying polypropylene or polyester pile and a nylon tricot inner lining. Another construction uses polyester-knit outer, absorbent polyamide velour, and foam inner layers. Gore-Tex and Sympatex are waterproof, breathable membranes laminated to a fabric—nylon in boots, for example. Scotchguard-treated material is also used for waterproofness.

Insole insulators and footbeds are of dense thermoformed polyethylene, polyurethane foam, or a foam and nylon sandwich. All provide an added layer for warmth, but some accentuate stiffness to lend more rigidity to the boot. Foams are used to pad tongues and collars and provide heel cushioning. Thermoplastics like Pebax are used to stiffen heel counters.

▶ Boot Sole Constructions and Materials

torsional rigidity—The resistance of a boot to twisting along its sole length.

Because of the arrangements between systems patent holders and their boot licensees, a finite number of companies provide soles for today's systems boots; thus materials and constructions are fairly standard. Pebax reigns supreme for top-level racing boot soles in dual density and tri-material Pebax/Rilsan/polyurethane. Rilsan, also used in downhill boot shells, enhances torsional rigidity, whereas the softer PU adds traction for walking. (**Torsional rigidity** is the resistance to twist along the boot sole length.) Hytrel is still used in some less technical performance boots, but it has gradually been replaced since 1984 by the stiffer, lighter weight Pebax that has made lower profiles possible. These soles are cemented with an adhesive to boot uppers by a pressurized heating process. Pebax is also used in a waffled, air-space design for added warmth in NNN-BC system soles from Rottefella.

There is more variety in recreational boot soles. Some are injected with Thermoplastic rubber or resin (TPR) and polyurethane foam (PU). This type of sole can be molded directly onto the boot. The upper sits on the mold into which the hot liquid sole material is injected. Once hardened, the boot is finished. Another method furnishes systems licensees with finished injection-molded soles to which they attach their boot uppers by a separate cementing process.

ulcanized rubber soles are applied to boot uppers in a one-step process. In this construction, the boot is positioned on the mold and a presized rubber blank is placed in the mold and exposed to pressure and 320 °F heat.

Multiple-density compositions meld properties that aren't inherent in the primary material. For instance, in a two-ply, two-material sole construction, a softer material is extruded through the stiffer, slipperier polyamid to create antiskid soles. Hytrel can be injected, so this is sometimes used in combination with TPR to achieve a stiffer sole.

Norwegian welt is a stitched construction used almost exclusively in the rugged telemarking and backcountry touring boots. The upper is sewn to lug rubber or Vibram soles. Steel and wooden shanks fortify midsoles. (See chapter 3, pp. 41-42 for a more thorough description of Norwegian welt construction.)

▶ Binding Materials

All bindings are constructed of metal or plastic parts, with preference dictated by end-use performance level, weight-to-strength requirements, and cost. Constructions for racing and sport cross-training bindings favor injection-molded polyacetal resins (such as the trademark Delrin) or aircraft aluminum alloy for toepiece hoods, throws, and steering ridges. Steel is used for pins, bushing axles, and other interface components for metal-to-metal precision and high fatigue strength. Newer systems bindings for recreation have Delrin or plastic heel plates, levers, ridges, cocking levers, and housings. Some housings are reinforced fiberglass. Flex plates are Hytrel; flex nubs are rubber. Springs as flexors are synthetic elastomere.

All 75-millimeter bindings have aluminum alloy bodies. Heavy-duty models use high-tensile 6061 T-6 aluminum bodies and case-hardened boron spring steel pins and bails for optimum strength and durability. Bails are graphite epoxy coated or nylon coated to reduce wear on boot soles. Rivets are stainless steel, and front throws are a polyacetate resin. Steering and heel plates are serrated metal. This quality construction is costly, so general touring 75-millimeter bindings are of lower grade aluminum that has an anodized coating. This coating not only protects boots but can be colored to match skis and boots.

▶ Boot and Binding Interfaces

By 1990 the newest boot and binding systems were polarized unlike anything since the glory days of the 75-millimeter systems. Each system remains proprietary—bindings will interface only with boots of the same system—but a definite pattern exists throughout. The following systems all espouse the fixed-axis interface principal that enables the boot to pivot like a door set into a hinge (see Figure 4.6). All position a closure device within the binding to regulate heel lift and provide ski retrieval. All address the significant importance of directional stability with their individualized steering ridge and sole groove assemblies. Technically, all interface designs reflect the importance of positioning the ball of the skier's foot at the peak of the catapult or flex. Systems

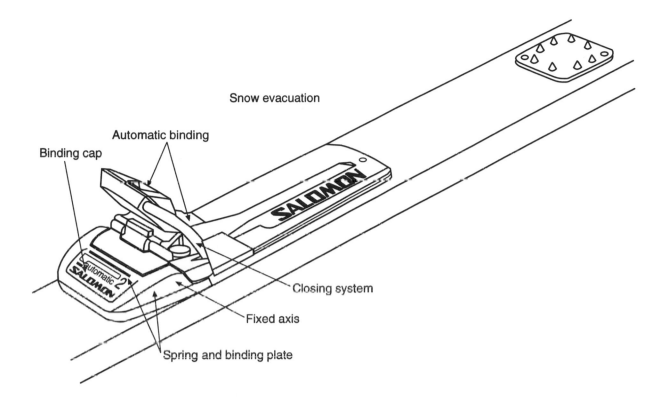

▶ **Figure 4.6** A typical fixed-axis binding system.

differ, however, in their structural interpretations of optimum location and design of the mechanical hinge, flexor, and sole attachment. In other words, how can each best achieve in construction what all resemble in theory?

The now defunct Adidas Skating Diagonal System (SDS) positioned steel pins within the side of the sole ahead of the toe. These drop into binding slots that activate a pressure bar achieving metal-to-metal contact. Two coil springs with softer, stiffer, longer interchangeable nipples govern flex. A single continuous sole groove mates with a ridge and wedged heel plate. This system was discontinued in 1991 when Adidas signed a license agreement with Salomon to produce Adidas boots on the SNS system.

Two companies emerge as design leaders producing bindings and compatible boot soles for an increasing number of boot manufacturers. They are Rottefella and Salomon. Rottefella New Nordic Norm (NNN) positioned a boot interfacing bar at the tip of the toes at zero pivot point where it was with 75 millimeter. In theory this positions the flex where the boot never leaves the steering ridges attached to the ski. The bar drops into a viselike grip that pulls the boot forward into the binding. Interchangeable rubber flexors compress with heel lift. This system has been superseded by Rottefella NNN-II.

The more rugged Rottefella New Nordic Norm Backcountry (NNN-BC) has wider grooves and a thicker pivot bar that is positioned on the boot 15 millimeters behind the location considered desirable in the NNN. The argument is that the new position directs more pressure onto the ball of the foot where the double steering ridge exists. This is a stable, stout system for off-track touring and recreational telemarking (see Figure 4.7).

Rottefella NNN-II replaced NNN for racing in 1990 and for recreational touring in 1992. This system has a locking device similar to NNN-BC. It draws the boot forward 3 millimeters into the binding; the sole pivot bar on the boot

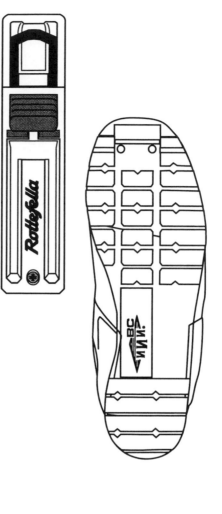

▶ **Figure 4.7** The Rottefella
NNN-BC (Backcountry).

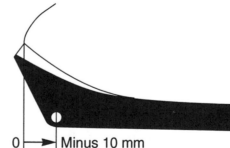

▶ **Figure 4.8** Locking
device of the Rottefella
NNN-II.

0 ⊢→| Minus 10 mm

is located 10 millimeters behind NNN under the toes, which positions the pivot point at −7 millimeters when placed in the binding. This improves edge control of the ski and conforms more to the natural striding movement of the foot (see Figure 4.8).

Salomon SNS Auto 2 has a D-ring interface unit of metal on the boot sole ahead of the toe and a very stiff spring flex regulator (Figure 4.9). A single steering ridge runs under the ball of the foot.

Salomon SNS Profil features a comparatively wide, graduated, raised, stabilizing ridge bar and a wide, deep, sole groove under the entire foot. In theory, this enlarged steering system assures constant boot contact at the ball and immediate total boot realignment for optimum lateral control of the ski. This system is shown in Figure 4.10. A buckle spring locks the system and inhibits

▶ **Figure 4.9** The Salomon SNS Auto 2.

▶ **Figure 4.10** Salomon SNS Profil.

free play. The interface bar is located at the tip of the toe (at zero pivot point). Flexors are interchangeable rubber plugs.

▶ A Look Ahead

All of these products attest to the exploration that is ongoing in boot and binding system development. At the moment, the swing of the pendulum favors the fixed-axis concept of interface. Stripped to their essentials, cross-country ski boots are very similar in construction and materials within each end-use category.

As for tomorrow, new materials, or an adjustment in skiing technique such as skating, will change construction and design. Designers and engineers are constantly creating the possibilities. Laboratory boot torture chambers gyrate with machinery that torques, twists, and otherwise tests the grit of every new design concept. Then expert skiers on some distant glacier synthesize the new technologies with practical on-snow observations, and the evolution of boot and binding systems moves ahead.

CHAPTER 5

Downhill Skis, Boots, and Bindings

Mark A. Smith, MS

The key function of the ski, boot, and binding complex is to most effectively and safely transfer the skier's movements to the ski. Skiers have a wide range of abilities and skiing styles (i.e., mogul, cruising, and racing) that require different equipment characteristics. This chapter details the basics of skis, boots, and bindings and also discusses the design differences for different types of skiing.

▶ Skis

In recent years ski manufacturers offered a massive onslaught of technological innovation in ski design. Most of this new technology has but a few goals: vibration dampening for enhanced comfort, increased control, and attainment of maximal speed.

Ski Categories

Despite the claim by manufacturers and ski enthusiasts that many different types of skis exist, there are two basic types of skis used by skiers: recreational and racing. It is true that most models have some distinguishing features that may be subcategories, but all can be placed within these two categories.

Recreational skis are designed for many different levels of skiers. There are separate models for beginner, intermediate, and expert recreational skiers. Also, skis in this category are designed for specific purposes such as cruising, mogul skiing, and powder skiing.

Racing skis are generally divided into three subcategories: downhill, slalom, and giant slalom. Downhill ski racers can exceed speeds of 70 miles per hour and make long looping turns. This type of ski is engineered for stability and so are the widest of all racing skis. Slalom skis are just the opposite. They are designed for quick, aggressive turns at much slower speeds (around 25 miles per hour). Giant slalom ski competition is faster than slalom, slower, and less lengthy than downhill and has more gates to maneuver. Therefore, giant slalom skis are a cross between the slalom ski and the downhill ski. It is designed to make moderate radius turns at high speeds. These types of skis must have both stability and flexibility, making them the most expensive ski to produce.

Ski Length

Ski selection is not only based on the type of skiing to be performed, but also the height, weight, physical strength, and ability of the skier. Generally, the taller, heavier, stronger, and more advanced a skier is, the longer the ski. Novice skiers, however, should use the longest ski that they are comfortable with. Short skis are actually less stable on varied surfaces and high speeds and are inferior for accurate turning and carving. Longer skis give just the opposite effect: They have more running surface on the snow, so they have greater stability and better turning characteristics.

Anatomy and Design

longitudinal flex—Often referred to as flex; it is the ski's degree of resistance to flex along a longitudinal axis (i.e., lengthwise).

torsional flex—Often called torsion, it refers to a ski's resistance to twisting along the longitudinal axis.

There are several design and anatomical similarities in all alpine or downhill skis. Figure 5.1 shows the anatomy of the general downhill ski.

All skis are designed to have some degree of flex—longitudinal and torsional. **Longitudinal flex**, called simply "flex," refers to the ski's resistance to deviate or bend along its longitudinal axis (i.e., along the length of the ski). Resistance to twisting is a ski's **torsional flex** (frequently called "torsion"). A ski with high torsional stiffness can transmit more energy to the tip and tail, creating sharper and quicker turns. Typically, skis that are easier to turn and have smoother skiing characteristics have softer torsion and flex, but they are often slower than stiffer skis.

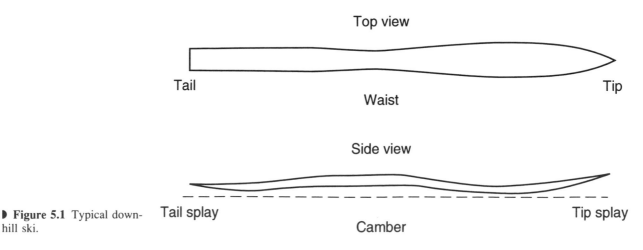

▶ Figure 5.1 Typical downhill ski.

tip—*The front end of the ski.*

splay—*The widest part of the ski that affects the ski's speed and stability and is located at the ski's tip.*

waist—*The narrowest part of the ski, usually located at the midpoint where bindings are mounted.*

tail—*The rear end of the ski.*

camber—*The amount of curvature a ski has. It can be seen when the ski is lying flat and when only the tip and the tail touch the surface.*

profile—*Thickness of the ski.*

sidecut—*The relative dimensions of the tip, waist, and tail of the ski.*

The front of the ski, called the **tip**, is always the widest part. It has an upward and outward curve called the **splay**. Different types of skis have varying amounts of splay. In general, skis designed for high speed and stability (downhill and giant slalom) have very little curve or splay; skis designed for sharper turns and slower speeds (recreational and slalom) have greater curve or more splay. The narrowest part of the ski is usually at the midpoint or **waist**. Bindings are mounted at the waist. For stability, high-speed skis have a wider waist than do sharper radius, low-speed skis. The rear of the ski is called the **tail** and is wider than the waist but narrower than the tip.

Taking a side view of a ski you will notice that the ski is curved. This curvature is called **camber**. If the ski were on a flat surface only the tip and tail would touch the surface. When the skier is mounted on the ski the camber flattens out, distributing weight along the bottom portion of the ski. Without a cambered ski a skier's weight would fall primarily over the ski waist. Camber greatly enhances control and turning by forcing the tip and tail into the snow.

Also in side view the ski's **profile** or thickness can be seen. All skis are thicker in the waist and gradually become thinner towards the tip and tail. Profile is a function of materials as it relates to camber. For example, lighter skis typically have more profile to enhance camber. Heavier skis like the older models made of metal had a thinner profile.

A top view of the ski reveals its **sidecut**, the shape of the ski determined by the dimensions of the tip, waist, and tail. Notice that the tip is the widest part of the ski, the waist is the narrowest. Sidecut also affects the turning capabilities of skis. High sidecut skis (i.e., relatively wider tip and tail) can make shorter, more aggressive turns. Conversely, skis with low sidecut are better at longer, more graceful turns.

Construction and Materials

There are basic elements common to all ski designs. The method of construction and the materials used varies and also influences the ski price. The following sections describe these different elements.

Core

core—*The centermost layer of the ski used to support the outer structural layers.*

The interior center part of the ski, called the **core**, is the layer of space between the structural layers of the ski and is used primarily to support the skis' exterior parts (e.g., the edges and base). Even though the core plays a minor role in the overall integrity of the ski, it does influence the ski's strength.

Core materials range from wood to foam to other proprietary materials. The early skis were made entirely of wood, but today only the core consists of wood. Wood cores can be made by laminating several thin strips of wood together, then planing the laminate into the desired shape. Or, a single piece of wood such as beech, ash, or spruce can be used. Core materials greatly affect the weight and price of the ski, so lighter and correspondingly more expensive skis are made from lighter tropical wood. For example, a firmer balsa-like wood called *okoume* is sometimes used. Wood-core skis offer a relatively high vibration-dampened ride.

Usually materials other than wood are used because wood is generally more expensive, and consistent wood-grain quality is hard to find. Polyurethane foam, for example, is the most commonly used core material today. This form is either molded or milled to size. Foam-core skis are noted for their light weight and more challenging riding characteristics.

Aluminum is another core material and is typically fashioned into a honeycomb pattern to make one of the lightest and strongest cores available. But aluminum honeycomb is even softer and livelier than foam-core skis. Because aluminum deforms permanently, soft skis or mogul skis are generally not made with this material.

Exterior Layers

The exterior portion of the ski consists of layers of laminated materials. These layers are built around the core to produce a finished ski. There are generally two laminating techniques: sandwich and torsion box (see Figure 5.2). The purpose of these exterior materials is to enhance the strength and vibration-dampening characteristics of the ski.

The traditional and oldest form of modern ski manufacturing uses a process called sandwich laminating. This is the easiest and typically least expensive form of construction. Sandwich-laminated skis also have more uniform flex than torsion box skis. Layers of fiberglass, carbon fibers, ceramic fibers, Kevlar, or metal are bonded (laminated) to both the top and bottom surfaces of the ski. More than one type of material can be laminated to any given ski depending on the manufacturer's intentions. In fact, most skis use at least two types of materials.

Torsion box construction consists of wrapping the same materials used for sandwich laminates, plus some manufacturers use aluminum to wrap around the core. This process is called "wet wrapping" because the exterior materials are soaked with resin then wrapped around the core. The ski is then placed in a mold and baked, a slow and expensive process. The flexibility of torsion box skis varies widely along the length of the ski. The advantage of this is in having the tip and tail firmer or softer than the waist depending on the intended type of skiing style.

Exterior Materials

Fiberglass is a popular and inexpensive material for a ski's exterior. It is a natural vibration dampener, is very resilient, and will not break except under extreme stress. Weight being equal, carbon fiber is twice as strong as fiberglass with regard to tension and has greater vibration-dampening properties. Carbon fiber is almost always used in combination with fiberglass.

Ceramic is a more recent and exotic material used in structural layering. It is actually a compound of metallic and nonmetallic materials. Ceramics can be much stiffer than an equivalent weight of fiberglass, but no stronger, so it is not used extensively despite its extreme stiffness which makes it very brittle.

Base Materials

base—The smooth gliding surface at the bottom of the ski.

The ski bottom is called the **base**. Its purpose is to allow the ski to smoothly slide over the snow. This movement actually causes the snow to melt along the base due to the skis' pressure on snow crystals. This film of melted snow

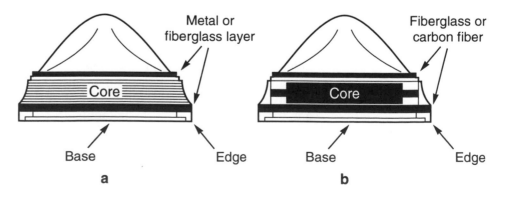

▶ **Figure 5.2** (a) Sandwich laminate and (b) torsion box constructions.

is called *meltwater*. The ski base has microscopic grooves that channel this water away. The molecular structure and the toughness of the base are important for control.

All modern skis use some type or grade of polyethylene on the base of the ski. The ski industry borrowed the use of polyethylene from the modern mining industry. Mining needed a slippery material with high abrasion resistance that could stand up to the cold. It was used in truck beds to make dumping muddy materials cleaner and easier. Polyethylene comes in many grades from a softer, low grade used for plastic bags to the harder, higher grades of which ski bases are made. High-grade polyethylene gets its toughness from the structure of the relatively long plastic molecules. Polyethylene grading is determined by molecule length—the longer the molecule, the tougher and faster the base and the higher the grade.

sintered base—A high wear-resistant base that is made from molten and compressed polyethylene.

Naturally, bases come in a variety of grades themselves. Less expensive skis have molecular lengths of less than 1 million atoms, whereas higher performance, **sintered-base** skis have about 3.5 million atoms per molecule. As you may remember from chemistry class, the number of atoms per molecule is its molecular weight. Higher molecular weight skis are less dense and more porous, which means they absorb wax better. But they also lose it faster, so they have to be waxed more frequently.

There are two types of base manufacturing processes: extrusion and sintering. The polyethylene of an extruded base is heated until it is molten, then it is forced through a die in the same form as the final product. Although extruded bases are the easiest to repair they are lower in density and molecular weight than sintered bases. Other disadvantages of extruded bases are lower resistance to wear and poor wax absorption.

To produce a sintered base, polyethylene powder is slowly heated under very high pressure. This process forces the polyethylene particles to bond together forming a crystalline structure. The molten polyethylene is then compressed into a shape and lastly shaved into the final form. The result is a finished product that is smoother when wax is applied, with very high wear resistance.

Other ski base materials are carbon-graphite, which are all black (polyethylene bases are clear). The benefits of carbon-graphite skis are unclear, but most ski manufacturers are unlikely to use this material because their names won't show on the ski bottom.

Edges

edges—Thin metal strips along the outside edge of the base.

Edges are the metal strips along the outside edge of the ski base, and there are two types: continuous and cracked. Continuous edges are the most common and easiest to manufacture and tune. This type of edge is simply one piece of metal running the entire length of the ski. Conversely, cracked edges have minute breaks along their length. These tiny breaks dampen vibration and hold better on hard snow.

Tuning

Tuning is a complex and controversial process that is intended to improve the performance of the ski and depends on the skier's skill, the snow conditions, and relative ski stiffness. Tuning consists of flattening the base, sharpening and beveling the edges, and waxing.

The base of the ski should be flat. However, untuned ski bases can form a concave or convex shape. Skis with concave bases (see Figure 5.3b) have erratic control characteristics and are very difficult to turn effectively. A convex base (see Figure 5.3a) is difficult to control because only a small part of the base's running surface is in contact with the snow. The optimum condition is a flat base, because its entire surface is applying equal pressure against the snow.

Edge sharpening and beveling is a very complex matter and considered an art by some in the profession. Beveling shapes an outside edge (i.e., the edge against the snow), so that either the bottom edge is not parallel to the snow and/or the vertical edge is not perpendicular to the snow. Edges that are not beveled are difficult to control in aggressive turns. Both the sides and the base portions of edges can be beveled (see Figure 5.4). Most skiers of all levels prefer a 90-degree side and base beveling. If edges are not beveled, the ski will have a tendency to "catch" the snow making turning very rough. The beveling process starts by tapering the base edge depending on the type of skiing and the skill of the skier.

Generally, beginning skiers only need about 1/2 degree of base bevel because they neither ski fast nor have the ability to ski their edges effectively. Intermediate skiers who are developing the ability to put greater energy into their turns have about 1 degree of bevel. Expert skiers typically use from 1 to 2 degrees of base bevel because of their higher skill level, thus faster skiers ski their edges at greater angles. Competitive skiers in the slalom and giant slalom are both experts, but the beveling they need is different because of speed and edge angulation. That is, the higher the speed, the greater the angulation of the ski on its edges; and the greater the angulation, the more beveling required. For

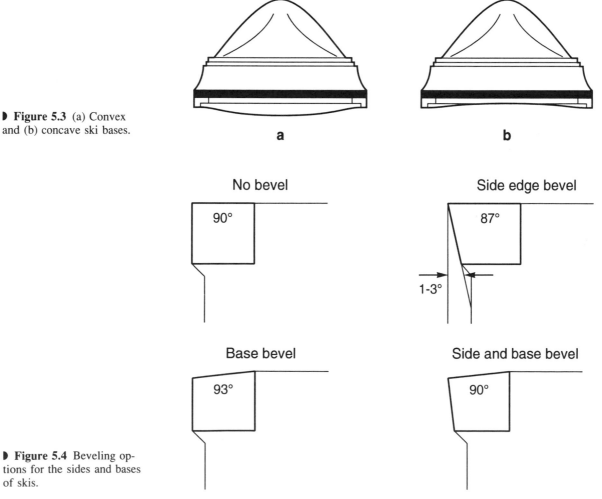

▶ **Figure 5.3** (a) Convex and (b) concave ski bases.

▶ **Figure 5.4** Beveling options for the sides and bases of skis.

example, a slalom ski may have 1 degree bevel, whereas a downhill ski could be beveled as much as 3 degrees.

The variables in base beveling are not only limited to skier ability, ski softness or firmness is also considered. Torsionally soft skis need less bevel because they tend to bow during turns, and too much bevel will cause loss of control. Conversely, stiffer skis use greater bevel. It is important to note that the more advanced skiers use stiffer skis. Lastly, a ski edge may be beveled on the side, which serves the purpose of creating an edge angle of 90 degrees.

After the edges are properly beveled, they are honed or sharpened to remove the burrs of dull edges and any left over from the beveling process. The result is better control and smoother turns. Edge sharpening technique is also highly personal, but the general rule prescribes edges progressively sharper from tip to tail (i.e., dullest at the tip and sharpest at the tail).

Waxing

The purpose of waxing is not to make the smoothest possible surface, but to create a uniform surface. Remember, the friction created by the ski over the snow melts a thin layer of water under the ski. A properly waxed ski makes the base glide easily over this meltwater. A process called *structuring* should be employed prior to and after applying wax. Perfectly smooth bases will not glide on snow as well as structured bases. A structured base has tiny ridges or grooves running from ski tip to tail. Its purpose is to break the suction force of a ski running over the snow. The ridges allow a small amount of air between the ski and the snow. Once applied, the hot wax should be scraped to a thin layer then structured with a soft brush.

▶ Bindings

The binding (Figure 5.5) has two functions: to hold the boot to the ski and to release the boot from the ski in a fall that could cause injury. Bindings hold the skier to the ski while traversing varied terrain, but it should also release the skier from the ski when movement's force approaches an injury-level potential. The binding is the most important skiing element for safety. As the level of binding technology evolved, the severity and incidence of ankle and leg injuries decreased.

Prior to modern downhill skiing, the binding held only the toe in place similar to today's cross-country ski. In the 1920s the heel was held by a cable to minimize lateral movement. But control was poor and this binding was quite dangerous, because the toe was bound firmly to the ski and could not be

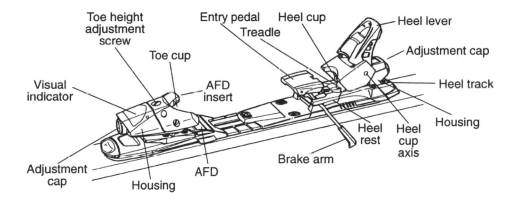

▶ **Figure 5.5** Typical ski binding.
Courtesy of Salomon.

But it was not until 1950 when Marker and Salomon introduced their version of alpine ski binding that releasable binding mechanisms were popularized. However, these bindings mandated use only with each proprietor's boots. That is, binding and boot makers did not make their products compatible with other manufacturers.

In response to this, an international standards group from Germany developed boot toe, heel, and sole thickness dimensions that, if complied with by all manufacturers would fit any boot in any binding. These standards were developed by Deutsche Industrie Normen, known widely as DIN. With the advent of DIN standards, advanced binding technology gained wide acceptance and enhanced the safety of the sport.

DIN standards have not only standardized how boots fit into the binding, but they have also standardized the adjustability mechanisms. The DIN scale for bindings is a numerical measure for a bindings release setting (see Table 5.1). DIN numbers correspond to the torque required to release a ski boot sideways from the binding toe.

The appropriate DIN setting corresponds to factors such as a skier's body weight, height, skiing aggressiveness, age, and boot sole length. World Cup racers ski very aggressively and require very high DIN numbers; children are shorter, lighter, and less aggressive so typically have DIN settings of 1 or 2.

▶ Boots

The first alpine ski boots were also climbing boots because in the early days the only way to ski down a hill was first to climb up it. The adaptation of the climbing boot to the present-day ski boot was slow but significant. One of the first modifications to the climbing boot was to laminate the sole for rigidity and apply a protective coating to the shell. Later, separate inner boots were introduced to provide better fit and support as well as warmth. For convenience, boots with buckles were invented to avoid untying frozen shoelaces.

Plastic-coated leather outer shells were the forerunners of the present-day plastic-shelled boots. Plastic-coated boots offered better weather resistance, greater support, and better rigidity for control. Even plastic-coated leather did not prevent the skier from leaning too far forward or backward. Skiers realized that correct ski position is essential to effective control, so boots were designed to be higher on the leg.

The next major evolution in ski boot design was the all-plastic outer shell. The rigidity of the all-plastic shell forced the skier's position over the top of the skis, more effectively translating the skier's movements to the ski. Discussed below are the characteristics of the modern ski boot.

Table 5.1 DIN Standards										
Category	1	2	3	4	5	6	7	8	9	10
	Body weight in pounds									
Beginner	40	60	90	110	130	150	170	190	210	230
Intermediate	—	50	80	100	120	140	160	180	200	220
Expert	—	40	70	90	110	130	150	170	190	210

Anatomy and Design Characteristics

Ski boots have three general elements:

- The outer shell
- The inner boot
- The fit and performance adjustments

There are also four basic types of ski boots: the overlapping closure, the external tongue, the rear entry, and the hybrid. Boot types actually reflect the characteristic of the outer shell design and so will be discussed in the outer shell subsection.

The Outer Shell

Most shells are molded from some kind of polyurethane, the material of choice because of its durability and low maintenance. This is the industry standard, and there is little variation in materials. But the variation in outer-shell design falls into four forms: the external tongue, the overlapping enclosure, the rear-entry, and the hybrid.

external tongue—An entry-level ski boot that has its tongue hinged to the toe of the boot, straps overlap the tongue and fasten shut.

overlapping enclosure boot—A snug-fitting boot characterized by cuff section straps overlapping the boot's shell to fasten.

rear-entry—A once popular boot design in which the boot could be easily entered and buckled from the rear. It lost its popularity because of poor fit.

hybrid—An overlap boot design that has several customizable fit adjustments.

External tongue boots are typically for entry-level skiers because they are easier to put on and take off. They are of a three-piece shell design characterized by a tongue hinged to the toe. The boot and buckle straps close over the tongue. **Overlapping enclosure** boots (Figure 5.6) are sometimes called the "traditional shell." Overlap designs don't look much different than they did 10 years ago. This design is used by more skilled skiers because of its snug fit. The overlap is usually a two-piece outer-shell design in which the cuff section wraps over the inner part of the outer shell reducing the volume within the boot between the shell, inner boot, and foot. The buckles are fastened on the lateral side of the boot. The **rear entry** design was very popular in the late 1970s and mid-1980s because of the comfort and easy entry it offered. Lately its popularity has diminished because its performance characteristics were inferior to other boot designs. To improve on the boot's performance many fit adjustments are employed; for example, a series of cables inside the boot for a more snug fit. These cables help customize the shape of the inner boot to the skier's foot. Lastly, the **hybrid** is the latest and fastest growing shell design (Figure 5.6). Hybrids combine the overlap design with the mechanical fit adjustments of rear-entry boots. But what is making them so popular is their release mechanism on the rear of the boot that allows the cuff to open for easy entry, exit, and walking. These conveniences combined with the performance attributes of overlap designs are likely to make hybrid boot designs the wave of the future.

Inner Boot

The inner boot is the medium between the foot and the outer shell. It is a combination of materials and different densities of foam over the contours of the foot. Based on the foot's contour and the skier's level of skill, a balance can be struck between comfort and response. For example, soft foam is used in more sensitive areas like the forefoot, instep, and ankle. Higher density foam, offering greater support and stiffness that translates a skier's movements more efficiently, is found in the front of the shin, back of the ankle, and under the heel.

Boots for novice skiers typically have more softer foam than high-density foam, because they usually want more comfort at the cost of performance.

▶ Figure 5.6 Two types of ski boots: overlapping enclosure (top) and a hybrid. Courtesy of Salomon.

injection molding—A low-cost technique for making inner boots.

preformed—The least expensive way to make inner boots, which takes component parts and sews them together.

Conversely, competitive skiers choose the most responsive, lightest boot possible. Compare the differences of a race car's light weight and responsiveness and a streetcar's comfort.

Inner boots can be manufactured by one of three processes: injection molding, preforming, or lasting. The **injection molding** process consists of stretching a lining material over a last or model foot form inside the mold. Some type of soft polyurethane is then injected into the mold and left to cure. Injection-molded inner boots are generally used in novice and intermediate boots, because they only offer one type of foam. But this type of construction yields a warm and leak-proof inner boot. A **preformed** inner boot is the least expensive construction method. A precut foam padding and less expensive component parts are sewn together by a machine from the inside out. Preformed seams may be sealed or unsealed. This form of construction is found in low-end novice boots. The most expensive and best designed inner boots are lasted.

Lasted inner boots are fashioned by stretching the components of the inner boot over the form of a foot and hand sewing the parts together. The seams have a waterproof seal applied to prevent water leakage. High-density foam and top quality components are generally used in this type of inner boot.

Fit and Performance Adjustments

All modern boots have some type of custom-fitting adjustments built into them. Some of the adjustments we'll discuss are forward lean, forward flex, cant, and heel height. Most adjustments can be done with a knob or a dial built into the boot itself; others require special tools. Fit and performance adjustments can dramatically improve a skier's balance, performance, and comfort.

The sophistication and variety of adjustments on a particular boot are price dependent. Generally, the more gadgets the boot has, the more costly it will be.

Forward Lean

The most common adjustment found in ski boots is forward lean. As its name implies, this adjustment changes the forward pitch of the boot's cuff. The purpose of forward lean is to force the knees and hips to bend or flex. Flexion in the knee allows more medial and lateral movement, which offers greater and more effective roll on the skis for edging. However, too much lean can force the skier into a position that is too low, thus putting too much strain on the thigh and hip muscles. Too little lean reduces your ability to edge the ski and make tight radius turns. Finding the appropriate level of lean is basically a process of trial and error.

Contrary to what you may think, skiers who ski steeper slopes and make aggressive, hard, edging turns prefer more forward lean. Likewise, less advanced skiers choose more upright stances. Increased forward lean lowers the skier's center of gravity and improves balance. As a result, taller skiers do better with more forward lean.

Forward lean adjusters come in three basic forms: finger nuts, ratchets, or plastic wedges. The most common, the finger nut, is located on the rear of a front-entry boot and is coupled with a threaded rod. As the nut turns it runs up or down the rod, resulting in the forward or backward movement of the boot cuff. Some boots have ratchets located on the rear of the boot. This mechanism is similar to a car jack. Last is the plastic wedge which works by selecting the desired wedge angle and placing it in the boot shaft.

Forward Flex

A forward flex adjuster varies the amount of a boot's ability to resist ankle flexion. Stiff forward flex (high resistance) allows more of the skier's energy to be transferred to the ski because the energy is not being absorbed by the flexing mechanism. However, some amount of flexion is necessary because the ability to flex the ankle in the boots enhances balance in rough terrain.

Forward flex should vary with the height, weight, and strength of the skier. Taller, heavier, and stronger people require little flex because they can impart more leverage against the boot. Shorter and lighter individuals, on the other hand, don't have the ability to bend the boot and thus need softer (more) flex.

Heel Height

This adjustment raises and lowers the heel height of a boot's sole. It is done by turning a threaded shaft that is connected to a wedge in the sole. As the heel is lifted, forward lean is increased. By this the Achilles tendon and the calf muscle are shortened (or at least the tension is removed). The result is greater ankle and hip flexion and mobility and a more snug boot fit.

Cant

Canting a boot involves changing the angle of the boot to compensate for bowlegged or knock-kneed skiers. This adjustment is only done once, as presumably the leg never changes. Conceptually, a bowlegged skier tips the boot and thus the ski outward. Naturally, skiing on the outside ski edges is very difficult. To compensate, the shaft of a boot is tilted inward to flatten the ski on the snow. For knock-kneed skiers a boot would be tilted outward.

The present goal and outlook for binding design is to develop bindings that can keep people skiing without getting them injured or compromising their enjoyment of the sport. Complexity of the bindings will likely increase, but those manufacturers that can keep them simple, lightweight, and safe will be the leaders in binding development.

The common theme of ski, binding, and boot design is specialization. Some critics say that many of the specialized subcategories are simply marketing gimmicks designed to entice people into buying the premium products. It is essential that consumers know their abilities and the types of skiing that they will be doing most and to exercise discipline by buying only the necessary ski equipment.

▶ Summary

Ski, binding, and boot technologies have undergone dramatic changes since the first multipurpose skis were introduced. These changes have occurred in response to the skier's demand for more comfort, control, and safety.

Boots are the primary component for comfort. Manufacturers have responded by designing boots that can be put on and taken off easily; that have simplified buckling, customizable fitting mechanisms, and heating elements; and that are easier to walk in. Based on the type of skiing, one or more of these elements is usually enhanced while others are compromised. Future trends in boot design will focus on perfecting each of these characteristics while reducing boot weight.

Ski designs have been divided into specialized categories. As skiers become more skilled, they are looking for a performance edge and specific control. That edge and control comes from specialized ski design. Skiers can find technologically advanced, highly tuned skis for slalom, giant slalom, downhill, powder, moguls, cruising, acrobatics, and general recreation skiing. Of course, there are sublevels for each of these categories. The key to specialized skis is dimensional and material design. Advances in future ski design will be in finding the particular blend of dimensional and material design that best suits both single-purpose and multipurpose skis.

Bindings are the safety element in skis. Their designs have also become specialized based on type of use.

PART II

Striking Implements

CHAPTER 6

Biomechanical Considerations for Striking Implements

Ellen F. Kreighbaum, PhD
Montana State University, Bozeman

The body consists of segments connected to each other in series. For most striking and throwing movements the segmental action begins with the base segments (the legs) and travels sequentially up through the pelvis, trunk, shoulder girdle, upper arm, forearm, and hand. When manipulated by the performer, the striking implement becomes one additional link in the series of segmental movements used to accelerate the sweet spot of the implement. The striking implement is considered the last link in the kinetic chain. Figure 6.1 illustrates the body segments used in a tennis forehand stroke.

▶ Creating Linear Velocity at the Sweet Spot

The purpose of the segmental movements is to accelerate the end point or sweet spot of the implement so that it is traveling at optimum or maximum speed at the time of impact with the object. There are two types of motion exhibited by a system: linear motion and angular motion. The body segments, and many times the implement, travel in angular motion; that is, they rotate around an axis of rotation located through the proximal end of the joint center. The place on the implement where the sweet spot is located is also rotating around an axis. The shortest distance between any axis of rotation and the sweet spot is called the **radius of rotation**. There is a radius of rotation between the sweet spot of the implement and the axis through the hip joint, the axis through the joints in the vertebral column, the axis through the sternoclavicular

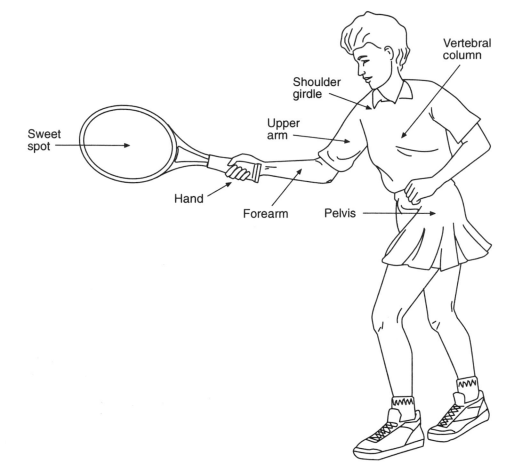

▶ Figure 6.1 Body segments used in producing a tennis forehand.

radius of rotation—For striking implements, the distance between the joint axes of rotation used in swinging the implement and the point at which the implement contacts the object being struck.

joint, the shoulder joint, the elbow, the radioulnar joint, and the wrist. Each joint has its own axis of rotation so there is a unique radius of rotation for each of those joints. Figure 6.2 illustrates the radius of rotation for several joints used in a forehand tennis stroke.

The sweet spot of the implement, the point at which the object is impacted, is rotating around various joints of the body in angular motion. However, when striking an object, it is more important to consider the linear velocity of that impact point, because the impact point of the implement will transfer its linear velocity to the object. The faster the sweet spot is traveling linearly then, the faster the object will leave the implement at impact. Figure 6.3a illustrates the displacement that the sweet spot of a tennis racket could have as seen from above.

The angular and linear velocities of the sweet spot are related. The tennis racket sweet spot (point B) in Figure 6.3b travels in a 50-degree arc. If it did this in 1 second, it would be traveling at an angular speed of 50 degrees per second. Likewise, the throat of the racket (point A) is traveling at 50 degrees per second, as is the tip of the racket (point C). If we were going to calculate the linear speed of points A, B, and C, we would see that in 1 second, these points travel different linear distances. Point A travels the shortest linear distance, and Point C travels the farthest. Thus, if the radius of rotation of Point A is 0.3 meters, Point B is 0.5 meters and Point C is 0.6 meters from an axis of rotation at the butt end of the racket, then we can calculate the linear speed of the three points by multiplying the angular speed by the radius of rotation:

angular speed (radius/sec) × radius of rotation (meters) = linear speed (meters/sec).   6.1

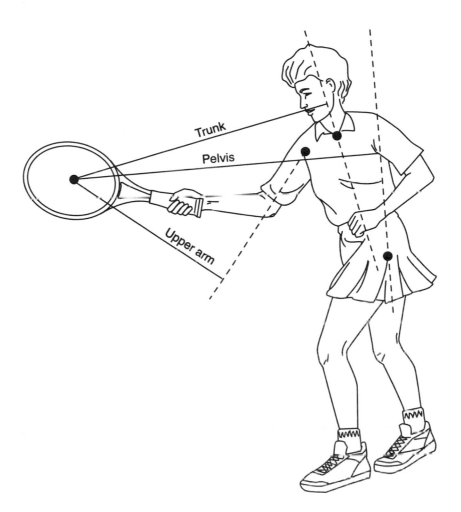

▶ **Figure 6.2** Radii of rotations for pelvis, trunk, and upper arm motions.

The farther the impact point is from the axis of rotation, the larger the radius of rotation; the larger the radius of rotation, the higher the linear speed. A point located farther out from the axis will have the greatest linear speed as long as the angular speed is the same. Thus, the longer the racket, the greater the linear speed of the sweet spot for a given angular speed. One important factor then is the length of the implement selected. Keeping the angular speed constant with a longer implement however may be too difficult.

▶ Creating Angular Velocity of the Implement

Imagine how you swing a softball bat. If you place your hands on the grip at the very end of the bat and swing, you feel the resistance of the bat to that swing. Then if you choke up on the bat, you feel a decreased resistance of the bat to that swing. The lesser resistance felt when swinging the choked bat is why you can swing it around faster. That is, you can cause it to rotate at a greater angular speed. As we saw in the previous section, the sweet spot on a longer bat will have a greater linear speed if the angular speed is constant. However, the longer bat may have a greater resistance to angular acceleration and consequently have a smaller angular speed, resulting in a lower linear speed. The contradiction may be better understood by knowing the mechanics involved.

The angular speed at which the sweet spot is traveling at the time of impact with the object depends on the angular acceleration that is given to it by the performer. The angular acceleration of the racket depends on three factors: the

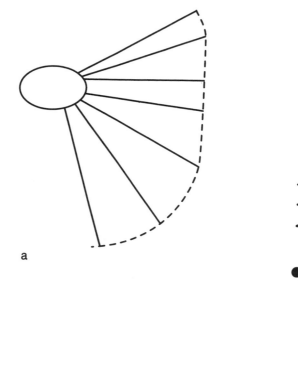

▶ Figure 6.3 (a) Path of sweet spot (dashed line); (b) rotational characteristics of a tennis racket during a forehand stroke.

magnitude of the muscle torques applied to the implement, the mass of the implement, and where that mass is located relative to the axis of rotation. For simplicity imagine that the wrist joint axis is the final axis of rotation for the bat.

Torque

Obviously, the person who can apply greater muscle torque to an implement causes it to accelerate more than one who has less torque to apply. The formula which shows this relationship is:

$$\alpha = T/mk^2 \qquad\qquad 6.2$$

where α = angular acceleration, T = torque applied, m = mass of the implement, and k = radius of gyration of the implement.

Mass

mass—The amount of matter in a body.

A second factor in an implement's angular acceleration is implement **mass**. From the equation, it can be seen that the greater the implement mass, the smaller the angular acceleration, because the mass is in the denominator. Mass may be calculated from the implement's weight, but it is not the same as the implement's weight. The formula for calculating an object's mass from its weight is:

$$m = W/g \qquad\qquad 6.3$$

where m = mass, W = weight, and g = gravitational acceleration.

Gravitational acceleration on Earth generally is 9.8 meters per second per second or 32.3 feet per second per second. Because gravity pulls on every particle of mass, the greater the number of mass particles, the greater the weight and vise versa. Gravity is constant, so every mass particle has the same force of attraction for the Earth. The resistive force to lifting the bat is the bat's weight; the resistance to accelerating the bat horizontally is the bat's mass.

Radius of Gyration

radius of gyration—A mea- sure of the distribution of a body's mass relative to an axis of rotation around which it is being rotated.

The final factor that influences an implement's angular acceleration is termed the **radius of gyration**. The radius of gyration should not be confused with the radius of rotation which was discussed earlier.

Recall that the radius of rotation is the distance between the point of impact or sweet spot and the axis of rotation (from the wrist, for example). The radius of gyration is also a distance. Imagine swinging a bat while gripping the handle. Feel the resistance of the bat to the swing. Next, swing the same bat by gripping the barrel end of the bat. Now feel the resistance of the bat to swinging. If the barrel end of the bat is brought closer to the axis at the wrist joint, then the resistance is reduced appreciably.

This resistance caused by the location of the bulk of the bat's mass is represented by a distance known as the radius of gyration. Simply identified, it is a distance that is always a little greater than the implement's center of gravity from the axis of rotation. The location of a bat's center of gravity, radius of gyration, and radius of rotation of the sweet spot are illustrated in Figure 6.4.

Rotational Inertia

rotational inertia—A mea- sure of a body's resistance to rotational acceleration.

The two properties of an implement, its mass and its radius of gyration, when multiplied make up what is called the implement's **rotational inertia** or its resistance to angular acceleration. The rotational inertia is calculated by the following:

$$I = mk^2 \hspace{3cm} 6.4$$

where m = mass, k = radius of gyration, and I = rotational inertia.

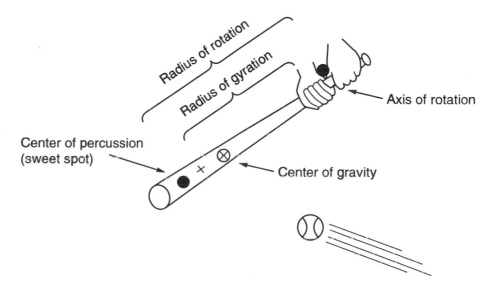

▶ **Figure 6.4** Physical properties of a bat.

With this relationship, we can substitute I for mk² and return to Equation 6.1 to find

$$\alpha = T/I. \qquad\qquad 6.5$$

Because the radius of gyration is a squared term in the equation, it has a greater influence on the rotational inertia than the mass.

In summary, to have the greatest possible linear velocity of an implement at impact with an object, you should maximize angular acceleration, maximize the radius of rotation, maximize the torques applied to the object, and optimize the implement's mass and its radius of gyration.

▶ Characteristics of Striking Implements

In the previous section the dynamics of swinging an implement were described, some of which were influenced by physical characteristics of the implement. A more specific discussion of those physical characteristics follows.

Mass and Weight

Mass (m) and weight (W) are two properties of implements that are often used interchangeably, but even though weight is related to a body's mass, the properties are really quite different. The mass of an object is the amount of matter in that object. Think of mass as being marbles or beans in a jar—the more marbles there are the more molecules of matter in the jar. Similarly, the more mass particles in a bat, the greater the bat's mass.

The force of gravity works equally on all the particles (or marbles) on Earth. The force of gravity works equally on all the particles (or marbles) on the moon. However, the force of gravity is different on Earth than on the moon, and therefore, an object on Earth will have a greater force acting on it than on the moon, even though there are the same number of particles in an object. Thus, an object's mass is *independent* of the gravitational force acting on it; that is, the number of marbles in the jar does not vary with gravity's pull. However, an object's weight does vary according to the gravitational force acting on it. Furthermore, if one jar has more marbles in it than another jar, for example, it will have a greater total downward force due to the sum of gravity's pull on each marble. Thus, it weighs more. Weight depends on the amount of mass (or in this example, marbles) in the system; the mass of an object is independent of its weight.

Weight also has direction associated with it. When you stand on a scale, your weight is directed downward toward the Earth's center, because the Earth's attraction to your mass is toward its center. Mass, unlike weight, does not have direction. Counting marbles in a jar may be done from any direction, and the number in the jar is still the same; mass is mass. Weight depends on the amount of mass in the system and the magnitude of the gravitational force acting on each mass particle. For all practical purposes, we can assume gravitational force is constant on the Earth, although technically it varies somewhat with location.

Center of Gravity and Geometric Center

The **center of gravity** (or center of mass) is an imaginary point that represents the balance point of an implement. Another way of saying it is that the center

***center of gravity**—The point at which a body would balance if it were supported at that point; the point at which the body's mass is assumed to be concentrated.*

***geometric center**—The center of volume of an object.*

of gravity is the place at which all the mass is equally distributed. Two factors affect the location of the center of gravity: the amount of mass and the location or distribution of that mass in the system. Imagine a teeter-totter with two children of equal weight on either end of the fulcrum: The two children will balance if they are sitting equidistant from that fulcrum. In this case, the fulcrum will also be the location of the **geometric center** or middle of the system. (Figure 6.5a illustrates this situation.)

However, if child A weighs more than child B, then to balance, the lighter child B must be farther away from the fulcrum than the heavier child (Figure 6.5b). In other words, the lighter person can compensate for less weight by being farther away from the fulcrum. If one were to multiply the weight of the heavy person by his or her distance from the fulcrum, it would equal the weight of the lighter person times his or her distance from the fulcrum.

In a golf club you can estimate the center of gravity's location by balancing it on your finger. Notice that the head end of the club, which has more mass in it and thus more weight, is closer to the finger than the grip end of the club, which has less mass or weight. The geometric center of the system does not change when the mass is redistributed but remains in the center of the system (see Figure 6.6).

Radius of Gyration

Remember that the radius of gyration is a measure of how an implement's mass is distributed relative to the axis of rotation. For a golf club we can assume that the final axis of rotation is located at the base of the index finger. The more mass located in the club head, the greater the radius of gyration; the more mass located in the shaft or grip, the smaller the club's radius of gyration. The greater the radius of gyration, the more difficult the club will be to swing. The radius of gyration is always a little longer than the distance of the implement's center of gravity from the axis of rotation.

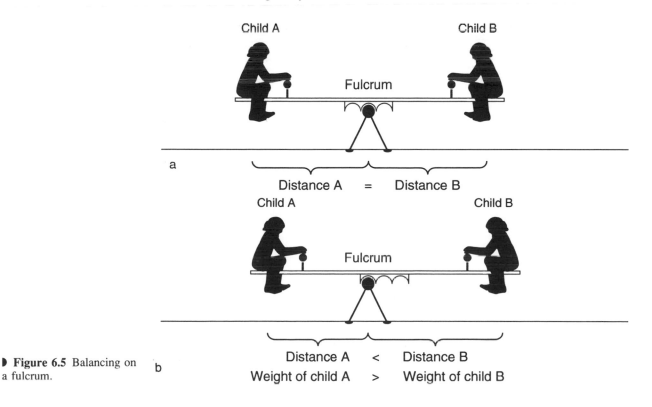

▶ Figure 6.5 Balancing on a fulcrum.

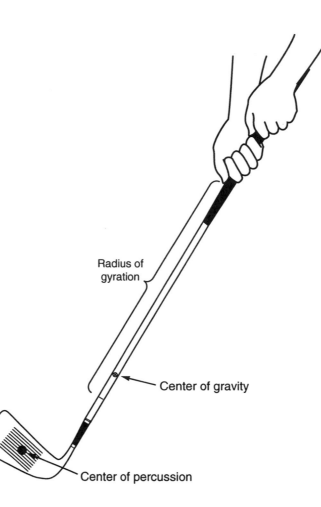

Radius of
gyration

Center of gravity

Center of percussion

▶ **Figure 6.6** The radius of
gyration is affected by an implement's mass and center
of gravity.

Center of Percussion

*center of percussion—The
sweet spot of a striking implement.*

The technical name for the sweet spot of a striking implement is the **center
of percussion** (shown in Figure 6.7), and it is dependent on the location of the
center of gravity and the implement's radius of gyration. It may be determined by
the following equation:

$$q = \sqrt{k^2/cg} \qquad\qquad 6.6$$

where q = the center of percussion from the axis, k = the radius of gyration, and cg = the distance of the center of gravity from the axis.

The center of percussion is always farther from the axis of rotation than the
radius of gyration distance. When the axis of rotation changes from the base
of the index finger to the wrist, the radius of gyration and the center of percussion
relocate themselves up the implement. The farther out to the end of the implement the center of percussion is located, the greater the potential linear velocity
of the impact point. (Recall that the greater the radius of rotation with the same
angular velocity, the greater the linear velocity produced.)

A more commonly known fact of importance about the center of percussion
is that an object struck there will not transfer vibrations to the hands at impact.
The effect can be easily seen if you suspend an implement on a rope from
the ceiling and then throw a ball at its center of percussion. The implement
will rotate around the grip end without the grip end's moving. But if you throw
the ball to the implement's center of gravity, then it will move in a linear

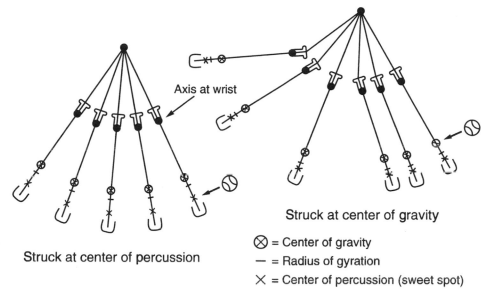

Axis at wrist

Struck at center of gravity

$\otimes$ = Center of gravity
— = Radius of gyration
$\times$ = Center of percussion (sweet spot)

▶ **Figure 6.7** The effects of the ball hitting the bat's center of gravity and center of percussion.

Struck at center of percussion

fashion (i.e., all parts of the implement move equally in a given direction). If struck off the center of gravity and the center of percussion, then the implement will rotate and move linearly at the same time. These motions are illustrated in Figure 6.7.

Interactions of Mechanical Variables

Because of the interrelationship of these mechanical variables, the designer must use each to best advantage. Changing the location of the center of gravity influences the location of the center of percussion. To reduce the radius of gyration so that the implement will be easier to accelerate, the mass must be moved closer to the axis of rotation. However, this also shortens the center of percussion, and vibrations will occur unless the impact point is moved closer to the hands as well. The designer of striking implements must consider all of these interactions. As you will see in subsequent chapters, different implement manufacturers address these dynamics in various ways.

▶ Applications of Biomechanical Parameters to Striking Implements

In the subsequent chapters you will read about the application of biomechanical variables to the selection and use of striking implement. The principles of anatomical function are common to all activities that use striking implements. In sports activity the human body organizes itself according to the overall performance objective of the activity (Kreighbaum & Barthels, 1990). Individual performance characteristics such as strength and size are also an integral part of the equipment selection process.

Tennis Rackets

The tennis racket is larger than either the badminton racket or the racquetball racquet and has a greater radius of gyration and radius of rotation than a racquetball racket. Among tennis racket designs there are differences in mass, radius of gyration, center of percussion, and so on. Any racket must be individually selected by a user according to her or his ability and purpose (i.e., strong-weak, beginner-intermediate-advanced, or recreational-competition player).

Racquetball Racquets

Racquetball is a faster game than tennis. The mechanical characteristics of the racquet include a shorter radius of rotation, a smaller radius of gyration, and a reduced mass. These mechanical characteristics allow for greater racquet acceleration so that the player can respond to a faster traveling ball.

Golf Clubs

From a motor learning perspective, golf is a very complicated skill. The length of the clubs and the fact that the club head sits at an angle to the shaft makes hitting the ball squarely a challenge for even the best skilled. Equipment manufacturers have designed clubs to enhance the performance of less skilled users. Club lengths are adjusted to the player's height, and the radius of gyration is increased and decreased around the club's shaft as well as relative to the wrist joint (the last joint segment rotation). The concentrations of the mass of the club shaft and that of the club head heel to toe and top to bottom are important differences to consider in selecting a set of clubs. A golfer's anatomical characteristics such as height, arm length, strength, and even the predominance of fast- and slow-twitch fibers in the upper extremity may influence which set of clubs is most appropriate.

Softball and Baseball Bats

Two characteristics used to select a bat are its mass (or weight) and its length. However, there is a third and probably more important characteristic, the bat's radius of gyration. This distribution of the bat's mass is critical for bat acceleration during the swing. Professional players may (illegally) hollow out their wooden bats and fill them with cork or another lighter material, attempting to reduce the bat's radius of gyration. This allows the bat a greater acceleration during the swing. A less complicated solution is to select a bat shaped more like a cylinder than one shaped like a bottleneck. The bottleneck bat has a greater radius of gyration and will be more difficult to accelerate.

▶ A Look Ahead

The next few chapters will present the specific design history of striking implements. Changes in material and design demonstrate the progress being made as biomechanical principles are incorporated into the design and manufacture of striking implements.

▶ References

Barham, J. and Krause, J. (1978). *Mechanical kinesiology.* Saint Louis: C.V. Mosby Co.

Kreighbaum, E. and Barthels, K. (1990). *Biomechanics: a qualitative approach for studying human movement* (3rd ed.). New York: Macmillan.

Plagenhoef, S. (1971). *Patterns of human movement.* Englewood Cliffs, NJ: Prentice Hall, Inc.

CHAPTER 7

Tennis Rackets

Carol Polich
Tennis Coach, Bozeman, Montana

The first real seeds for today's tennis game were planted in the 13th century in France. At that time the palm of the hand rather than a racket was used. There have been several theories suggesting how the word "tennis" originated. One theory proposes the French word "tenez" (which loosely translated means "to play") was shouted at the beginning of a match. During the 14th century, wooden paddles were introduced, and eventually the handles were lengthened, the face was hollowed out, and strings were added by the 16th century (see Figure 7.1).

The game was brought to England and became an aristocratic pastime. Originally, the game was played indoors using walls and roofs as well as a net. During the mid-18th century, the strategy of court tennis was to use low, slicing shots. Therefore, rackets were shaped with off-center heads that made it easier for players to scoop up the ball and fling it. To shape the racket head this way, a long strip of flexible wood was softened and slowly bent. Holes were drilled into the wood. The result was a frame that broke rather easily. Because of this breakage, head sizes were small and strings were made from silk, or gut (made from calf or sheep intestines) and strung at low tensions, so as not to put too much tension on the frame (Figure 7.2).

By the 1880s tennis was very much the accepted pastime on both sides of the Atlantic. The game, now being played outside, was called "lawn tennis." Rackets at this point had larger heads, and balls made of rubber were giving the game more bounce. In the 20th century, tennis equipment changed drastically. This chapter looks at the changes made in the design and construction

▶ **Figure 7.1** A 16th-century racket.

of rackets and strings during the last 100 years, with emphasis on the latter part of the century.

▶ The Development of Rackets

Rackets are key to the game of tennis. The lighter and more powerful the rackets, the better a player may perform. Two areas greatly impact racket construction: the materials used and design and construction features. In addition, techniques, styles, and new trends of play are important in choosing the right racket. Some rackets are built head heavy for ground strokers, and some are head light, allowing quicker maneuverability for a serve and volley style of play.

Materials

Changes in the materials used for rackets did not occur until the late 1960s when technology began to skyrocket. New materials were applied to the construction of tennis rackets, beginning a series of relatively rapid developments in racket materials.

Wood

In the first US Open final in 1968, Arthur Ashe defeated Tom Okker using a wooden racket. At that time, using a wooden racket was not out of the ordinary; today, wooden rackets are virtually obsolete. Since the beginning of tennis, wood had been the dominant material in racket construction. Most frames were made from laminated wood, that is, wooden strips bonded and bent together. Because of wood's porous nature, it naturally absorbs shock and vibration, making it less stressful on the arm.

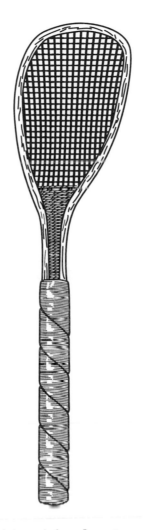

▶ **Figure 7.2** Mid-18th-century racket.

Wood is a natural material, and therefore the type of tree and its growing conditions have much to do with the wood's structure. Thus, strips selected for use in a racket were closely inspected and chosen. Some of the best woods used for rackets were: ash, beech, maple, birch, hickory, and mahogany. Many of these woods were imported from various countries. For example, a famous English-made racket used a combination of American hickory, English ash, Nigerian obeche, and West African mahogany.

Why use so many different woods? By placing stiffer and harder woods (maple, mahogany, and birch) in strategic places in the frame, a stiffer racket is produced. The softer and more resilient the wood (ash, for example) the more flexible the racket. The type of wood used also influenced racket weight and was used to change cosmetic appearance (e.g., mahogany gives a very attractive outer finish). Because wood is a natural substance, no two rackets play or feel exactly the same. Unfortunately, wood is not very durable, so industry introduced the metal rackets.

Metal

In 1967, aluminum and steel rackets were introduced. Aluminum frames were stiffer, providing more control, and were lighter weight than wood. Steel frames were heavier but gave less ball control. Combining these two materials gave rackets more durability and power, but they lacked shock-absorbing qualities because of their design.

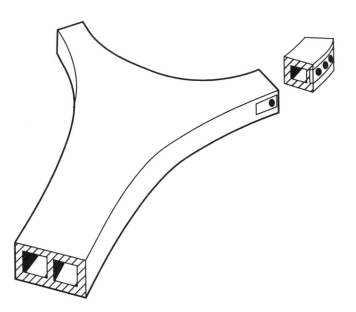

Figure 7.3 "I-beam" construction.

Composite

The next significant new material in the early 1970s was fiberglass. Manufacturers developed the first composite racket by combining fiberglass fibers with aluminum. To lessen the weight of a fiberglass racket, companies designed a hollow-core frame in an "I-beam" construction. Some frames were left with this hollow-core design; others were filled with a foam to help absorb vibration (see Figure 7.3).

In the mid-1970s a huge leap in material construction was seen with the use of graphite. Graphite is extremely light, stiff, and strong and is made of carbon fibers, so it also damped vibrations in the frame caused by ball impact. Today, graphite is still the most widely used material in racket construction. Since 1985, ceramic, a silicon derivative, has been used in frames. It has even better damping qualities than graphite and is usually used in combination with graphite.

Construction

There are basic construction features common to all racket types. But the application of high-tech materials and design innovations have changed today's overall racket construction, giving the player many racket choices.

Sizes

With stronger materials like aluminum and graphite, manufacturers were able to experiment with frame sizes and shapes that wood did not allow. Head size was increased without increasing racket weight. In 1976 Howard Head introduced his oversized, aluminum Prince Classic with a playing area of 110 square inches (opposed to the traditional 70 square inches), and in 1982, the superoversized Weed with 132 square inches of hitting surface was on the market. Today's player can choose from five racket sizes: traditional, midsize, supermidsize, oversize, and superoversize (see Figure 7.4). The mid- and oversized rackets are the most popular and allow for a larger sweet spot (the area of the hitting surface that provides maximum power with the least vibration).

Wide-Body Rackets and Shapes

In 1988 an aerodynamic, wide-body racket was introduced. The head frame was now wider than the standard width of previous racket heads. Again, the

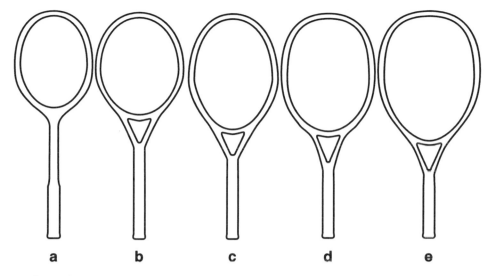

a. Traditional, up to 80 sq. in.
b. Midsize, 81-90 sq. in.
c. Super midsize, 91-100 sq. in.
d. Oversize, 101-110 sq. in.
e. Super oversize, 111 sq. in. and above

▶ **Figure 7.4** Some common racket sizes.

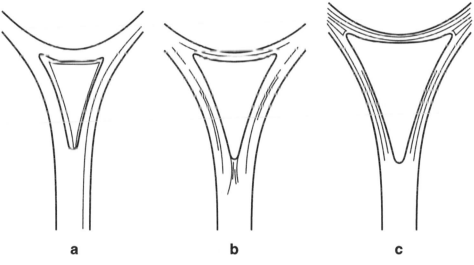

▶ **Figure 7.5** Racket throat shapes may be (a) boxy traditional, (b) rounded, or (c) aerodynamic.

idea was to alleviate vibration and soreness in the arm. The wide body design allowed new profiles in racket frames. There are three common characteristics:

- The frame has an aerodynamic design. When viewed as if hanging from a peg on the wall, the frame has a slim, streamlined appearance in the shaft and head. Refer to Figure 7.5 for an illustration of the throat shape of these rackets.

- The head frame is wider than conventional rackets when viewed from the side.

- There is an increased stiffness resulting from these new dimensions that gives the racket increased power. Instead of flexing at impact and storing energy, the frame resists bending and returns power more efficiently to the ball through the strings.

With an aerodynamic design, the frame can move through the air with less air resistance than a box-shaped frame (Figure 7.6).

There are four new wide-body configurations, each with a different kind of tapering to the frame (Figure 7.7). With each new tapered frame, stiffness and flex in the frame head will fall in different areas of the frame. For example, illustrated in Figure 7.7, the constant-taper frame will be stiffer in the upper part of the head while flexing in the throat area. The reverse constant-taper will be stiffer in the throat and shaft. The dual-taper frame is currently the stiffest frame on the market with very little flex; and the varied-tapered frame has most of its flex in the center of the head. Companies are experimenting with what each feels to be the best design.

Vibration-Free Innovations

One of the primary concerns of today's tennis player is excessive racket vibration. With the decline of wooden rackets that were almost vibration free, and with the production of rackets using space-age materials that make them stiffer, there has been an increase of overuse injuries of the arm such as "tennis elbow." Because of consumer demand, many new string devices have been created to help dampen vibration, thus saving the player's arm. Aware that these string devices cannot stop the vibration from the frame itself, manufacturers have designed rackets that combine power, control, and feel with little vibration to the tennis arm (e.g., the wide-body frame which we have previously discussed). Whether the frame is thick or thin, some of the more forgiving fiber materials being used in these frames

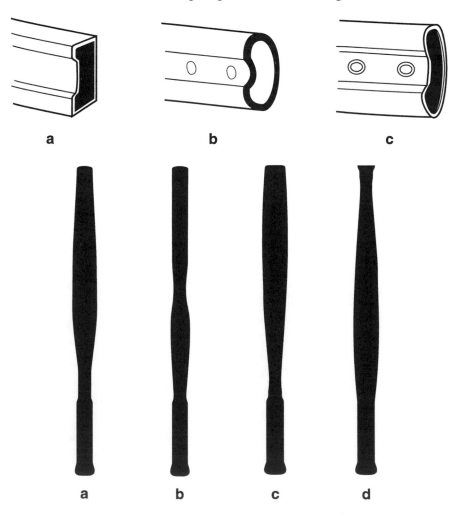

▶ **Figure 7.6** Frame designs have evolved from (a) boxy traditional to (b) aerodynamic with a foam-filled core and (c) aerodynamic with a hollow, wide body.

▶ **Figure 7.7** Wide-body frames with (a) dual taper, (b) varied taper, (c) constant taper, and (d) reverse constant taper.

are ceramic, which is light, resilient, and durable; Kevlar, known for its strength and absorption quality; and twaron, which also helps to absorb vibration.

Another damping method for vibration-free rackets has been used in handle construction. Foam-constructed handles have given way to new ideas such as Spalding's *sensathane*, a softer, shock-absorbing compound used in conjunction with foam. In Prince's constant-tapered system rackets there is a rubber pallet under the synthetic grip that helps absorb shock and vibration and allows the hand to squeeze into the handle. This cushion-grip system absorbs shock 85 percent better than traditional grips. Companies have also experimented with more dense string patterns in frames as well as softer string tensions to help cushion the ball's impact.

Grip Size

The proper grip size is crucial for controlling the racket. There are different methods to figure the correct grip size for the hand. One measures the distance from the second, long crease in the palm to the tip of the ring finger, using the hand that grips the handle. The standard measurement is generally between 4-1/4 inches and 4-5/8 inches (Figure 7.8). If the measurement is between sizes (i.e., slightly greater than 4-3/8 inches and not quite 4-1/2 inches), then you should consider the larger grip. The larger grip usually helps with racket control if your hand is comfortable with that grip size.

Playing Characteristics

Every racket plays differently. The following characteristics should be considered when buying a racket to best match your playing style.

Stiffness and Flexibility

A frame's flexibility depends on how much it will give in the head and throat of the racket. A more flexible racket is often desired if you are a "ground stroker" and want powerful ground stokes, because the frame will flex and recoil causing a trampoline type of action. A stiffer frame, often used by a "serve and volley" type of player, allows for a quicker ball rebound off the frame because it does not flex as much.

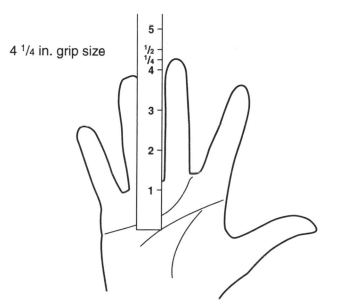

4 1/4 in. grip size

▶ **Figure 7.8** Calculating grip size.

Weight and Balance

Balance is determined by the distribution of the racket's weight in most cases, from 12 to 14-1/2 ounces unstrung (strings add about 3/4 ounce to the racket's weight). If the racket balances evenly at its midpoint, or geometric center, it is said to be evenly balanced. If the head dips, it is head heavy; and if the head rises, the racket is head light.

The player who plays a baseline game and has well-controlled ground strokes, might use a head-heavy or evenly-balanced racket, which would add more speed to the ball. The head-light frame is more often used for a serve and volley game, because it can be maneuvered more quickly for quicker play when coming to the net.

New Trends and Gimmicks

Various manufacturers have experimented with new frame designs. The consumer should be aware of some of these new, nonconventional designs on the market. Following are three innovative ideas that really never caught the public eye.

The Chris racket developed in the mid-1980s was designed to alleviate arm problems by increasing shock absorption within the frame. This racket was more stable because of its innovative convex throat design. Stability increased when more mass was placed away from the center of the racket, which also increased the radius of gyration. The result is less twist, especially with off-center shots. Because this racket design has a wider bridge at the base of the head, allowing for 75 percent of the mainstrings (vertical) to be strung through it, a more natural shock-absorbing action was created.

During 1987 another revolutionary frame style was designed: The Rival gives exceptional control with a design based on physics and principles of the human hand. That is, the mid-to-lower points of the frame including the throat were much wider than the top of the frame—a shape similar to the hand. These innovations improved the torsional stability of the Chris racket with its broad head design. In other words, with a mis-hit shot, the racket would not spin as easily in the hand.

Another racket innovation claimed to help eliminate tennis elbow by using a curved-handle concept designed by Sentra. It fits the natural contour of the player's hand which then eliminates shock, wrist fatigue, and tennis elbow.

▶ Characteristics of Strings

The question always arises, "What kind of string should I get for my racket?" In this era of new, space-age materials, the types of strings are numerous. Therefore, a professional racket stringer should consider the following points about your play:

- How do you hit the ball (i.e., with lots of spin, softly, or is your game power oriented)?
- How frequently do you play during the week, and for how long?
- What kind of "feel" do you like on the ball with string response (stiffer or more forgiving)?
- What type of surface do you play on, and do you mostly play inside or outside?

Giving consideration to these questions, you can decide what kind of string and tension to apply to your racket.

There are two categories of strings, gut and synthetic (made from nylon). Because of larger head rackets, industry was forced to improve string quality: The string has to be longer and pulled more tightly for these large rackets, so the string has to be more durable.

Twenty years ago natural gut was the standard string used by most players. It comes from the intestines of sheep or young cattle and consists of a bundle of thin strands of natural fibers that are twisted together to form the string. Gut's superior energy transfer yields more power than most synthetics, and with its natural fibers it will absorb vibration better than nylon string. Nylons cannot compare with the control, feel, resiliency (springiness), and response that gut offers. Most gut strings are coated to prevent breakage, to lock out moisture, and to make the string more lively or to respond more quickly. An uncoated gut offers better ball control and spin due to its rough surface. On the other hand, this uncoated gut does not play as long as synthetic string. Gut fibers deteriorate more quickly because humid weather conditions can cause a loss in tension; these strings can also break from any additional friction caused by dirt from the court surface. Making gut string is also an involved process, and the resultant high price ($25-$40) discourages many consumers from buying it.

Consequently industry had to create a quality nylon string. Today, most nylon strings are from a multifilament type of construction. The wrapped, multifilament string has thin strands of synthetic fiber wrapped around a mono-filament center core (Figure 7.9a). The multiwrapped multifilament design has several nylon fibers double-twisted around the monofilament core, and they run clockwise and counterclockwise giving added strength (Figure 7.9b). Synthetic gut is coreless and is made using the same process as natural gut with twisted fibers.

The thickness of strings, determined by how many fibers are twisted together, is expressed in gauges of which there are four: 15, 15I (light), 16, and 17. The lower the number, the thicker the string, with the 17-gauge string being the thinnest. The 15-gauge string is fairly obsolete; 15L is the most durable but the stiffest in playability. The 16- and 17-gauge strings have the most resiliency (springiness), but their thinness sacrifices some durability.

When is it time to restring a racket? Many casual players go 2, even 3 years without replacing their strings. What they don't realize is that strings lose their tension and resilience, which results in a reduction in their ability to deform and impart energy to the ball. Strings need replacing before they break. A racket sitting in the closet over the winter will lose string tension. It's like a

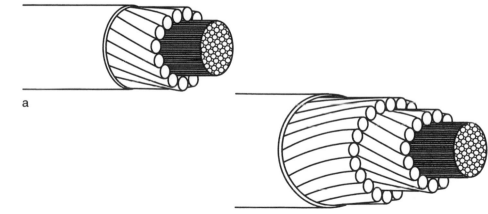

▶ **Figure 7.9** (a)Wrapped multifilament string; (b) multiwrapped multifilament string.

rubber band losing its elasticity after being stretched out over a period of time. Regardless of how often you play, a racket should be restrung at least twice a year. Another rule of thumb is to restring the racket during a year, as often as you play during a week. For example, if you play four times a week, restring your racket four times a year.

Strings break for several reasons. Players who frequently hit with topspin often have string wear. A topspin hit creates friction between the strings themselves which will cause breakage; also, playing outside where more dirt collects on the ball (and on the strings as well) increases friction, decreasing string life.

Today's strings, just like rackets, come in a multitude of colors, thicknesses, and unique shapes and textured surfaces to help impact spin on the ball. Refer to Figure 7.10.

Which string is right for you? Here is a quick overview:

Power—Power is increased when the strings are loosely strung and of a thinner gauge. When the ball strikes strings that have looser tension, the strings deform, storing energy (a trampoline effect), and fling the ball with greater speed as they reform.

Feel (sensitivity)—Thinner strings are more lively or have more springiness whereas a thicker string does not give as easily.

Control—Thicker and higher tensioned strings increase control. The tighter the strings, the more the ball flattens out against them causing a gripping of the ball for more control.

It is difficult to have all three with one choice, and that's where you as the player must find a type of string and magnitude of tension that best suits you.

Before stringing, consider what materials are used to make the racket—they range in stiffness, size and string gauge—and contemplate how it is made.

Approximate string tensions are listed below. The consumer and/or the stringer must choose and consider also the manufacturer's recommended tension.

Appropriate String Tensions		
Tension	**Midsize racket**	**Oversize racket**
Loose	54-56 lb (string tension)	62-65 lb
Medium	57-61 lb	66-69 lb
Tight	62-68 lb	70-75 lb

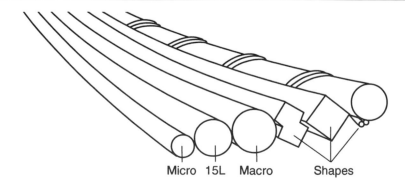

Micro   15L   Macro   Shapes

▶ **Figure 7.10** Various string shapes.

▶ Summary

With rackets changing from wood to metals to space-age materials, the game of tennis has changed, too. Today's high-powered composite rackets, with larger heads that provide a greater sweet spot, are evidence that tennis has become a game of power and speed. In men's professional play, the game is now one of 125 mph serves and a possible return! For viewers this is not the most entertaining of matches and certainly does not show the technical skill required in tennis.

Manufacturers continually redesign the rackets with new materials, weight, head size, and frame width. Today's time frame for redesigning rackets is every 2 years, so what was a perfectly great racket 2 years ago is now outdated by the newest model.

Just remember that the racket that is properly strung, feels good, and doesn't cause you elbow problems could be one you bought 3 years ago. Keeping up with trends is not always the best trend to follow.

▶ References

Day, K. (1988, August). Racquet smarts: What you need to know today. *Tennis*, pp. 61-66.

Day, K. (1988, June). Six expensive new frames. *Tennis*, pp. 48-51.

Day, K. (1988, July). From bales to balls. *Tennis Buyer's Guide*, pp. 26-28.

LaMarche, R.J. (1988, March). It's time to restring! 5 steps you need to know. *Tennis*, pp. 36-37.

LaMarche, R.J. (1988, April). The year's hot trends. *Tennis*, pp. 65-70.

Leonard, T. (1989). A graphic racquet glossary. *Racquets*, a supplement to *Tennis Buyer's Guide*, pp. 4-10.

Schweid, J. (1988, August). Gutless doesn't mean worthless. *World Tennis*, pp. 22-23.

Sparrow, D. (1988, June). The inside story of gut. *World Tennis*, pp. 60-61.

Sparrow, D. (1988, July). A shift to stiff. *World Tennis*, p. 35.

Fiott, S. (1978). *Tennis Equipment*. Radnor, PA: Chilton Book Company.

CHAPTER 8

Racquetball Racquets

Kim Koski, MS
Montana State University, Bozeman

Racquetball, a relatively new sport, has existed under a governing body since 1968, when the International Racquetball Association (which evolved to the American Amateur Racquetball Association) was formed and national rules were standardized (Wong, 1988). That same year, the first international racquetball tournament was held in St. Louis, Missouri, which later became one of the hotbeds in the United States for this fast-growing sport. Bud Muehlcisen, a dentist and one of the pioneers of racquetball, won this tournament; he was the first player to use an aluminum racquet in tournament play. Until that time, players had been using wooden racquets (Wong, 1988).

Many people were actually enjoying a form of racquetball as early as 1920. Referred to as paddleball, this game was popular until the late 1950s and was played with a solid wooden paddle that weighed as much as 350 grams. To make the paddle lighter and more responsive, holes were drilled in it; this eventually led to the development of a new design with a frame and strings (see Figure 8.1).

Joe Sobek, a former tennis and squash pro, is considered the father of racquetball and is credited with inventing the first actual racquetball racquet. Because he could not find adequate squash competition and tennis was not played during the winter, Joe sought a sport that could give him a good workout year-round. Although Joe was also an avid paddleball player, he contended that the heavy wooden paddles made the game too slow. Joe designed a metal racquet frame and contacted the Magnan Racquet Manufacturing Co., which agreed to make 25 racquets at Joe's expense in 1950. Other manufacturers soon copied the idea using wooden frames, which started the misconception

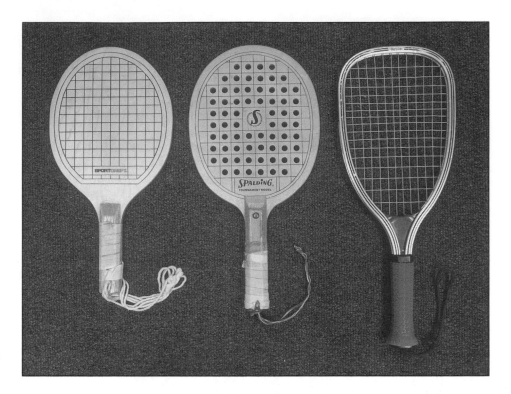

▶ **Figure 8.1** Three frame constructions of racquetball racquets.

that the impetus for racquetball was a sawed-off tennis racquet. From that beginning, modern sport technology turned racquetball into a multimillion-dollar business (Sobek, 1988).

With the advent of the men's pro tour in 1973, racquetball was established to stay. The first women's pro tour followed in 1975, and in 1981 racquetball made its first appearance in the World Games. As the sport grew in popularity and began to receive international coverage, competition between racquet manufacturers became more intense. The next major breakthrough in racquet manufacturing occurred in 1979, when the first hand-laid composite racquets were introduced (Sobek, 1988).

The next innovation came 5 years later in 1984, when the mid- and oversize racquets appeared on the market. By 1985, these racquets had become so popular that the rules of racquetball were changed to allow their use in tournament play.

Racquetball has emerged as a fast-paced, exciting game in which players of all abilities and skill levels can participate. Sporting goods companies manufacture a new line of racquets annually to encourage players to upgrade their racquets to the latest designs. It is here that we will begin our discussion of racquetball racquets.

▶ Racquets

The average player might find it difficult to point out any major differences between racquetball racquets, but a number of them exist. These factors affect quality, performance, and price.

Sizes

The rules of racquetball dictate the racquet size. Including the guard and all solid parts of the handle, the racquet may not exceed 21 inches long. There are no restrictions on racquet width.

Figure 8.2 The three sizes of racquetball racquets: standard, midsize, and oversize.

Three basic racquet sizes are available on today's market: the standard size, midsize, and oversize (see Figure 8.2). The midsize and oversize racquets have become popular in recent years because they help many players improve their performance. The increased length in turn increases the string area and enlarges the "sweet spot," which causes the racquet to be more forgiving on off-center hits.

A midsize racquet gives a player a longer reach (about 2 inches) and has 73 to 85 square inches of string area. This increases the sweet spot by about 63 percent over the standard size. Oversize racquets also increase the reach by two inches in addition to being wider. Total string area is between 86 and 94 square inches, with the sweet spot being 80 percent larger than the standard. Both midsize and oversize racquets increase a player's power while improving accuracy (Davis, 1982).

The one advantage a standard-size racquet has over midsize and oversize racquets is its greater maneuverability. The larger the racquet, the more unwieldy it becomes on the court, particularly in the corners. However, most players feel that the advantages of the midsize and oversize racquets far outweigh this factor (Yellen, 1987).

Construction

The three types of construction used in the manufacture of racquetball racquets are depicted in Figure 8.3: metal, injection-molded composites, and hand-laid composites.

Metal racquets are the least expensive and range in price from $20 to $50. There will always be a market for metal racquets because of their low price and great durability. The frame is formed using solid bars or hollow tubes of aluminum or steel—the same alloys used to build an aircraft. For the most part, metal racquets are a stiffer racquet than injection-molded composites and therefore generate more power. This is ideal for a beginning player, as it allows them to mis-hit the ball and still impart enough force to hit the front wall.

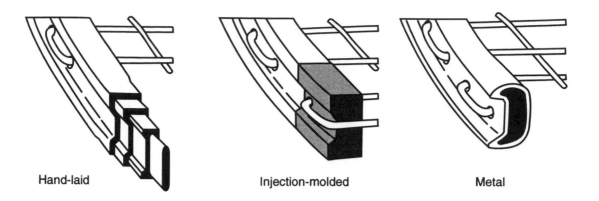

Hand-laid   Injection-molded   Metal

▶ **Figure 8.3** The three types of construction of racquetball racquets.

A full range of flexes can be produced in a metal racquet, but the degree depends on the frame design. Different tubing configurations, that is, of hollow or solid designs, will have an effect on the frame's flexibility. Although a player can choose the degree of flex he or she prefers, a particular racquet gives the same responsiveness at every point on the frame.

Injection-molded composites are the second most expensive racquet available today and cost somewhere between $45 and $125. This price increase over the metal construction is due to more than one type of material's being used for manufacture. A number of different materials are mixed together, injected into a mold, then baked and dried. Usually the fibers of graphite, ceramic, nylon, and fiberglass are used and are ground or chopped into a powder before being injected into the mold. This type of racquet, like the metal, will also respond the same at every point along the frame; but because of the mixture of materials being used, it is a more flexible racquet than the metal models (Yellen, 1987).

Hand-laid composites are the most expensive racquets manufactured and are priced from $75 to $265. With this method a solid core is constructed, then layers of different materials are wrapped around the frame (commonly graphite, boron, Kevlar, ceramic, and fiberglass). By combining these materials, it is possible to make the racquet stronger, lighter, or more flexible at key locations along the frame, which in turn gives the racquet more versatility. For example, it can be stiff at one point, but flexible in another area, depending on what material is laid at each specific point. Certain areas can be reinforced for strength, but not at the cost of additional weight. Overall racquet durability is increased due to the variety of materials used. From an advanced player's point of view, a composite racquet is preferred over racquets using other construction methods (Toljagic, 1987).

Composite Materials

We have mentioned the various types of materials used to manufacture racquet-ball racquets, but why have they been chosen for use? Each material has a specific quality that makes it essential to racquet construction.

Graphite is a form of carbon (black in color) and one of the lightest materials available. This material has allowed manufacturers to decrease overall racquet weight. Usually graphite is the material used in the greatest proportion in the construction of hand-laid composites. Graphite is also known for being a stiff material, so it helps to eliminate vibration and optimizes the power a player is able to get from the racquet.

Fiberglass was one of the first materials used in constructing racquets, but it has lost popularity since the evolution of racquetball from a game of finesse to a power game. One of the most flexible materials, fiberglass, gives a player more control, but at the expense of power. Because it is easily bonded to other materials, it is still commonly used in small proportions in hand-laid composites, giving those racquets the flexibility they need in specific areas.

Boron is used primarily to strengthen areas in the racquet designated as high stress. Known for being 10 times stronger than tungsten steel, it is found in the more expensive, hand-laid composites.

Kevlar has a shock-absorbing quality that is referred to as "vibration damping." A stiff material, Kevlar's shock absorption quality has made it a valuable commodity.

Ceramic was introduced primarily because of its bonding properties. Like fiberglass, it is easily bonded to other materials but has the additional trait of being more responsive according to advanced players. Not all players are able to distinguish this quality.

Weight and Balance

On the average, higher quality racquets now weigh between 205 and 235 grams, due primarily to the variety of materials now available (Davis, 1982). With a lighter frame, it is possible to swing slightly faster, react more quickly, and feel less arm fatigue. Conversely, using a heavier frame slows your movement reaction time (because more time is needed to swing the racquet). The advantage of the heavier racquet lies with the player who is looking for additional power.

Anything lighter than 205 grams presented problems, because players began experiencing elbow and arm injuries in the effort to generate more power by overswinging at the ball (Davis, 1982). On the other hand, racquets weighing more than 235 grams were not practical because of the speed required in the game of racquetball. Players were not able to accelerate the racquet quickly enough to keep up with the game.

Because of the small legal weight range of racquets, greater importance lies in the balance of the racquet (how weight is distributed throughout the frame). Recall that the measure of mass distribution is called the radius of gyration and is related to the axis of rotation at the wrist and forearm. The introduction of hand-laid composites made it possible, for example, to weight the racquet at the top of the frame making it "head heavy," or to weight it at the "throat" or bottom of the racquet, besides weighting it evenly throughout (as with injection-molded or metal construction). A head-heavy racquet will be more difficult to accelerate and will feel heavier although it is not. A head-light racquet will be easier to accelerate and can be moved at a faster velocity. It will feel lighter although it is not. All racquets feel a little different when the player hits the ball. A player chooses by personal preference, but the differences between the feel of racquets lies in their different weight distribution.

Shapes

Before midsize and oversize racquets became popular, manufacturers tinkered a lot with the racquet shape to enlarge the sweet spot, giving players that extra advantage. Since the advent of the larger framed racquets, only two shapes are now popular—the *teardrop* and the *quadriform* (see Figure 8.4).

Differences in the two shapes are minute, with the basic variation being the position of the sweet spot. The sweet spot of the teardrop frame is located higher on the frame. Because it is farther away from the handle, the additional

▶ **Figure 8.4** Presently popular frame designs: teardrop (left) and quadriform.

leverage (radius of rotation) is said to add power. The quadriform style centers the sweet spot, and therefore adds control at the sacrifice of some power. Many players choose a racquet shape according to the types of games they play.

Flex

flex—A common term for stiffness of the racquet.

The final characteristic that will be discussed is a racquet's **flex**, which describes the flexibility, or the stiffness of a racquet. Most manufacturers encourage players to look for a racquet that has the flex characteristics that match up with their skill levels and game plans. This means that a player who hits the ball hard will want to purchase a stiff racquet, whereas a player who looks for more control or "touch" would want a more flexible frame.

With a stiff frame, the ball will not contact the racquet for very long, so a player gets more punch on a shot. Although a stiffer frame results in more power, a player must be skilled enough to control a shot, or the additional power is not much of an advantage. Conversely, the more flexible frames have more "give," so the ball stays on the racquet longer giving players added accuracy.

It is for these reasons that some manufacturers will rate racquet flex on a 1-to-5 scale. Recommendations are then made to players according to skill level, with advanced players using a racquet with a flex of 1 to 2; beginning and intermediate players should probably choose a racquet with a flex of 3 to 5.

Grips

There are two factors that determine the proper grip for any player: size and material. With a grip that is properly sized for a player, he or she should be able to wrap the hand around it so that the middle finger just contacts the base of the thumb. Most companies make a range of grip sizes—from 3-11/16 inches to 4-1/8 inches—to accommodate hands of all sizes (Turner, 1982).

Three basic materials are used to make grips: leather, rubber, and synthetics. To choose a grip type, you must first decide whether or not you will use a glove. A better feel is obtained when no glove is worn, but with heavy sweating a player usually experiences a lot of racquet slippage, which results in a loss of control. The residue of sweat on the grip (salt) also tends to make the grip more slippery the next time you play.

Although some players choose not to wear gloves, the majority of players will use gloves to increase the firmness of their grips. The gloves now on the market are so thin that a player really doesn't lose much feel. The only drawback is that once the glove becomes very wet, it must be exchanged for a dry one, so a ready supply must be kept on hand. This, coupled with the fact that all gloves wear out and need replacing, can add up to quite an expense.

Both leather and synthetic grips can be used with or without a glove. The advantage of a synthetic grip is that it has a cushioned backing that helps absorb shock and vibration on mis-hits. Rubber grips are most commonly used by players wearing gloves. They provide the best grip when the glove is slightly wet because the combination of the damp leather against the rubber provides additional tackiness. This type of grip will not usually be used without a glove, because the rubber can irritate the skin and cause blisters.

▶ Strings

Nylon string is the most commonly used material to string a racquetball racquet. Due to the nature of the sport, gut is not an appropriate material; it is not durable, and particularly when it gets wet it has a tendency to disintegrate at a faster rate (Hice, 1987). Nylon monofilament is the most suitable because of its durability, and there is rarely a drop in the tension after a player uses it several times (Baudman, 1988).

Racquet string tension is normally recommended by the manufacturer according to the frame shape and materials for maximum racquet effectiveness. In general, racquets strung at higher tensions will give players more control, whereas the loosely strung racquet tends to add power.

At both ends of the spectrum there comes a point of no return. In other words, if the string tension is too high, you end up losing control because the string becomes so board-like that the ball rockets off the strings so fast a player has no chance to control the shot. Conversely, if the tension is too low, the "spaghetti effect" results, meaning the ball lies on the strings so long that most of the power is sacrificed. On the average, standard-size racquets are strung at about 8 to 32 pounds, while midsize and oversize racquet tensions range from 22 to 50 pounds. Some manufacturers will recommend a range of tension varying from 3 to 10 pounds when stringing a racquet. A player might experiment with various tensions until he or she finds the one that is appropriate for the game.

As the shape and size of racquets has changed in recent years, so have the stringing patterns in order to accommodate these changes. When the throat piece feature was removed from some racquets, the longitudinal main strings extended down farther on the frame, once again increasing the size of the sweet spot (Davis, 1982).

Ektelon's sunburst pattern is less dense than most racquets, with the idea of increasing the feel of the racquet, because the strings can act independently of one another. Omega patented the Mad Raq design that added a diagonal set of strings to the conventional main and cross strings, thus giving more string contact with the ball to increase control. Pro Kennex instituted its own design

▶ **Figure 8.5** Pro Kennex micro string system.

which is called the *micro string system* using a smaller gauge (thinner) nylon string and a greater number of strings, creating a more dense pattern (see Figure 8.5). With more strings the company reduced the tension, but not at the expense of power. Neither the Mad Raq pattern nor the micro pattern proved to be extraordinarily popular, and the manufacturers of both have discontinued these models.

▶ Summary

Over the years, racquetball has continued to increase in popularity. The year 1993 marked the 25th anniversary of the American Amateur Racquetball Association, and a pro tour now exists for both male and female athletes. Racquetball has been included in the World Games and in the Olympics as an exhibition sport. National tournaments are held annually for which participants must qualify by winning regional tournaments.

Because of the sport's popularity, organized racquetball has worked to include players at every level. Rule modifications have been made to generate interest among and include people at the junior level and people who are physically disabled. Age divisions range from 8 years and under to the Grand Masters, for those 80 years and older.

As touring pros continue to promote the game through clinics and exhibitions, new players are regularly enticed to learn the game. The future of racquetball appears to be secure, and it will continue to evolve as sports technology improves.

▶ References

Boudman, J. (1988, May). Is it time to restring your racquet? *National Racquetball*, 17(5), p. 6.

Davis, R. (1982, October). Racquets of the future. *Racquetball Illustrated*, 5(7), pp. 22-24.

Hice, R. (1987, June). Look ma, no strings! *National Racquetball*, 16(5), pp. 24-25.

Sobek, J. (1988, November). The father of racquetball. *National Racquetball*, 17(11), p. 22.

Toljagic, M. (1987, August). Frame by frame: String doctors at work. *National Racquetball*, 16(8), pp. 24-26.

Turner, E. (1982, October). Everything you always wanted to know about the grip. *Racquetball Illustrated*, 5(7), p. 25.

Wong, K. (1988a, June). The St. Louis revolution—secret of the JCAA. *National Racquetball*, 17(6), pp. 6-8.

Wong, K. (1988b, July). The St. Louis revolution—the source of fire. *National Racquetball*, 17(7), pp. 34-38.

Yellen, M., McKinney, C., & Swain, C. (1987, December). Standard, mid-size or oversize—what works best? *National Racquetball*, 17(12), 19-20.

CHAPTER 9

Golf Clubs

Mark A. Smith, MS

Perhaps in no other sport has the evolution of its equipment had so much impact on the game's advancement and its popularity than golf. Technological advances are at the heart of this evolution and have increased the two most sought-after attributes of golf: distance and accuracy. Yet golfing is still a highly skill-based sport.

Many of us find golfing nothing more than an exercise in frustration. Mark Twain once called it "a good walk spoiled." Nevertheless, it is one of the world's fastest growing sports. Billions of dollars a year are spent on golfing equipment, instructional videos, and golfing lessons. Still sports technology seeks that perfect match between golfer and club.

▶ History

The word "golf" originates from the German world *kolbe*, which means club. But the origins of the game itself are much less clear. The Flemish claim golf's origins stem from the game of *chole*, where the French maintain that *jeu de mail* is the ancestral game of golf. The ancient Romans even have a claim for golfing roots with a game called *Paganica*, which means "a game of countrymen."

Whatever its origins, it is widely agreed that the Scots were the first to organize and play golf the way we know it today. An Act of Scottish Parliament in 1457 is the first documented reference to the sport. This Act made it unlawful

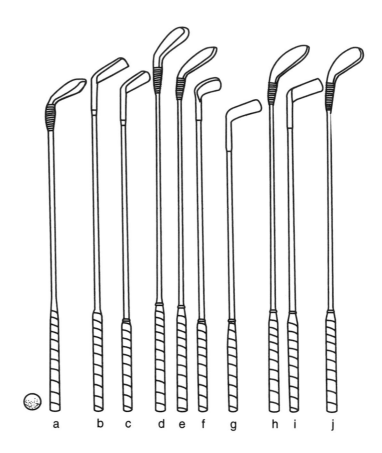

▶ **Figure 9.1** While the designs of American golf clubs haven't changed much since the early days, the names are far different. Shown here are designs depicting the (a) wooden putter, (b) cleek, (c) mashie, (d) driver, (e) short spoon, (f) niblick, (g) iron putter, (h) long spoon, (i) sand iron, and (j) brassie.

to play golf while at war with England. Apparently, the Scottish government didn't want its young men to neglect their military training.

During organized golf's early era, balls were fashioned from leather spheres stuffed with goose feathers, which was called a *feathery*. Clubs were crafted from wood and bone. Typical golfers usually would carry a few more balls than they thought they might lose and two putters—a driving putter (for approach shots) and a green putter. The green putter was much the same as it is today except for materials. The tools were perhaps crude but very expensive, making it a "gentleman's" game. In fact, a ball alone sold for the price of a common man's daily wage.

Figure 9.1 shows the basic set of American clubs in golf's early days. As you can see, the designs are familiar but some of the names are not. This chapter will outline the recent evolution of golf clubs and discuss their anatomy, construction, materials, purpose of design, and mechanical properties.

▶ Club Anatomy

There are three major components of a golf club: the head, the shaft, and the grip. Figure 9.2 illustrates the anatomy of a golf club. The other parts shown in this illustration will be discussed in their respective sections.

Two basic concepts about club design, length and swing weight, must be discussed before the specifics of the head, shaft, and grip are detailed.

Length

One of the first things you learn about golf clubs is that the longer the club, the flatter the club head is and the farther the ball will travel. Club length plays

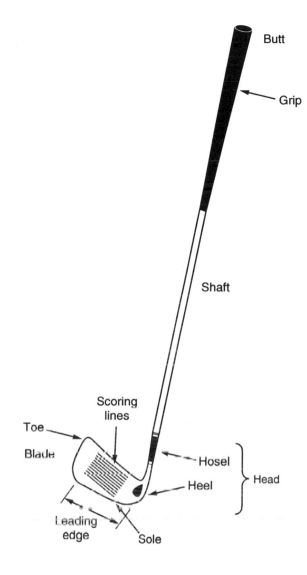

▶ Figure 9.2 Anatomy of a golf club.

a greater role in distance than does the angle of the club head, which influences the loft of the ball. The standard lengths of men's and women's golf clubs are shown in Table 9.1.

Longer clubs naturally put the golfer farther away from the ball. It is the angular speed of the club head at this longer distance that transfers velocity to the ball. Recall that linear velocity equals angular velocity times the radius of rotation. Thus, the angular acceleration of a longer club head will produce greater linear velocity than a shorter club.

Swing Weight

swing weight—A golf club's weight distribution.

Swing weight is a little more complicated and much less understood by most golfers. This concept has been put into practice for over 50 years; it gives a uniform balance to a set of clubs by systematically distributing the weight of a club. Figure 9.3 shows how both total weight and swing weight are measured. As you can see, swing weight is dependent on total weight and is the measurement of a club's weight distribution at an established distance from the grip end of the club.

The point at which the club is measured is the fulcrum. Fulcrum points can be either 12 or 14 inches from the grip end of the club. Swing weight is

Woods	Men's length	Ladies' length
Table 9.1 Custom Fitting Table—Standard Lengths for Woods and Irons		
1	43"	42"
3	42"	41"
4	41 1/2"	40 1/2"
5	41"	40"
6	40 1/2"	39 1/2"
Irons	*Men's length*	*Ladies' length*
2	38 1/2"	37 1/2"
3	38"	37"
4	37 1/2"	36 1/2"
5	37"	36"
6	36 1/2"	35 1/2"
7	36"	35"
8	35 1/2"	34 1/2"
9	35"	34"
PW	35"	34"
SW	35"	34"

PW = Pitching wedge
SW = Sand wedge
Note. These lengths are generalized. Many manufacturers vary these lengths.

typically characterized by letters ''C'' or ''D'' (which describe the fulcrum distance 12 and 14 respectively) and a number in ounces required to balance the club on the fulcrum. Table 9.2 outlines some typical swing weight configurations. Note that the stiffer the shaft flex, the higher the swing weight. This will be discussed more thoroughly under the section on shaft flexibility.

Generally, swing weight is nothing more than a unique and systematic way to assess the balance of the club. Club manufacturers make entire sets of clubs so that the balance among clubs in a set is alike. But, swing weight is only one element in the feel of a club. Other characteristics like club-head design, shaft flexibility, and grip play important roles as well. These characteristics are discussed below.

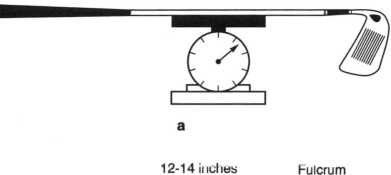

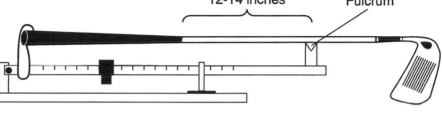

▶ **Figure 9.3** Measuring (a) total weight and (b) swing weight.

Table 9.2 Custom Fitting Table—Swing Weight Range by Shaft Flex

Shaft flex designation	Recommended swing weight range	Average
L–Ladies	C0-D0	C7
A–Flexible	C7-D3	D0
R–Medium	C9-D5	D2
S–Stiff	D0-D6	D3
X–Extra stiff	D2-D8	D5

Note. Shafts designated with C are more flexible than shafts designated with D.

▶ Club Heads

The design or shape of the golf club head distinguishes the irons from the woods and has undergone changes with the introduction of new technology and materials. Both club-head design and its materials have remained virtually the same until the mid-1960s. Prior to this time the club heads forged had design limitations. The forging process heats metal so that it is pliable and can be hammered or pounded into the desired shape. (Horseshoes, for example, are forged.) Automation and forging technology improved the quality of forged clubs over the years, but new processes give today's clubs superior performance.

Irons manufactured by this forging technique can't match the playability of most present-day clubs that are cast in molds. Forged clubs, commonly called *blades*, are still made, but most of today's clubs are investment cast into molds.

A cast club is made by pouring molten metal into a cast and cooling it until solid. It is this process that allowed club manufacturers to perfect the perimeter-weighted club and enlarge the so-called "sweet spot" (that area on a club face that when hit produces little or no vibration on the hands). Casting allowed the metal to be shaped around the club's perimeter and increased the effective hitting area of the club face, thereby enlarging the sweet spot. Naturally, more accomplished golfers had little trouble consistently hitting the sweet spot, but most golfers improved their game when using cast clubs.

perimeter weight—added mass around the perimeter of a club designed to impart more lift on the ball.

Perimeter weighting also puts more mass at the bottom of the club head thus lowering the club's center of gravity, which more effectively forces the club face under the ball, resulting in more lift. Most beginners' clubs are designed with more bottom perimeter weighting to assist in lifting the ball higher in the air.

Loft

loft—the angle of the striking face of the club.

Club-head **loft** is the angle between the horizontal plane of the bottom of the club head and the plane of the club-head face itself. As seen in Figure 9.4 club-head loft decreases with the length of the club. The loft of irons is fairly rigidly established. However, recently some club manufacturers have been decreasing the loft of their irons to give golfers the impression that they can hit their irons farther.

A set of irons consists of a one iron (which has the least amount loft and is the longest) sequentially through the nine iron, the pitching wedge, and the sand wedge (which has the highest loft and is the shortest club). Naturally, club heads with shallow loft (e.g., the one iron) keep the ball lower to the ground when hit. This, coupled with club length, imparts greater horizontal normal force on the ball when it is hit. Thus, distance is increased.

As club-head loft decreases so does club length. Club heads with greater loft impart two characteristics to the ball: height and spin. Height is increased because the normal force of the club head hitting the ball approaches a more vertical angle. Higher lofted club heads impart more backspin on a ball as well. Backspin is created when the club head and the ball connect. All club faces except putters are grooved. As the club face strikes the ball, the club face is still moving downward through the arc of the swing; the grooves momentarily grip the ball and force backspin on it. Backspin is the characteristic that enhances

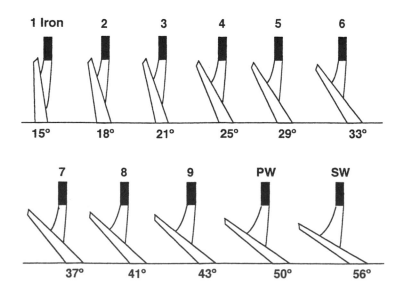

▶ **Figure 9.4** Typical loft of irons.

the "feel" of club head hitting the ball. It also offers more control and accuracy in shot making. Recently, there has been some controversy over whether square grooves on the club head give the golfer "too much" spin, control, and accuracy over the ball.

The Putter

Putters have more variations in design and modification than any other club—because putting is the make-or-break element of the game. It is also the club that requires the most amount of feel. The recent trend in putters is toward a bigger mass and more perimeter weighting. Perimeter-weighted putters are sometimes called *cavity-backed putters*. The increased mass and perimeter weighting also increases the sweet spot.

Alignment is crucial in putting, so most putter shafts are a few degrees off vertical. The purpose is to put the golfer's eyes directly over the ball, so that when the putter hits the ball, it is hit in the center of the putter. There are thousands of different putter designs and hypotheses on how to putt. Putting is a skill so personal and so based on feel that an entire book could be written on this topic alone.

Materials

Club manufacturers are experimenting with a variety of metal alloys and nonmetallic compounds to increase club-face performance. The more exotic materials include the increasingly popular beryllium copper and graphite, and the most intriguing is ceramics. Each of these materials has unique attributes. For example, most of the older, forged clubs were some type of steel that had a stiffer feel. Beryllium copper clubs are considered softer because they grip the ball on the club face, allowing greater control.

Woods

Wood clubs include the driver or 1 wood, the 3 wood, and sizes up to 14. Woods like irons are numbered in descending order by length and loft. That is, the driver or 1 wood is longer and has less loft than a 3 wood. The loft and length characteristics of woods are exactly the same as those discussed for irons. As Figure 9.5 shows, the driver typically has a loft of 7 to 11 degrees. Shorter woods like the 3 wood and up have a higher loft of 14 to 17 degrees.

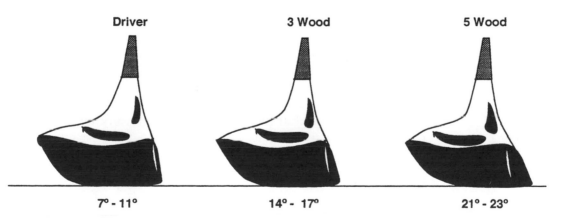

Driver	3 Wood	5 Wood
7° - 11°	14° - 17°	21° - 23°

▶ **Figure 9.5** Loft ranges in woods.

More technologically advanced woods also have incorporated the concept of perimeter weighting. The more popular metal woods of today are, as the name implies, made from a metallic outer shell. These club heads are hollow with an inner core consisting of various materials ranging from styrofoam to a cardboard or plastic honeycomb composite. The cross-section of a metal wood reveals unevenly distributed metal throughout the club head (for the same reason it is done in iron club heads).

The older wood designs of the modern era were typically thinly layered wood pieces bonded together into the shape of the club head and finally laminated with either a hard coat of paint or some other laminate. The most popular type of wood for this process was persimmon, the wood of choice because of its combined hardness and resilience.

Along with the length of the shaft, the shape of the club head is also important for its distance-producing effect. The relatively massive shape of the wood club head is another simple application of physics to produce a desired effect (in this case distance).

▶ Shafts

The shaft is the unifying element of the club. It bridges the golfer's hands to the club head. It wasn't until the 1930s that steel was used for the shaft. Although steel is still the standard, more exotic materials are being introduced such as graphite, fiberglass, aluminum and titanium.

Prior to the 1930s shafts were fashioned from wood; those of the early Scots were hazel. By the 19th century, ash was used most extensively. However, hickory would subsequently became the standard because of its combination of toughness, rigidity, and resiliency.

The introduction of steel clubs was another revolutionary change for golf. Steel added more power to shot making coupled with greater control. Also, their ability to be mass produced to exact specifications allowed manufacturers to offer steel-shafted clubs as a matched set, one with a consistent likeness and feel throughout each club in the set.

A sophisticated and costly technique that can produce this consistency in feel uses resonate frequency matching which measures a shaft's resonate frequency using an oscillating machine. Shafts with similar frequencies are grouped and may become part of a single set of clubs.

Materials

Graphite shafts have offered mixed results since their introduction in the late 1960s. Graphite weighs less but has torsional problems; that is, these graphite shafts would twist during the swing which made them very inconsistent. Advances in graphite composites and weave patterns in the 1980s solved these problems, now making graphite shafts very popular.

Like graphite, titanium also offers light weight, even lighter than steel, and pound for pound is much stronger and stiffer than steel. Titanium also has none of the torsional problems of graphite had in its early introduction. However, it is expensive and the shaft is simply too stiff for most golfers who prefer some type of steel shaft.

Flexibility

Steel shafts are hollow to reduce weight and increase flexibility (a variable characteristic). Shafts come in a variety of flexes: very flexible, flexible, ladies' flex, medium or regular flex, stiff, and extra stiff. Based on a golfer's physical characteristics such as strength, swing, and body height, shaft flexibility is chosen. Golfers who are taller, stronger, and have a greater swing arc typically tend to generate more club-head speed and usually select the stiffer shafts. Conversely, golfers who are shorter, relatively weaker, and have shorter swinging arcs (i.e., slower club-head speed) will often select a more flexible shaft.

Again, a longer swing arc or a longer shaft (greater radius of rotation) creates more linear velocity and thus more velocity transfer when the ball is hit. A flexible shaft compensates somewhat for a golfer of lesser strength because the acceleration of the club head increases dramatically as the club head approaches the bottom of the swing. This occurs because a shaft with higher flexibility is bending at the top of the swing; as the swing progresses downward the hands stay ahead of the club head until the reflex action of the shaft begins. The club head begins to accelerate even more at the bottom of the swing. This sudden acceleration of a flexible shaft is a whip-like action that produces more club-head acceleration than a stiffer shaft would. The compromise for high flexibility is consistency and control.

▶ Grips

The interface between the club and the golfer's hand is the grip. Early grips were made of sheepskin or leather. Originally, grips were intended to cushion the hand against the impact of the ball. Clubs were held differently then—by the palms rather than the fingers as in today's technique.

Leather has always been a very popular grip because of its cushioning properties and the hands' ability to grip it. However, today most grips are made from a rubber composite. This type of grip is much cheaper than leather and is easier to manufacture to exact specifications.

Grip size is an important element for an effective hit. For example, a grip that is too large for a hand can reduce hand movement during the swing, which frequently forces the club face to aim right of the target. A grip too small can force too much hand movement, resulting in club-face alignment left of the target.

▶ Summary

The modern-day set of clubs is far more technologically advanced than even those in the 1950s. These advances in club design technology coupled with those in manufacturing and mass production have propelled golfing into the fastest growing sport in the industrialized nations.

We have discussed how the evolution of the club has changed the game. We also have discussed how characteristics like club length, loft, shaft flex, and swing weight interact. These elements are golf basics and are unlikely to change, but their use and the advancement of newer technologies will always push golfers in their quest for greater distance and accuracy.

CHAPTER 10

Baseball and Softball Bats

Gale C. House, PhD
School District of Philadelphia

A baseball bat at first appearance seems to have changed very little during the history of the sport itself. Even with the introduction of metal bats, its flared-cylinder design with a knob at the end farthest from the barrel appears unchanged. A closer examination reveals numerous variations in this basic design.

Manufacturers of wooden bats, either on their own or at the request of individuals (such as major league players), have introduced some variations in bat construction. These include removing the knob, varying the thickness of the handle, and altering the shape of the barrel (e.g., with longer flare, with a "milk bottle" design, or by scooping out the end).

The development of metal alloy bats has permitted an even greater variety in design—as well as introducing the "ping" sound at ball contact. With regard to distribution of mass, metal bats allow for more variability by changing the thickness of the metal in different areas of the bat. Metal bats can withstand the forces of impact better than wood and are capable of hitting a ball farther than wood. They can be drilled, filled, or angled, unlike wood.

Major league baseball may eventually see the end of wooden bats. The difficulty in supplying the quality wood necessary for the number of ash bats currently used and broken each season may necessitate a controlled-design, composition baseball bat for use in the major leagues (Gammons, 1989). Experiments with ceramic composite materials have produced bats that sound and perform more like wood than other composite bats.

In recent years the game of softball has become a showcase for the special-design metal bats. The sport of softball began in the 1880s as indoor baseball and originally used baseball bats to hit a 16-inch soft ball rolled up in a boxing glove. The game evolved to outdoor fields and an identity of its own (ASA, 1993). Softball today encompasses fast pitch and slow pitch, single-sex and coed teams, and nearly as many bat choices as there are types of players.

The obvious function of a baseball or softball bat is to generate the game's offense. Some of a bat's physical properties can be manipulated by manufacturers to enhance the batter's success in reaching this goal. However, success occurs only if the coach or batter properly matches bat parameters with the batter's physical prowess. An understanding of the physics of a swinging bat and the variations in bat designs available is necessary to make the best choice of bat.

▶ Rules

The legality of a bat varies with different rule-making bodies. In major league baseball a bat:

- must be wooden, one piece or laminated;
- may not be more than 42 inches long or more than 2-3/4 inches in diameter;
- may have a grip-improving substance added to the 18 inches above the knob;
- may be cupped at the barrel end; and
- may not be colored, unless approved by the Rules Committee, as black bats are (Official Baseball Rules, 1993).

College teams who play baseball under NCAA jurisdiction may use wooden or metal bats. Wooden bats must conform to the major league bat and must also have a line marking the 18 inches from the knob end. College players may also use nonwooden bats as long as the knob is permanently attached and the bats have been approved by the NCAA Rules Committee (NCAA Baseball Rules, 1993).

Some nonprofessional leagues, in which many professional prospects play, have banned metal bats because hitting prowess with the metal bat may not be indicative of ability with the wooden bat required in the Majors.

The Amateur Softball Association of America (ASA) has opened its arms to a great variety of designer bats (see Gimmicks below). The Rules Committee of the association has approved bats with angular handles, liquid centers, perforated barrels, three-sided barrels, and scooped ends; in a rainbow of colors; and with knurled finishes (see Figure 10.1). The bat may be constructed wholly or in part from a variety of materials including aluminum, plastics, graphite, ceramics, magnesium, or wood. A softball bat is legal and stamped with ASA approval as long as it is safely constructed to meet size restrictions and does not have any "special design features to enhance hit distance" (*The Official ASA Guide* and *Playing Rules*, 1993). The bat may not exceed 34 inches in length, 38 ounces in weight or 2-1/4 inches in diameter at the barrel. Safe construction includes such features as a permanently attached knob, a closed barrel end, and a safety grip in place.

▶ Materials and Construction

Traditionally, baseball and softball bats have been made from wood. The introduction and acceptance of aluminum bats opened the door to creative bat designs that attempt to enhance the mechanics of batting.

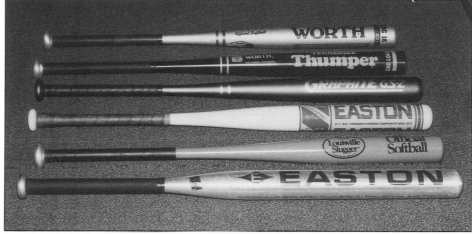

▶ **Figure 10.1** Examples of legal softball bats. From the top: knurled surface (Worth-SBC16), scooped end (Worth-SBC29), graphite (Worth-GSZ), ceramic/carbon/composite (Easton-SC1), orange color (Louisville Slugger-125LSB), and 16-inch barrel length (Easton-S93436). (Bats courtesy of Hauff Sporting Goods Co., Sioux City, Iowa.)

One-piece wooden bats are usually made from ash because it is a hard and resilient wood. (Some Little League bats are made from maple, but this wood is not sufficiently durable for major league play.) The lumber from an ash tree is cut into 40-inch segments. If the grain is of acceptable quality, it is then split into quarters, hewn into cylinders, and dried by air, kiln, or microwave. The cylinder is placed on a lathe and turned to the shape of a model or computer-programmed design.

Laminated bats are made from blocks of wood formed from two or more layers of wood bonded together with adhesive. The grain of each wood layer is parallel to the length of the bat. No other substance besides wood and adhesive may be included in the lamination. This block of laminated wood is then turned on a lathe to create the desired bat form.

Construction of aluminum, graphite, steel, ceramic, and magnesium composition bats includes milling the material into a tube, cutting the tube into appropriate lengths, and molding the tube into a flare according to a prototype. The barrel end is scaled, the knob end is welded on, identifying markings are screen-painted on the bat, and a safety grip is attached. Most metal bats used in the United States have some type of foam inserted into the barrel before it is closed to reduce the ''ping'' sound resulting from impact. (Bats shipped to Japan are made without the foam insert; the Japanese prefer the sound associated with ball impact.)

The choice of materials for a bat's composition determines some of its qualities. With aluminum the weight distribution along the length of the bat could be altered. Graphite and carbon fibers add strength and stiffness. Ceramic composits produce a sound at ball impact which resembles the ''crack'' of a hit with a wooden bat (Linson, 1989). All of the composition bats damp the vibration and therefore the sting of the bat at impact.

▶ The Physics of Bat Design

The function of a bat is to impart momentum to the ball through impact with it. The physical properties of a bat (see Figure 10.2) that vary from one bat to another and that influence the physics of the hit are: its mass (measured by its weight), the location of the center of gravity, the location of the center of percussion, the length of the radius of gyration, and the hardness and stiffness of the material (House, 1988).

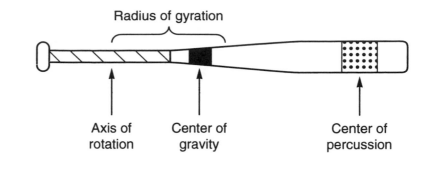

▶ Figure 10.2 Bat parameters.

Mass or Weight

momentum—A quantity of motion of an object equal to the mass of the object multiplied by its velocity.

A "long-ball" batter wants to swing a heavier bat so that more momentum can be transferred from the bat to the ball (Barr, 1970). **Momentum** equals mass times velocity. The momentum of the bat is a function of its mass (weight)—which can be varied up to the legal maximum in softball or the practical maximum in baseball—and the velocity with which it is swung. The ball's mass (weight) remains constant (unless it is saturated while playing in the rain). Therefore, when the momentum from a heavier and/or faster moving bat is transferred to the ball, the bat will have greater velocity and the ball will travel farther and faster. Unfortunately, as the mass of the bat increases many batters find that their ability to accelerate the bat (generate bat velocity) decreases, which negates the advantage of greater bat mass in generating bat momentum.

Center of Gravity

center of gravity—The point at which all of the weight of an object is concentrated.

The **center of gravity** or center of mass refers to the point at which the bat can be balanced in a horizontal position. A bat's center of gravity depends on the distribution of the mass of the bat. In practical terms, when a batter judges the "feel" of the bat, she or he is really referring to the location of the center of gravity. A bat that feels balanced has a center of gravity located at its geometrical center, whereas a bat that feels barrel-heavy has its center of gravity closer to the barrel end than the knob end (i.e., more of the weight is distributed toward the barrel end of the bat).

Bat manufacturers adjust the distribution of mass in several ways while maintaining the same bat weight (Hersch, 1986). With wooden bats, a cylinder can be reshaped to add a knob, or remove it, or a fat handle can be tooled down to a thin handle to distribute more weight to the barrel end. The construction of metal bats allows the manufacturer to "load" the bat nearly anywhere along its length by increasing the thickness of the cylinder wall, or by altering the density of the metal along the barrel. Thus end-loaded bats have more weight in the barrel end and less in the handle end, creating a bat that feels barrel-heavy. Why is this an advantage, and why are manufacturers end loading so many metal bats? The answer is to move the sweet spot, or the center of percussion, toward the barrel end of the bat.

Center of Percussion

Any batter can tell you that hitting the ball at the sweet spot sends it farther and doesn't sting your hands. When the ball and bat meet at a point other than the **center of percussion**, or sweet spot, the batter's hands feel the sting, especially on a cold day. The sting comes from the bat's rotation and is created

center of percussion—The point at which a striking implement can impact with another object and yield no reaction force at the axis of rotation.

harmonic node—The point of no disturbance of a standing wave.

axis of rotation—The point at which the impact reaction torques are equally distributed. For a batter, this point is the most distal part of the two hands.

by not hitting at the center of percussion. Also, some of the bat's velocity is lost moving the handle against or out of the hands, but when the ball is struck at the center of percussion there is no rotation, and all of the bat's velocity is transferred to the ball, which results in the greatest postimpact velocity (Weyrick, et al., 1989).

There is a second sweet spot on a bat that is about 1 inch from the center of percussion (Brody, 1985), which is the result of the harmonic motion of the bat's natural oscillation. A ball hit at the **harmonic node** of this oscillation will produce no sting or vibration at the batter's hands. Researchers indicate that the sweet spot area, which includes both the center of percussion and the harmonic node, is larger on an aluminum bat (Bryant, Burkett, Chen, Krahenbuhl, & Lu, 1977).

The center of percussion should be located toward the barrel end of the bat because of the relationship between the distance from the **axis of rotation** (defined by Noble [1985] as being the most distal part of the hands on the bat) and the linear velocity of any point on a rotating object. That is, the greater the distance from the axis, the faster the point will be moving, because linear velocity is directly proportional to the length of the radius ($v = r\omega$). Since the center of percussion is the desired point of contact between bat and ball, the center of percussion should be located as far up the barrel as possible (longer "r") so that maximum linear velocity (greater "v") can be imparted to the ball.

Even though there are some exceptions, the practice of end loading the bat does move the center of percussion closer to the barrel end of the bat, resulting in greater ball velocity when the sweet spot is hit. Greater ball velocity occurs because no velocity is wasted in vibration or rotation, and because the distance from the axis of rotation to the sweet spot is greater.

Radius of Gyration

radius of gyration—The distance from the axis of rotation to the point where the object's weight is concentrated.

The fourth parameter that is important in bat selection is the distribution of the mass or weight with respect to the axis of rotation.

Try to swing a bat first by its handle end, and then turn it around and swing it by the barrel end. You will notice that, although its weight is unchanged, the bat is harder to swing from the handle, because more of the bat's weight (which is in the barrel) is distributed farther from the axis of rotation when swinging from the handle. This parameter is called the **radius of gyration**, a distance that represents where the weight is concentrated with respect to the swing axis (defined earlier as the axis of rotation).

In practical terms, we are talking about how hard it is to swing the bat fast or how much resistance the bat has to being swung (or accelerated). In numerical terms, hard and easy function as a square of the radius of gyration. So, if two bats had the same mass and one had a radius of gyration of 4 (mass concentrated closer to the handle) and the other 8 (mass twice as far from the handle), then the second bat would be four times as hard to swing ($4^2:8^2$ or 16:64). If the bat is hard to swing, you will not be able to generate as much velocity (angular or linear), or impart as much momentum to the ball. Therefore, if the bat's center of percussion is moved too far from the axis of rotation by end loading, the advantage gained will be more than offset by the resistance to rotation created by this weight placement.

A way to shift the center of percussion toward the barrel end of the bat without increasing the radius of gyration has been demonstrated by Noble and Eck (1986): By loading the bat at the knob end (i.e., adding a relatively heavy metal knob), the center of percussion (the harmonic node) is moved farther out to the barrel end. This strategy increases linear velocity by having the sweet spot a greater distance from the axis of rotation while concentrating the weight close to that same axis. This greatly reduces the bat's resistance to being swung, in effect making it easier to generate greater angular velocity.

The radius of gyration may also be reduced by scooping out some of the material in the barrel end of the bat creating a cupped effect. Cupped bats—both wooden and metal—have up to a 1-inch-deep curved depression in the end of the barrel. This reduces the amount of mass farthest from the swing axis, decreasing the radius of gyration and making the bat easier to swing.

Hardness and Stiffness

coefficient of restitution—An index of elasticity; a nondimensional ratio of the velocities of two colliding bodies after and before collision.

The harder the material of which the bat is composed, the more energy (momentum) transferred to the ball during impact, because of the greater **coefficient of restitution** between the bat and the ball. In other words, less energy is lost due to bending at impact with a stiffer bat. (The coefficient of restitution is a function of how quickly an object that deforms in a collision can restore itself to push away from the contact.)

Ash is a hard, yet resilient wood. It is able to withstand the force of impact with the ball (most of the time) and retain its shape after numerous impacts. Some players have tried questionable methods to increase a wooden bat's hardness: for example, refrigerating, scratching out the dark grain and replacing it with pine tar (which is illegal), or rubbing it with a soup bone or soda bottle (a ''boned'' bat) (Gutman, 1990; Schrier, 1987).

hardness—Resistance to pressure; firm, rigid, unyielding.
stiffness—Difficult to bend; rigid, not flexible.

Nonwooden bats can be manufactured from metal alloys of greater **hardness** and **stiffness** than wood. Batters achieve greater distance with alloy and composition bats. Ceramic coatings present the hardest surfaces. Graphite fibers added to a bat create the stiffest bat, as well as the most expensive.

▶ Gimmicks

Some manufacturers have gone beyond the traditional and created bats with special features that may or may not improve a player's ability as a batter (see Figure 10.3). These special designs are seen mostly in softball bats because the ASA Rules Committee has approved their use. Some of these designer bats may have more influence on a batter psychologically than mechanically. The advertising claims that accompany these bats may also be misleading.

▶ **Figure 10.3** Gimmick softball bats. From the top: ''Broadsider''—barrel triangulated into three surfaces (Broadsider Sports Co.), ''Tidal Wave''—water moves 12 to 14 inches within the barrel (Spalding), ''Whizz''—180 small holes drilled into the hollow barrel (Marshall Clark Corp.), and ''Zapper II''—S-shape of the handle places barrel in front of the hands during the swing (Easton).

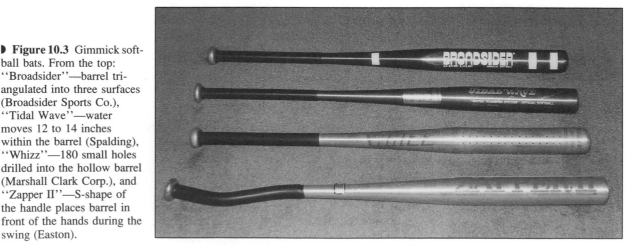

Three-Sided Barrel

The manufacturer of the Broadsider three-sided bat claims that it has a "new geometry for line drive power." Placing the flatter surface toward the pitcher at contact is supposed to increase the chance of hitting a line drive. The success of this claim depends largely on the rotation of the hitter's wrists and the amount of spin on the pitch.

The Broadsider is also advertised as having a "220% greater sweet spot for the ultimate in power and control." This means that the sweet spot is more than two times greater on a flat surface than on the round surface of the traditional bat. However, because this increase is perpendicular to the length of the bat, it does not move the sweet spot closer to the end of the bat, making its usefulness questionable.

Fluid Filled

centrifugal force—Force that tends to move a rotating object away from its center of rotation.

Have you seen the Tidal Wave II? It contains a fluid in the barrel and is legal for softball because it is welded closed and cannot be easily altered. The theory is that while waiting for the pitch, the fluid is nearer to the hands, lessening the radius of gyration. Once the bat begins to swing, **centrifugal force** pulls the fluid out to the barrel end to load the end and moves the sweet spot farther out the barrel. The movement of the fluid supposedly makes it easier to initiate the swing and then creates a longer radius to the sweet spot. The time it takes the fluid to move compared to the speed of the bat swing could make it impractical.

Pressurized Air

The Bombat features pressurized air inside the bat that supposedly enhances a hitter's power and propels a softball farther. The theory is that the increased air pressure inside increases the coefficient of restitution between the bat and the ball. For instance, an overinflated basketball bounces higher than an underinflated ball does. It is difficult to imagine the amount of air pressure necessary to restore or to prevent the deformation that may occur in an aluminum bat or how long the restoration might take.

Knurled Surface

turbulent flow—A fluid flow having random fluctuations of velocities and pressures.

Several bat designs sport a rough surface (knurled) around the barrel, which theoretically affects batting in several ways. First, the ball tends to stay on the rough surface slightly longer, allowing the bat to do more work on the ball (i.e., to apply force to the ball for a longer time resulting in greater ball velocity). Secondly, the knurled surface increases the amount of friction between the bat and the ball creating more spin on the ball. A ball hit in the air with greater backspin will travel farther, whereas a ball hit on the ground with greater topspin will stay low and maintain more of its horizontal velocity after the first bounce. Thirdly, the rough surface may work like dimples on a golf ball to reduce the **turbulent flow** behind the swinging bat and, therefore, allow it to be swung faster. Some batters used to sand or file their bats to rough up the surfaces and increase the ball contact time, especially useful for bunting. This action is considered altering the bat and is illegal unless the manufacturer knurls the surface and it meets ASA specifications.

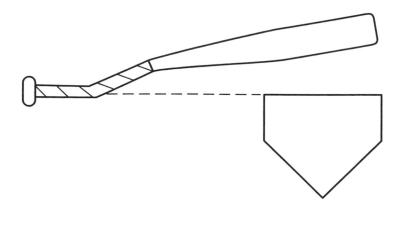

Figure 10.4 Angled handle bat. A right-handed batter contacting the ball out in front of the plate would hit toward left field.

Perforated Barrel

The Whizz bat is designed with numerous small holes through the barrel end. Air is supposed to flow through the bat to reduce form drag. It makes a whizzing noise as it passes overhead! The air enters the bat through the holes thereby reducing the air pressure against the front of the bat; but once inside, the air may increase the pressure against the back wall of the barrel. Perhaps nothing is gained.

Angled Handle

Two companies include in their equipment lines softball bats with an angle in the handle. These bats purportedly allow the batter to make contact out in front of the plate (see Figure 10.4). If a batter typically swings late (because of poor timing, or insufficient muscle torque for the weight of the normal bat) the angled bat handle may change some of a right-hander's right-field foul balls to fair balls. However, by the same reasoning a normal hitter will probably pull more balls foul. Rather than relying on a gimmick design, correct technique and a bat with appropriate weight and radius of gyration should help a late-swinging batter.

▶ Summary

Today's manufacturing technology has generated creative designs in baseball and softball bats constructed from a variety of materials. Some of these bats have features which, from a mechanical point of view, should enhance a batter's ability to hit the ball harder and farther. The bats that produce good hits are constructed from a harder material with a greater weight that is distributed more closely to the handle and in such a way that the sweet spot is directed farther toward the end of the barrel. These design characteristics improve, respectively, the coefficient of restitution, the quantity and distribution of mass, the radius of gyration, and the center of percussion of the swinging bat.

It is difficult for the consumer to determine the mechanical characteristics of a bat by feel alone. Understanding the biomechanics of swinging a bat for successful contact can establish some guidelines for matching the proper bat to the individual batter.

▶ References

Adair, R.K. (1990). *The physics of baseball.* New York: Harper & Row.

American Softball Association. (1993, August-September). In the beginning. . . . *Balls and Strikes SOFTBALL*, pp. 38-39.

Barr, G. (1970). *Here's why: Science in sports*. New York: Scholastic Book Services.

Brody, H. (1985). The sweet spot of a baseball bat. *American Journal of Physics*, **54**, 640-643.

Bryant, F.O., Burkett, L.N., Chen, S.S., Krahenbuhl, G.S., & Lu, P. (1977). Dynamic and performance characteristics of baseball bats. *Research Quarterly*, **48**, 505-509.

Gammons, P. (1989, July 24). End of an era. *Sports Illustrated*, **71**, 17-23.

Gutman, D. (1990). *It ain't cheatin' if you don't get caught*. New York: Penguin Books.

Hersch, H. (1986, April 14). The good wood. *Sports Illustrated*, **64**, 66-68.

House, G.C. (1988). Designer softball bats. In M.J. Adrian (Ed.), *National Coaching Institute applied research papers* (pp. 16-21). Reston, VA: National Association for Girls & Women in Sport.

Linson, S. (1989, April). The new softball bats: Great at the plate. *Women's Sports and Fitness*, **11**, 86.

NCAA: Baseball rules. (1993). Mission, KS: National Collegiate Athletic Association.

Noble, L. (1985). Empirical determination of the center of percussion axis of softball and baseball bats. In D.A. Winter, R.W. Norman, R.P. Wells, K.C. Hayes, & A.E. Patla (Eds.), *Biomechanics IX-B*, (pp. 516-520). Champaign, IL: Human Kinetics.

Noble, L., & Eck, J. (1986). Effects of selected softball bat loading strategies on impact reaction impulse. *Medicine and Science in Sports and Exercise*, **18**, 50-59.

The official ASA guide and playing rules. (1993). Oklahoma City: Amateur Softball Association of America.

Official baseball rules. (1993). St. Louis: Sporting News.

Schrier, E.W., & Allman, W.F. (Eds.). (1987). *Newton at the bat: The science in sports*. New York: Charles Scribner's Sons.

Weyrich, A.S., Messier, S.P., Ruhmann, B.S., & Berry, M.J. (1989). Effects of bat composition, grip firmness, and impact location on postimpact ball velocity. *Medicine and Science in Sports and Exercise*, **21**, 199-205.

PART III

Personal Fitness Equipment

CHAPTER 11

Biomechanical Considerations for Personal Fitness Equipment

Ellen F. Kreighbaum, PhD
Montana State University, Bozeman

The reasons for exercising are varied. Several of many reasons are psychological well-being, calorie expenditure, rehabilitation, increased muscular tolerance for skill acquisition, and injury prevention. Your reason for exercising has some influence on what type and duration of exercise you choose. The following chapter will point out several aspects of exercise that should be taken into consideration before selecting an exercise routine.

▶ Aspects of Fitness

There are five aspects of fitness you should consider before selecting the activities of your routine: flexibility, muscular strength, muscular endurance, muscular power, and cardiorespiratory fitness. A well-rounded program includes exercises for each of these, whereas rehabilitation programs, for example, focus only on joint flexibility muscular strength and endurance. Exercises for increasing physical tolerance, which enhances ability, should include the specific demands of the skill to be improved. Marathon running training focuses on cardiorespiratory and muscular endurance, whereas gymnastics training focuses on muscular power and flexibility.

Flexibility

flexibility—The range of motion of a body part.

Flexibility is defined as the total range of motion through which a single articulation can move in one plane (range of motion is usually measured in degrees). The limitations to flexibility are bony restrictions, musculotendinous limitations, ligamentous restrictions, and tissue or clothing bulk. If a joint of the body were forced to the end of its range of motion without any tissue restrictions, some joints would show bone contacting bone.

If the elbow, for example, were forced into hyperextension and had no ligaments or tendinous structures to stop the motion, the olecranon or end of the ulna would contact the olecranon fossa or depression on the humerus, possibly causing it to break or chip. This situation is unlikely but serves to demonstrate restrictions caused by bony processes in some body joints. Usually, ligaments or muscle tendons will prevent the joint from moving too far in a given direction. Muscle tendons cannot always be stretched far enough to allow full range of motion. Exercises can help extend the flexibility of the joint.

Muscular Strength

muscular strength—The maximum amount of force that can be generated by a muscle or muscle group.

Although it is nearly impossible to measure muscular strength directly, how much weight you can lift is measureable. **Muscular strength** is specific to the position of the joint and the muscles being used for any given exercise. For example, when you perform a forearm curl, your strength changes throughout the range of motion, being less on either end of the range and greater in the middle. We usually measure strength by using the one-repetition maximum concept; that is, the maximum amount of weight a person can lift one time and one time only without resting. This of course is specific to the lift being performed. Someone may be stronger performing a forearm curl with the palm facing upward than with the palm facing downward.

Muscular Endurance

muscular endurance—The ability of a muscle or muscle group to repeatedly exert less than maximal force against a resistance.

Muscular endurance involves the number of times a person can lift a resistance. The resistance is submaximal of course. In continuous activities like cycling and rowing, you usually drop the resistance setting to 60 to 80 percent of the one-repetition maximum level and attempt to increase the number of times the weight is lifted. As with the other aspects, muscular endurance is specific to the position of the joints and muscles in question.

Muscular Power

power—The ability of a muscle or muscle group to exert force quickly; explosive ability of a muscle or group.

Power is explosiveness; it involves not only the amount of force being used but also how fast that force is applied. Kreighbaum and Barthels (1990) classify power events into either force dominated (heavy resistances must be accelerated in a short period of time), like throwing shot put, or speed dominated (lighter objects must be accelerated in a short period of time) like swinging a badminton racquet. Both aspects of power, force and speed, may be trained. A frequent training error is to focus on only the force aspect.

Cardiorespiratory Endurance

cardiorespiratory endurance—The ability of the heart, vascular system, and

Cardiorespiratory endurance involves the system's efficiency at exchanging oxygen for carbon dioxide. The more you can supply oxygen to the tissues carrying away waste products, the greater your cardiorespiratory endurance.

lungs to provide oxygen to the body's tissues and carry away waste products over the course of a continuous, physically stressful activity.

Events that rely heavily on this system are those involving a relatively light load and a long duration, such as a marathon run.

▶ Overload and Specificity Principles

overload—To exert the body more than usual in order to increase its ability.

In order to increase the ability of the system to work at a higher level, an **overload**—or pushing beyond the normal limits—is applied in training. If flexibility is what you desire, the joint range of motion must be pushed beyond its current range. If muscular endurance is what you want, then the muscles must be asked to work at a given load using a greater number of repetitions.

The overload principle is used with a given movement and with specific muscles. Overloading the elbow flexors will not enhance the performance of the elbow extensors. Overloading the elbow flexors within a limited range of motion will not necessarily enhance their performance over their entire range of motion. The necessity of working a system in the exact movement pattern, range of motion, position, speed, and so on is termed the **specificity principle**. For general fitness activities, work as many joints and muscles as possible over the entire range of motion without emphasizing any one aspect over another (e.g., strength over speed of movement, or the endurance of muscle contraction to the exclusion of strength work).

specificity principle— Effective training is produced when overloading the body or its parts in the exact manner (position, speed, etc.) for which you are training and when directed at the exact aspect of fitness one desires.

▶ Biomechanics of Exercise Modes

In the following chapters several methods of achieving fitness are discussed. Because there are many ways to reach fitness goals, you may use a diverse array of equipment. In this section, biomechanical principles are presented for the different modes of exercise activity. Table 11.1 shows the fitness equipment most likely to help develop each aspect of fitness.

Aerobic Exercise Equipment Principles

Repetition of an activity over and over is the key to aerobic fitness improvement. However, the resistance associated with this repetitive movement is also important. For example, false casting a fly fishing line continuously may not cause an increase in your heart rate, although it may cause sore muscles. However, if you use the upper body to row a shell vigorously for an extended period, your heart rate will increase, besides producing muscle fatigue if you're not used to that activity.

Moreover, a performer's fitness state will also determine the aerobic benefit. A crew athlete accustomed to rowing a shell extended lengths of time may not obtain the aerobic benefit of someone unaccustomed to that same level of activity. Thus, when evaluating aerobic exercise equipment, you must consider individual differences in users' aerobic fitness levels and the differences in the muscular endurance of the specific body parts being stressed. In lap swimming for aerobic fitness, if your upper body musculature is in a low muscular endurance state, then you may be unable to continue swimming the length of time necessary to produce aerobic effects (because your muscular endurance is not great enough to go on that long).

Surface and treadmill running require minimal amounts of muscular endurance, so the performer may continue to a state of cardiovascular overload.

Table 11.1 Equipment Most Likely to Help Develop Each Aspect of Fitness

	Flexibility	Muscular strength	Muscular endurance	Muscle power	Cardiorespiratory fitness
Road and track bicycles			X		X
X-C ski simulators	Somewhat		X		X
Stationary bicycles		May	X	Somewhat	X
Treadmills			Somewhat		X
Rowing machines	Somewhat		X	Somewhat	X
Jump ropes			X		X
Stepping machines		May	X		X
Stretching, pulling, or pushing devices	May	May	May		
Resistance training equipment		X	May	X	
Canoes Kayaks Rafts	Somewhat		X		Somewhat
Rebounders			X		X
Parallel turn simulators	Somewhat		Somewhat		

However, the stair climber and the rowing machine may tax the muscular endurance of the legs and the upper body, respectively, so that direct aerobic benefits may not be forthcoming immediately. Even the jump rope is very stressful to the upper body, and the bicycle is very stressful to the lower body. For either, aerobic benefits may not be reached until muscular endurance in those respective muscle groups is increased.

Muscular Endurance

Muscular endurance is increased by repetition of a movement or a series of joint movements against about 60 percent resistance of the maximum strength of those muscle groups. To determine your starting point for building muscular endurance, you must know your present level of muscle endurance. For some, the continuous casting of a light fly rod and line will be 60 percent of their maximum strength; for others, the same motion may be 20 percent of their strength. Muscular endurance will be increased in the former but maybe not in the latter. In other words, 60 percent of a lesser value is less than 60 percent of a greater value.

Numerous activities increase muscular endurance. Rowing, cycling, weight lifting, and stair climbing all fit this category. But remember the specificity principle, muscular endurance is specific to the muscle group being worked. Working on the lower body muscles on a stair climber does not increase muscular endurance for the upper body muscles. A rowing machine probably affects muscular endurance for more muscles than other single activities, because you pull with the arms, push with the legs and extend the back against a resistance.

Muscular Power

Power involves the speed of movement as well as the force with which the movement is performed. When you work out on a rowing machine, a weight machine, a bicycle, or just about any exercise machine and focus the workout on increasing your performance speed, you are working on power. Research shows that increased strength does increase speed, but it is not necessarily true that the greater your strength, the faster you move. Increasing your speed to move a constant weight should be the goal. To the author's knowledge, there are very few if any machines designed for power training.

Muscular Strength

To increase muscular strength, apply the overload principle. As you increase muscular strength in a muscle group, you must increase the resistance against which the muscle group works. For those at the lower and middle level upper body muscular strength, the use of rowing machines is advisable. For those already fairly strong in the upper body who want even greater strength, a weight-lifting device would be warranted. Similarly, for those at the lower and middle level lower body muscular strength, the use of stair climbers would increase lower body muscular strength. However, if one is at the upper levels of muscular strength, a weight machine or free weight exercises designed for the lower body would be advisable.

Flexibility

There are few if any devices designed for increasing flexibility alone. As with many other aspects of fitness, achievement depends on where you start. For example, an inertial band applied to a body segment can coax it to a greater range of motion which stretches the muscles on the opposite side of that joint. Mostly, the inertial band is used for resistance to increase muscular strength or endurance; however, if used to provide the force for returning the body part to a position beyond the starting position, it can be a flexibility device. For the most part, there are no exercise devices designed to increase range of motion. One must devise his or her own stretching program.

▶ A Look Ahead

In the following chapters the authors present the history, materials, and design characteristics of bicycles, watercraft, aerobic fitness equipment, and strength training equipment. Using the principles and information presented in this chapter and the information presented by these authors, you should be able to assess fitness levels and prescribe the device or devices necessary to achieve the aspect and level of fitness desired.

▶ References

Kreighbaum, E., & Barthels, K. (1995). Biomechanics: A qualitative approach for studying movement. Boston: Allyn & Bacon.

CHAPTER 12

Bicycles

Rebecca Carson, MA
Lewis Palmer School District, Monument, Colorado

The purpose of this chapter is to acquaint the reader with today's bicycle. There have been many changes in the basic bicycle design. The most notable changes have occurred in frame materials, drivetrain components, such as the addition of suspension, and construction methods. This chapter will discuss the anatomy of a bicycle, bicycle types, materials, and construction methods used in bicycle design so that the reader may understand basic bicycle components and be aware of the many innovations taking place in the bicycling industry. We hope a better understanding helps the reader make intelligent decisions when purchasing a bicycle or bicycle parts.

▶ Anatomy of a Bicycle Frame

The bicycle as we know it today has looked basically the same for the past 100 years. Figure 12.1 illustrates the basic frame design. The main triangle consists of the top tube, the seat tube, and the down tube. The rear triangle is made up of the seat tube, and chainstays, and the seat stays. At the farthest point away from the seat tube on the seat stays are the dropouts, which provide a slot for the rear wheel axle. Both the main triangle and the rear triangle are attached to the bottom bracket shell. Bicycles with this frame design are said to have a diamond frame.

There are two exceptions to the diamond frame: the mixte frame and the ladies' frame—neither has the top tube (see Figure 12.2). The ladies' frame looks identical to the diamond frame without a top tube. The mixte frame looks similar to the ladies' (no top tube) but has an additional down tube, or two

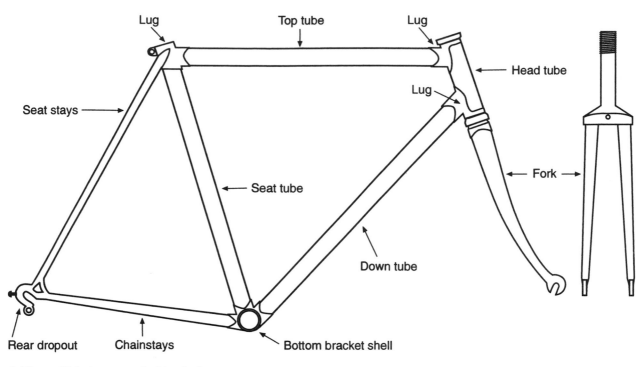

▶ **Figure 12.1** Anatomy of a bicycle frame.

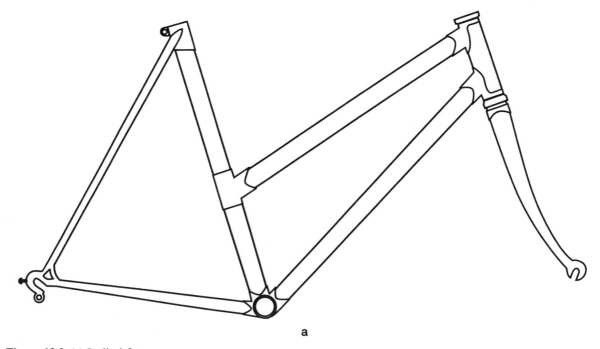

a

▶ **Figure 12.2** (a) Ladies' frame.

smaller tubes running parallel to the down tube. The diamond frame is superior in strength to either of the other two types because of the stability afforded by the top tube.

The tubes of the bicycle are joined and reinforced by brackets or specially shaped sleeves called lugs (Figure 12.3). Lugs provide additional material and surface area for brazing or welding, thereby joining and strengthening the tubes. Lugs and the joining of the tubes will be discussed in more detail later in the chapter.

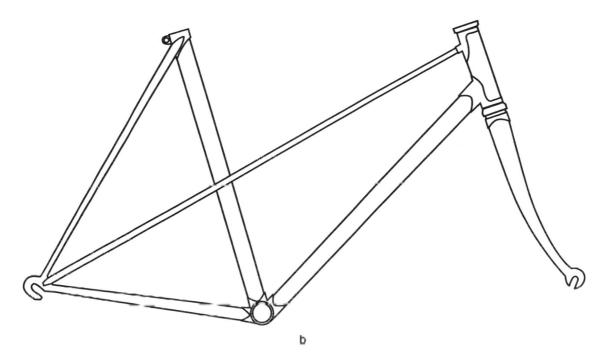

▶ **Figure 12.2** (b) Mixte frame.

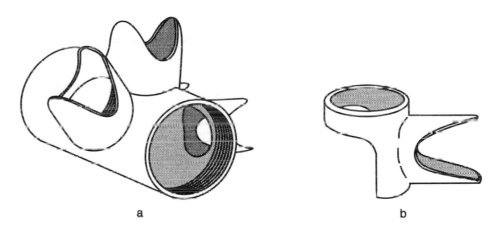

▶ **Figure 12.3** A (a) bottom bracket shell and a (b) lug.

At the front end of the bicycle is the traditional fork, consisting of a fork crown, fork blades with dropouts, and a steering column. The steering column goes through or sits in the head tube and is secured by means of the headset assembly. The head tube is also attached to the down tube and the top tube.

Figure 12.4 shows the individual parts of the fork. Like the dropouts in the rear, the front dropouts provide a slot for the axle of the front wheel.

▶ Frame Design

Many bicycles look very similar, but there are distinguishing features that separate one bicycle from another. Frame geometry plays an important part in determining a bicycle's performance qualities. Bicycle types are determined by both frame design (discussed in this section) and specific parts (discussed later) found on the bike. Therefore they can be grouped as follows: touring, sport/triathlon, racing (road and track), and all terrain. A subgroup of the all-terrain bike is the ''cross'' bike—a bike with characteristics of both the all-terrain bike and the road bike.

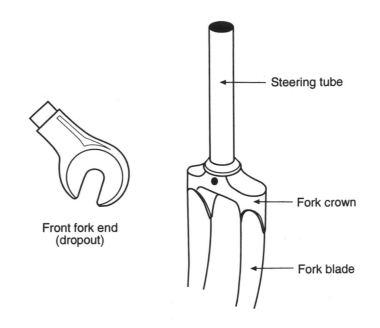

Figure 12.4 The steering tube, fork crown, fork blade, and dropout make up the fork.

Design Objectives

There are several objectives in frame design. One is to distribute the rider's weight to effect a desired result, which varies according to the intended performance of the bicycle. For instance, a touring bicycle, designed for stability and comfort, is built with a long wheelbase and shallow angles to ensure good handling and a comfortable ride.

Another objective in frame design is to ensure the transfer of power from rider to machine. To achieve this, the points of contact on the bicycle (handlebars, seat, and pedals) must fit the rider. Any bike's height measurements will determine the size of the rider able to ride a given bike. Any dimension having to do with the length of the bike (wheelbase and chainstay length) will affect its performance characteristics.

Bottom Bracket

bottom bracket—One part of the crank assembly housed in the bottom bracket shell at the bottom of the seat and down tubes; it consists of an axle, bearings, and a race to house the bearings.

The diamond frame design has allowed frame builders to create many variations to achieve a desired outcome. The **bottom bracket**, housed in the bottom bracket shell, is a bike's center of gravity. Figure 12.5 shows the bottom bracket assembly.

Once the wheel diameter has been determined, the builder will use the bottom bracket as the starting point in assembling the frame. The design of the bottom bracket will influence the handling characteristics of the finished product (e.g., a bottom bracket built low to the ground makes a more stable bicycle). Placement of the bottom bracket, however, is limited to a distance leaving ample clearance for the pedals. In contrast to most touring bicycles and some racing bicycles,

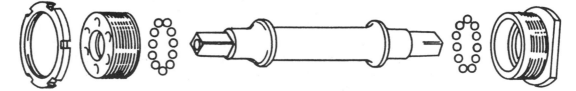

Figure 12.5 Bottom bracket assembly.

many all-terrain bikes come with a high bottom bracket to allow additional clearance in off-road situations.

Wheelbase

After choosing the bottom bracket height the builder can decide on overall wheelbase length, the distance from the front axle to the rear axle (see Figure 12.6). In determining overall wheelbase a builder must allow for space between the front wheel and the down tube. This is especially important when steering, so that the pedals don't hit the front wheel. Also, a rider may want to add fenders to the bike and therefore may need more clearance between the front wheel and the down tube and between the rear wheel and the seat tube. Taking into account these considerations, wheelbase length between bicycles will vary from 38 to 44 inches (Stevenson, 1982).

A bicycle with a short wheelbase will accelerate quickly and respond quickly to the rider's movements. A track racing bicycle and most road racing bicycles have short wheelbases. In contrast, a bike with a long wheelbase is slower to respond but provides a more stable and comfortable ride. Touring bikes, most recreational bikes, and some all-terrain bikes have wheelbases at the long end of the spectrum. However, as all-terrain bikes have grown more popular and many wheelbase lengths have become shorter, giving these bikes more maneuverability and quicker response.

An important part of the wheelbase length is the length of the chainstays—this is usually about 16 to 18 inches (Stevenson, 1982)—or the distance from the bottom bracket to the rear axle. Refer to Figure 12.6 for this measurement.

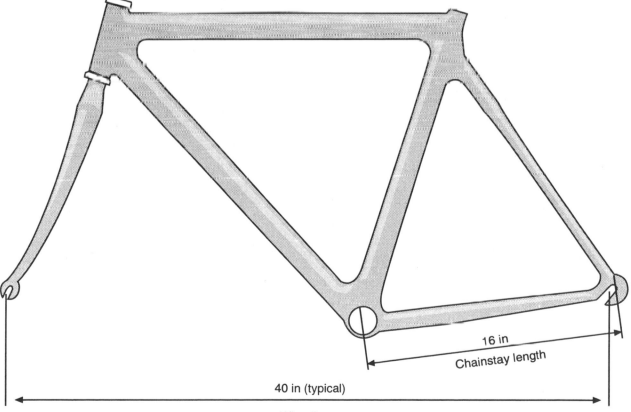

▶ **Figure 12.6** Wheelbase and chainstay length.

This dimension affects the "ride" of a bike. Two factors will influence this design: the handling qualities desired and wheel clearance. The chainstay length needs to be a little longer on an all-terrain bike to accommodate a larger tire. A touring bike will likely have longer chainstays for stability. A bicycle with shorter chainstays, usually a racing bicycle, will accelerate faster and allow for more direct transfer of power to the rear wheel than a bicycle with a longer chainstay.

Frame Angles

Frame angles, another aspect of frame design, also contribute to a bicycle's "ride." Figure 12.7 illustrates the bicycle angles. The seat tube will affect road shock or the absorption qualities of a bicycle. The steeper the angle, the rougher the ride; the more shallow the angle, the more shock absorbed. However, a steeper angle more efficiently transmits power from rider to machine. The head tube angle in combination with the **rake** (bend) of the fork will determine how the bicycle steers. See Figure 12.7 for trail, the distance that the front wheels contact point is behind the intersection of the steering axis and the ground (Delong, 1974).

rake—Amount of bend in the fork blades.

The steeper the head tube angle, the easier the bicycle is to maneuver, but it may be harder to control. The effect of a steep head tube is a very quick, almost nervous turning front end. A more shallow head tube angle makes the bicycle more shock absorbing and easier to handle, but less responsive. The

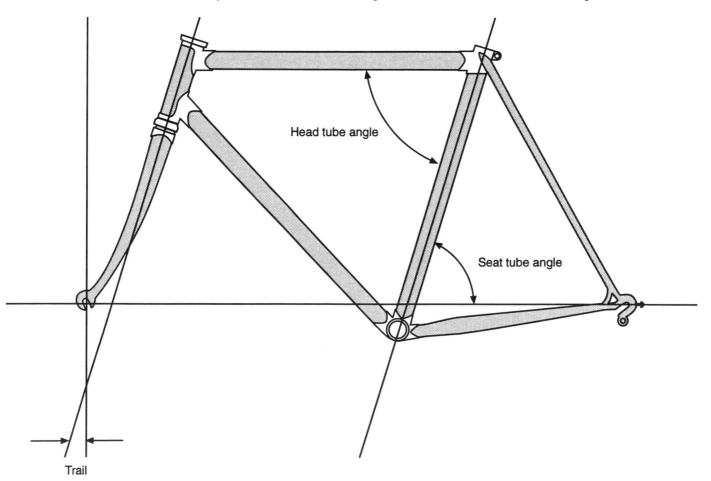

▶ **Figure 12.7** Head and seat tube angles and trail affect maneuverability and control of the bike.

head angle and the rake combine to determine the amount of trail a bicycle will have—more trail means greater stability.

On a standard road bicycle, head and seat angles will vary between 72 and 75 degrees; many combinations are possible according to the ride desired. An exception is a very small frame, which may have angles as steep as 77 degrees to achieve the right size top tube for the smaller rider. All-terrain bicycle angles may be from 68 to 75 degrees. More all-terrain bicycles are being made with steeper angles to accommodate the ever-growing group of racing off-road riders. Angles therefore are one feature that differentiates one bicycle from another.

Frame Size

Bicycle size is determined by the length of the seat tube and the relationship between that measurement and the length of the rider's legs. Top tube length also is important in fitting the rider with a bike. There can be variations both with seat tube length and with top tube length. A rider may choose a position that is more stretched out than normal, or may choose to sit more upright than normal. Either is determined partially by top tube length.

Racers will typically choose a frame with a seat tube length as small as possible, while still providing some comfort. Choosing the smallest frame possible reduces bike weight and gives the racer a stiffer frame because of shorter tubes. With more off-road racers, more all-terrain bikes will have a shorter seat tube relative to top tube length. This ensures maximum safety when mounting and dismounting in a racing situation and, like road racing frames, saves a little weight, providing a stiffer, more responsive frame.

Types of Bicycles and Their Frame Designs

In reviewing the types of bicycles and how frame design contributes to specific desired characteristics, the following summary can be made: Touring bikes have a long wheelbase, shallow angles, and a fair amount of trail for a stable, comfortable ride. Racing bikes have a short wheelbase, steep angles, and little trail for a quick, responsive ride. Sport/triathlon bikes and cross bikes fit somewhere in between these two with the intention of offering a bike that is both comfortable and reasonably responsive.

With such a large continuum of frame lengths, it can be extremely difficult to identify a bicycle type. All-terrain bikes will vary according to their specific function. There are models with extremely long wheelbases and shallow angles for slow, comfortable cruising. There are others that are designed with the racer in mind, so they have a short wheelbase and steep angles. And there are still others that have a very high bottom bracket, short wheelbase, and steep angles for trails riding. Choosing the best bicycle for you is determined mostly by how and where you will use the bicycle. For the serious cycling enthusiast, that may mean owning several bicycles instead of just one.

▶ Frame Materials

elasticity—The ability to deform and reform with a change in forces; a metal modulus of elasticity shows how it will deform under stress.

To discuss materials we must define several properties of materials. **Elasticity** is the ability of a material to respond to an encountering force by changing its shape and returning to its original shape after the force is taken away. The point beyond which a material cannot return to its original shape is its **elastic limit**—once reached, it becomes permanently bent and therefore weakened (Stevenson, 1982).

Another property to consider is a material's breaking strength; that is, a measure of force required to cause material failure altogether. Elasticity is better known as stiffness, and breaking strength is better known as strength (Stevenson, 1982).

Formation of Tubing

alloy—A substance with metallic properties that is comprised of two or more chemical elements of which at least one is a metal.

butted tubing—Tubing or spokes made thicker at the ends than in the middle.

The majority of bicycle frames are made of high-grade **alloy** steel. There are many other materials appearing on the market now, but steel is still the most widely used. A true tube, as opposed to a pipe, is formed from a solid, pierced ingot of steel. The metal is drawn over a mandrel so the metal form doesn't change and so that there are no seams or joints (Stevenson, 1982). Most quality tubing is made thicker at the ends, called butting, to increase tube strength. Most bicycles, even those in the $200 range, will have **butted tubing**.

Depending on the number of times the diameter is changed, the tubing is referred to as either double-butted, triple-butted, or quad-butted (Hayduk, 1987). There is also splined tubing, which incorporates a series of ridges at critical areas in the bicycle such as near the bottom bracket shell. Tubing can be aero-shaped, round, square, or triangular. Manufacturers have different theories on which shape of tubing is the best for a certain application. A bicycle may incorporate more than one shape of tubing.

Chromoly

The strength of good tubing comes from the combinations of materials used. The most common uses a combination of chromium, molybdenum, and manganese; hence the name *chromoly*. Today even a low-cost bicycle will have some chromoly. Manganese molybdenum is of slightly inferior quality to chromoly and is often found in very inexpensive bicycles and in the fork or rear triangle (stays) of moderately priced bicycles.

There are different gauges of chromoly tubing; each company has its own variations. The standard for years was Reynolds 531 tubing. Ten to 15 years ago the standard steel racing bicycle frame weighed 5-1/2 pounds. In the late 1970s Reynolds introduced the tubing 753 with thinner walls which meant a subsequently lighter frame (4 pounds). The weight saved was an obvious advantage and the tubing proved to be as strong, if not stronger than the 531. It could not, however, withstand as much stress, because it was not as resilient.

Aluminum

With the increased use of aluminum as a material for bicycles, the same complaint (lower resiliency) surfaced. Many criticize the use of standard-gauge aluminum tubing because it cannot be stressed the way a standard-gauge steel frame can. One solution has been to use oversized aluminum tubing. Aluminum alloys have been used in the bicycling industry for years but have never been as widely accepted as now. Gary Klien introduced the first oversized aluminum tubing bicycle in the early 1970s, but the cost was too prohibitive for most people. Since then many companies have mass-produced oversized aluminum tubing bicycles. By increasing the tube diameter without increasing wall thickness, stiffness is retained and weight is reduced. Conversely, increasing tube wall thickness without changing the diameter will produce the same result. Both methods and combinations of these are used (Hayduk, 1987; Stevenson, 1982).

Titanium

Titanium is another material being used more and more. There are currently several titanium bikes on the market or in research development. Although more research with titanium is necessary, you can buy a titanium bike—but high production costs make this kind of bicycle very expensive.

Fibers

Carbon fiber and boron fiber are the latest materials in the bicycling industry. Again, their popularity is limited by cost and the fact that they have not been proven yet. Fiber frames do not result in a significantly lighter bike, but there is a potential for greater stiffness and a higher strength:weight ratio than with either steel or aluminum. The fibers are woven together and then are incorporated into a tube by embedding the fibers in resin. The tube fibers run longitudinally, at opposing angles, or both depending on the particular manufacturer. Much research remains to determine the best method of laying down the fibers. In some cases the fibers are laid in resin, then the whole assembly is wrapped with a metal wire. A disadvantage with fiber tubes is that they are an amalgam of two different materials that have different physical properties; therefore the tubes may behave unpredictably under stress (Stevenson, 1982). Many of these composite frames are bonded together with glue, much like aluminum frames with standard diameter tubing.

Heating of Materials

The heating of materials is an extremely sensitive process. Welding and brazing must be controlled to retain a material's original strength. For example, welding titanium requires an oxygen-free environment. If oxygen is present the weld becomes susceptible to brittleness (Hayduk, 1987; Kukoda, 1989).

Strength to Weight and Stiffness to Weight

composites—A material made by combining two or more materials with different characteristics in order to provide a more useful product for a specific application.

To summarize, we are concerned with two different ratios when comparing frame materials. One is the strength:weight ratio, the other is the stiffness:weight ratio. Steel, aluminum, and titanium have a similar stiffness:weight ratio, especially when using oversized aluminum tubing. The **composites** are about six times as great as the others in the stiffness:weight ratio. In comparing strength to weight we need to clarify how strength is influenced in different products. In coherent materials (metals) it is the composition of the metals that determines strength. An example is the amount of carbon used in steel frames: the more carbon the greater the strength. In aluminum the addition of magnesium or zinc produces a stronger material. With the composites, strength is related to how the materials are bonded together and how the fibers are laid down (Hayduk, 1987).

Pros and Cons of Materials

Here is a breakdown of the pros and cons of different materials used in the bicycling industry:

Steel alloys— pros: reliable, inexpensive, and durable with predictable handling

cons: other materials have the capability of being lighter

Aluminum alloys— pros: light weight, shock absorbent, and comfortable

cons: susceptible to breakage as the result of cracking or chipping; will fail catastrophically, not gradually

Titanium alloys—   pros: has the capability to be as stiff as steel, yet is stronger, lighter weight, and more shock absorbent with a higher bending strength

cons: expensive, hard to find (limited supply); the diameter of tubing commonly available is very flexible, hard to weld, and hard to machine

Composites—   pros: highest strength: weight ratio and stiffness: weight ratio of any of the materials used

cons: unproven, expensive, and problems with bonding

▶ Construction Methods

The main triangle of the bicycle, its foundation, is a fairly simple structure and receives a lot of attention in design. In addition to deciding angle steepness, bottom bracket height, and tube length, the builder selects the type of tubing and what method to use for joining the tubing. In most cases the builder works in one area exclusively, either building custom steel, aluminum, or other alloy bicycles, or working in a production unit where materials and methods are predetermined.

On most good-quality bicycles the tube ends that are fitted together must join precisely so that no gaps are present. The process of creating this fit is called **mitering**. Figure 12.8 illustrates a mitered tube.

mitering—A process that makes tubes acceptable to one another; the end of a mitered tube fits against another tube with no gaps.

Mitering can be done by hand or machine, using either a lathe or hole saw to cut the tubes for an exact fit. With hand cutting, or with a hole saw the tube ends are carefully filed until an exact fit is achieved. After the tubes have been mitered they are either welded together, or a **lug** is slipped over the two joining tubes, and the whole joint is brazed together.

lug—A specially shaped sleeve that provides extra material and surface area for joining two or more tubes together to make a stronger tube joint. Lugs can be external or internal.

Most high-quality steel bicycles are lugged. Lugs are of three kinds: stamped and welded, forged, or investment cast. Forging and investment casting will be found on most high-quality bikes. Usually, the fork (dropouts) are cast or forged, the bottom bracket is investment cast, and the remaining lugs will use any of these three methods. Stamping and welding offers an advantage in some situations where there is a need to reshape the lug or accommodate tube length and angle changes. In general, however, it is the least expensive process and produces the lowest quality of lug. The lug that joins the rear triangle to the seat tube is an example of a stamped, welded lug (Hayduk, 1987).

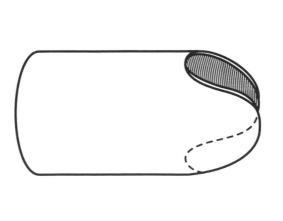

▶ **Figure 12.8** Mitered tube.

Some bicycles don't use a lug for some joints; rather, two tubes are welded together. The extra material used in certain kinds of welding ensures that the joint is adequately held together. In both situations the materials must be heated in a precise manner so the material retains the greatest possible strength. For aluminum bicycles the standard procedure is to heat-treat the frame once the welding has been finished. This treatment is necessary because welding weakens the material. By heat-treating the frame the builder can reinstate a material's original strength. Many aluminum frames are welded together without the use of lugs, and still other materials are joined together using lugs and aerospace adhesives (Hayduk, 1987). This will be discussed in further detail later in the chapter.

The rear triangle was discussed at the beginning of the chapter. Refer to Figure 12.1 to locate the rear dropout. Figure 12.9 shows a larger view of the dropout in various forms.

Dropouts are usually horizontal with the opening pointing forward on a road bicycle, and horizontal with the opening pointing backward on a track bicycle. The reason becomes clear when trying to remove the rear wheel of a track bicycle. On such a bicycle with very short chainstays there is little room between the seat tube and the rear wheel. It is therefore easier to remove the wheel by pulling it back than by pushing it forward. Some road bicycles may have vertical dropouts if the wheel position is not going to change. High quality dropouts on road bikes have a screw adjustment for the rear axle and an attachment point for the rear derailleur. This screw adjustment centers the rear wheel or changes its position; the attachment point for the derailleur makes a better shifting drivetrain.

▶ Suspension

Over the years bicycle component designs have borrowed from motorcycle technology. The most successful carryover has been in the area of suspension. While bicycles that are fully suspended (front and rear) are still a bit costly for most riders, bicycles with front suspension can be purchased for as little as $350. Suspension forks alone cost anywhere from $150 to over $600.

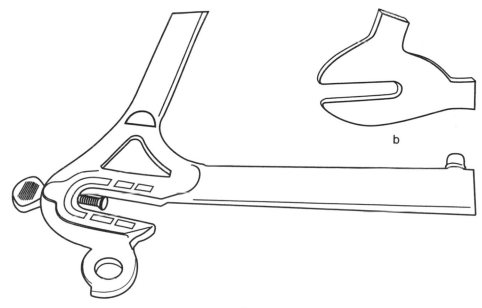

▶ **Figure 12.9** (a) The horizontal rear dropout and (b) the rear track dropout.

a

Since the recent technological development of suspension seems to be here to stay, a breakdown of bicycle design types and their springing systems is necessary. The bicycle's internal workings are usually classified by one of or a combination of the following: air/coil, coil spring, or urethane bumpers. Design types available are these: telescopic, parallelogram, springer, steerer tube, leading link, and upside down. It is critical to choose the brand, design, and springing method of your bicycle carefully because no two forks perform alike.

The air/coil springing system was the first to appear on the market. Air pressure makes the springing effect possible, and the oil provides a damping effect. A coil-spring fork is one in which the coil spring (spring for suspension effect) is housed in hydraulic oil, which provides the damping effect. Forks with urethane bumpers use elastomer, elastopolymer, or foam bumpers for their spring.

Overall designs are more varied. The telescopic design is the most widely used. One part of the fork slides over another part of the fork, providing a telescoping effect when the bicycle hits a bump. Parallelogram forks have a rigid fork attached to two parallel arms on either side of the fork. When the bike hits a bump, the rigid fork moves upward, causing the arms to move and the springing design to compress. Springers have rigid fork legs. On the bottom end of these legs are small linkage arms to which another rigid fork connects; it runs nearly parallel to the first fork. At the top of this fork is the springing device, usually a coil spring. Leading-link forks also have rigid fork legs. A swing arm facing forward joins with these legs, holds the front wheel in place, and pivots against the legs, providing the suspension effect. The suspension system on a steerer type design is an integral part of the bicycle, the internal workings being housed in the steerer column. Finally, an upside-down fork is similar to a telescoping fork except that the way the tubes slide together is reversed (the tube that normally fits into the other tube is now over it). Whatever the springing system, a rigid fork is always used. These forks cannot be purchased independently.

Before making a purchase, here are a few things to consider:

- Will my existing bike modify appropriately to be able to use a suspension fork?
- What is the cost of the fork?
- Is the amount of travel, or spring, in the suspension adjustable?

▶ The Drivetrain

The most complex of all the bicycle components, the drivetrain is a collective group of parts responsible for moving the bicycle mechanically. Housed in the bottom bracket shell is the bottom bracket assembly, which is actually a square-ended axle. Like other axles on a bicycle it has either a cup and cone arrangement or a sealed bearing arrangement. The cranks or crank-arms slip onto either side of this axle and are secured by a bolt or nut, which is threaded onto either end of the axle.

The right-handed side of the axle has either one, two, or three chainrings, depending on the type of bicycle, and are the front driving cogs. The chainrings are round, or oval shaped. Ovalized chainrings are found on some all-terrain bicycles, the theory being that the ovalized shape helps the rider get through the recovery phase of the pedal stroke more quickly and back into its power phase. Another chainring innovation uses the addition of a small kidney-shaped cam that supposedly acts much like the ovalized ring. Another innovation with the crank assembly or the bottom bracket assembly is the use of titanium for the axle of the bottom bracket.

Attached to the crank arms are the pedals. The traditional pedal or cage pedal can be all steel, steel and rubber, or any combination of alloys. On racing bicycles the pedal assembly usually includes a clip and strap, which keeps the rider's feet from moving around. Recent technology has produced the clipless pedal, which is similar to a ski binding. Figure 12.10 shows the difference between the two systems. The clipless pedal system has almost replaced the traditional pedal for racing bicycles and is widely used on all-terrain bicycles as well.

Clipless pedal systems are made of plastics and alloys and allow for increased blood circulation in the feet during cold-weather riding. The clipless design allows for only small amounts of lateral movement in the foot, making it a good choice for riders with knee problems. These pedals are generally heavier than traditional (racing) pedals and do not provide as much clearance. Both of these problems are being addressed and exceptions are on the market. Once you master the system, you can get in and out of the clipless pedal faster than the traditional pedal.

The chain transfers the front chainring motion to the rear wheel of the bicycle with the help of the *freewheel*. The **freewheel** is a cluster of smaller driving

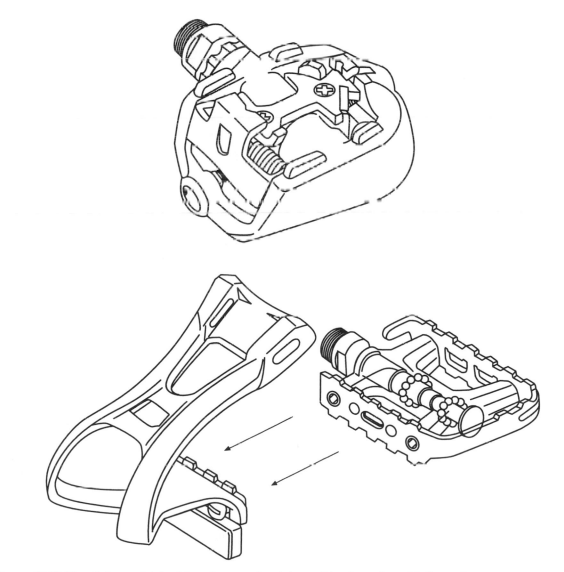

▶ **Figure 12.10** The clipless pedal (top) has almost replaced the traditional step-in pedal (bottom).

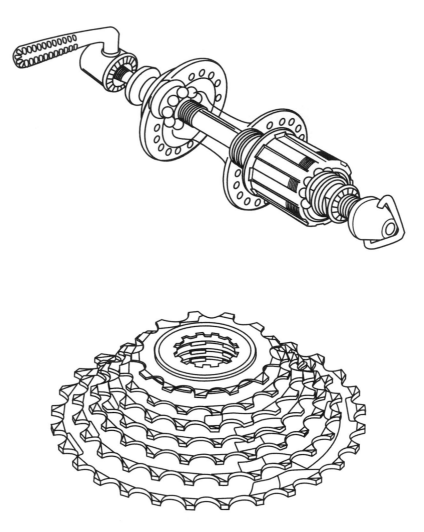

▶ **Figure 12.11** (a) Cassette hub (top) and freewheel (bottom) work together to move the rear wheel.

freewheel—A group or cluster of small chain-wheels or cogs attached to the rear hub, an important part of the drivetrain (cranks, chainwheels, chain shifters, derailleurs, or free-wheels).

derailleur—Bicycle compo-nent responsible for mov-ing the chain from one cog to another (rear derailleur) or from one chainwheel to another (front derailleur).

cogs (5-8) held together on the freewheel body. The entire freewheel assembly is mounted on the rear hub. The freewheel body may be part of the hub, in which case the cogs are slipped onto the hub (a cassette hub). Figure 12.11 shows a freewheel and a cassette hub.

The freewheel is a ratchet mechanism that allows the wheel to move forward when pulled by the chain and yet continues to rotate when the chain is not moving (i.e., when the rider is not pedaling). In contrast, track bicycles have no freewheel but have a single cog in the rear and a single chainring in the front. For this reason a track bike can be ridden forward and backward but cannot coast.

Finally, for bikes other than track bikes there are the parts that make up the shifting assembly. A pair of shift levers can be found on the down tube of most racing bikes (these are used in combination with the brake levers on most racing bikes) and on the handlebars of most all-terrain bikes (see Figure 12.12).

Shifting also can be accomplished using bar-end shifters, that are housed in the end of each handlebar, or in grip shifters—very similar to the throttle on a motorcycle—installed over the end of each handlebar. Cables run from the shifting mechanism to the front and rear **derailleurs**. By manipulating the shifters and either taking up or letting out slack in the cable, the derailleur moves, taking the chain with it. Derailleurs come in various styles, but for the most part are very similar. In general the cage length of both the front and the rear derailleur is determined by the span of gears being used. A bicycle with a wide range of gears has a derailleur with a longer cage than one with a small

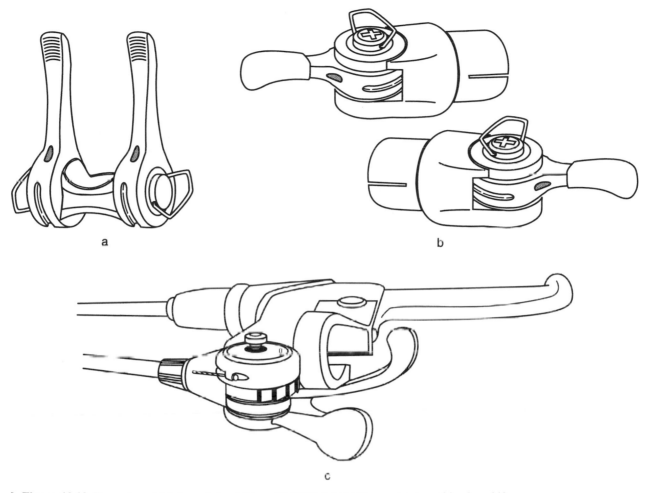

▶ **Figure 12.12** Examples of (a) down tube shifters, (b) handlebar shifters, and (c) combination shifters.

range of gears. Figure 12.13 compares a short-cage rear derailleur and a long-cage rear derailleur.

In recent years there have been many innovations in the drivetrain assembly. The two most notable changes are indexed shifting and automatic shifting. Indexed shifting enables the rider to shift solidly from one gear to another without fumbling for the right spot on the shift lever. This is made possible by notching it inside. When the shifter is moved, it falls into the appropriate notch; the derailleur moves the chain, thus putting the bicycle in another gear. This convenient innovation has simplified the frequently intimidating art of shifting and has made cycling more appealing to many people. It is found almost exclusively on road and all-terrain bicycles purchased in specialty shops. More recently, one manufacturer put the shifting mechanism on the brake lever so that riders can shift and brake by moving their hands.

Some racers and traditionalists still prefer the nonindexing (or friction) systems, where you simply "feel" with the shift lever until you are in the right gear. Most shifters offer an indexing and a nonindexing mode. Many of the bigger component manufacturers have now introduced indexed shifting on front derailleurs, systems that drop the chain back down the freewheel with the touch of a button. There are also smoother shifting systems made possible by a change in the tooth shape of either the chainwheels or the rear cogs. These improvements, positive and helpful to the rider, still have small problems to correct.

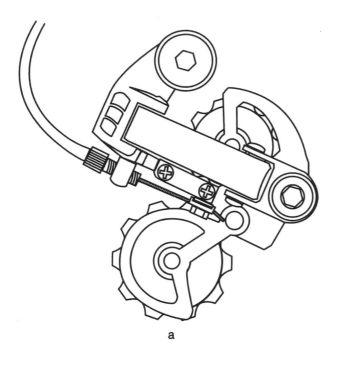
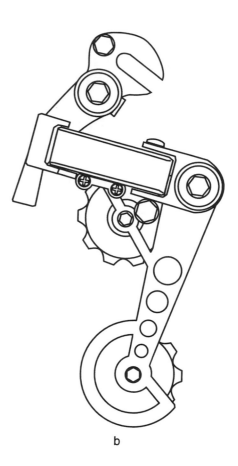

▶ **Figure 12.13** Short (a) and long (b) rear derailleur types.

Another new change, the automatic shifter, shifts for you, but among the several versions available you are required at least to push a button! This system is unlikely to take the place of manual shifting in the case of racing bikes, but these systems are already being seen on all-terrain bikes and touring bikes.

▶ Brakes

Brakes are of three basic types. Coaster brakes house the brake assembly in the hub. The weight and the design of this brake make it unsuitable for high-performance bicycles. The caliber brake is either a side-pull brake, a center-pull brake, or a variation of the two. Figure 12.14 compares the side-pull brake with the center-pull brake.

The side-pull caliber brake (Figure 12.14b) works by applying the brake lever. When this happens, a cable connecting this lever to one of the brake arms pulls against that brake arm. This brake arm then pivots and connects with the other arm, and as a result of the increased cable tension the two arms compress against the rim. Brake pads, usually made of a rubber composite, attach to the brake arms and touch the rim. It is the friction of the pads against the rim that slows the wheel down.

The center-pull caliber brake (Figure 12.14a) works similarly. The brake cable attaches to a cable carrier, which is attached to two brake arms. The cable transfers force applied by the brake levers to the brake arms. Variations of the center-pull brake are the U brake, the roller cam brake, and the cantilever brake. Both the U brake and the roller cam have similar mechanisms as the

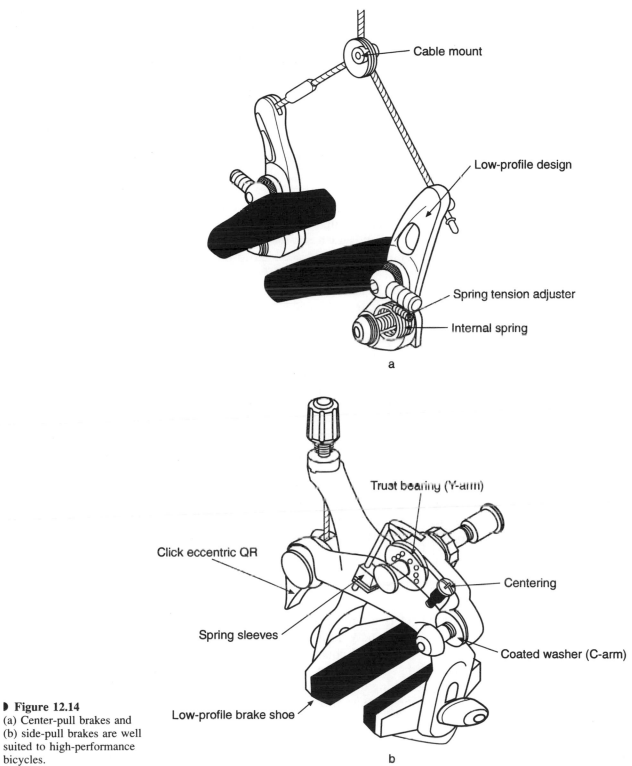

Cable mount

Low-profile design

Spring tension adjuster

Internal spring

a

Trust bearing (Y-arm)

Click eccentric QR

Centering

Spring sleeves

Coated washer (C-arm)

Low-profile brake shoe

b

▶ **Figure 12.14**
(a) Center-pull brakes and
(b) side-pull brakes are well
suited to high-performance
bicycles.

center-pull, but the roller cam uses a small roller that sits between the two brake arms to facilitate their compression against the rim. A type of center-pull brake widely used on all-terrain bikes is the cantilever brake. Brake shoes attach to an arm that joins directly with a boss on the fork blade or rear seat stay. A piece of cable wire connects to both brake arms and a cable hanger unites this piece of cable wire to the cable originating from the brake lever. Tension applied to the cable causes the arms to compress against the rim. Since there is no solid cross bridge, there is the possibility of flexing with this system (Delong, 1974).

The center-pull caliber braking system is the most popular system for all-terrain bikes. It has many desirable qualities: It is light, easy to maintain, and has adequate stopping power. Recent changes to this particular brake system have caused manufacturers to improve their overall products. Brake bridges add stability and strength to the brake because a bridge, or yoke, sits behind the brake arms and attaches to the same bosses as the brake arms. The popularity of suspension forks has also added to the demand for brake bridges because their fork legs are incredibly stiff. When vertical arms became available (for the cantilever brake), products also improved. Vertical arms provide increased leg clearance for the rider and increased braking power because of their position relative to the rim.

The disc brake has been in development for years. Although it has many uses, manufacturers are still refining it. Disc brakes are activated by a cable-and-lever setup, or a hydraulic setup. Hydraulic brakes work on the same principle as cantilever brakes. A closed hydraulic system filled with fluid provides a hydraulic pulse when the brake lever compresses a piston. That hydraulic pulse pushes the brake pads against the rim. Although hydraulic brakes are heavy, require a special hub, and need more maintenance than other braking systems, they are excellent in wet conditions and have great stopping power.

Just as in choosing many other bicycle components, selecting the right brake is based largely on its intended application. Disc brakes are often found on tandem bicycles because of their stopping power. Cantilever brakes and side-pull brakes are found almost exclusively on road bicycles.

▶ Wheels

The wheel is a simple and amazing piece of engineering. A properly built wheel is extremely strong and can be used for a long time. The hub is the wheel's center and contains either a solid or hollow axle. Most high-quality bicycles have a hollow axle and a quick-release mechanism that works like a clamp, securing the wheel to the bicycle dropouts. Figure 12.15 shows an axle with a quick-release mechanism.

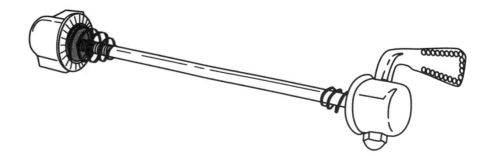

▶ **Figure 12.15** Quick-release skewer.

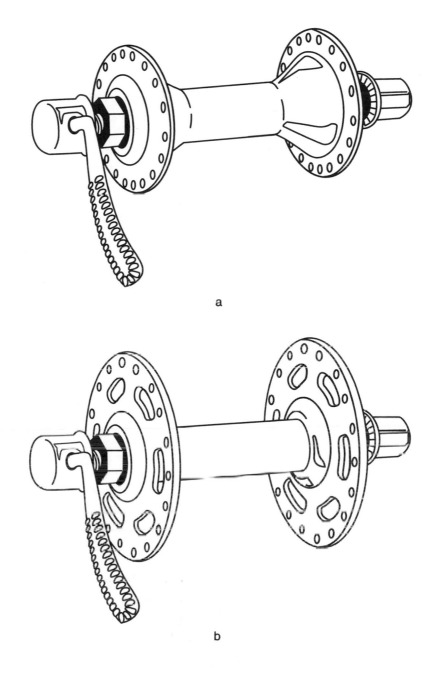

a

b

The biggest advantage of the quick-release mechanism is that it allows for a fast wheel change. Track bicycles almost always have a solid axle, which uses nuts to secure the wheel to the dropouts. A hub flange is where the spokes are attached to the hub, which will have either low flanges or high flanges. Figure 12.16 illustrates the two types of hubs.

The high-flanged hub makes a stiffer wheel; the low-flanged hub cuts weight marginally and helps contribute to a more comfortable ride. A cassette hub, mentioned earlier in the drivetrain discussion, holds the entire freewheel assembly (see page 148).

Spokes connect the hub to the rim and come in various lengths usually made of zinc or stainless steel. Stainless steel resists corrosion better than zinc, but both are equally strong. Spokes are either straight-gauged, double-butted, or bladed. Double-butted spokes can reduce the weight of the wheel slightly. Bladed or ovalized spokes are more aerodynamic than the other two types.

There are five possible spoking patterns that describe the spokes' relationship to the hub. The spokes on a radially spoked wheel will not cross each other at all; instead they go directly from the tub to the rim. The other four patterns are one-cross, two-cross, three-cross, and four-cross. In a one-cross pattern each spoke crosses another on its way from the hub to the rim. In a two-cross pattern each spoke crosses two others on its way from the hub to the rim, and so on. A three-cross pattern is the most common. A four-cross pattern is frequently used on touring bikes and tandems to offset the added weight of a bicycle packed for touring, or the weight of two riders in the case of a tandem. The disc wheel (one without spokes) is essentially a radially spoked wheel and is a common wheel design today due to its aerodynamic properties. Disc wheels are used mainly on track bicycles and have some road racing applications.

A wheel rim can be either a clincher rim or a tubular rim. Another name given the tubular rim (or tubular tire) is a ''sew-up,'' because the tube is sewn inside the tire. Clincher rims are generally heavier and sometimes sturdier than tubular rims. Figure 12.17 shows the cross-section of a clincher rim and a tubular rim.

Most high-quality rims are made of aluminum alloys. The steel rim is becoming virtually obsolete. Tires match the rims. Therefore we have clincher tires and tubular tires. Until recently clincher tires have been much heavier than tubulars and unable to hold as much pressure as tubulars. The clincher tire's edge is a wire bead and it is literally wired onto the rim. A tube, separate from the tire, is mounted between the rim and the tire.

A tubular tire is actually a tube and a tire in one. It is glued to the rim with a special glue. Inexpensive tubulars are made by vulcanizing a tread onto a cotton casing. Better ones are hand-glued to the casing, which is either cotton or silk. The tubes of both clinchers and tubulars are made of butyl or latex. Tubulars are still lighter and more responsive than clinchers. They are more expensive than clinchers and are harder to change and repair.

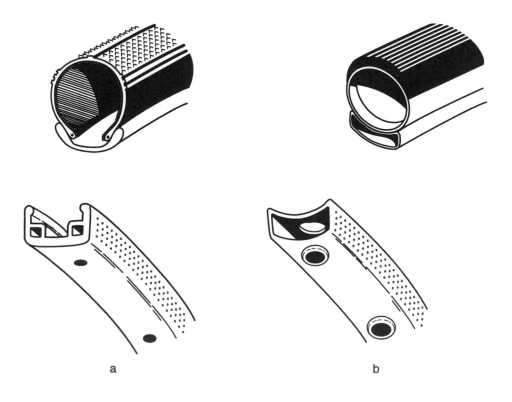

▶ **Figure 12.17** (a) A clincher rim and (b) a tubular rim.

a   b

▶ Stems, Handlebars, and Saddles

We have covered the wheels, brakes, and drivetrain. These are the main components of the bicycle. However, one could not ride a bicycle without the stem, the handlebars, and the saddle. Stems come in various extension lengths and various vertical lengths. Quality will depend on materials used and stem design. Figure 12.18 below illustrates a basic stem. Recently, a flex or suspension stem was introduced. It has a pivot point and a spring system (where the horizontal and vertical points intersect) to allow for flexing.

Handlebars come in different sizes and shapes, depending on the size of the rider's hands and how the bars will be used. A touring bar, known as a "drop bar," has an upsweeping bend starting from the center of the bar and curving around and back toward the rider. The particular upsweeping middle of the touring bar was designed primarily for comfort. A racing bar is similar but without the upsweeping design—it is flat along the top portion. A track bar has no flats on the top, because the rider almost always uses the dropped portion of the bar. Bars on an all-terrain bicycle are usually flat or have a slight rise from the center—again depending on a rider's needs. These bars do not curve around like the drop bar.

Anyone who spends much time reading bicycle publications is aware of the changes that have occurred in handlebars. The most widely used innovation is the triathlon bar, so named for its first use by triathletes attempting to cheat the wind. It is basically a closed bar which when attached to the existing bar extends out in front of the bicycle, allowing the rider to assume a more aerodynamic position. Many variations of this bar now exist, including several versions for all-terrain bicycles. Another change in handlebar components for all-terrain bicycles was the addition of bar ends. Their design mimics the hand position created by brake lever hoods found on road bike brakes. A single piece of bar attaches to the end of either side of the traditional bar. The length, materials used, and ergonomical shape of this bar vary. Chromoly and aluminum alloys are the most widely used materials, but titanium bar ends can be purchased for $140 to $175. Bar ends may be C shaped, L shaped, or completely straight (a zero-degree bend). Lengths range from a few inches to over 8 inches long.

There is little variation among saddles. The extremes are probably found on racing bicycles and exercise bicycles. A racing saddle will be long and narrow to allow more variation in positioning. Saddles designed for women are a recent addition; they are shorter and wider to accommodate the difference in pelvic

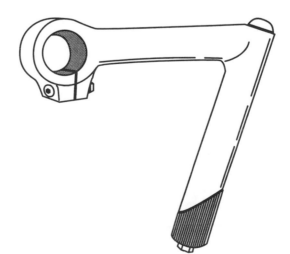

▶ **Figure 12.18** Basic road stem.

structure between men and women. Many women racers still choose a traditional saddle because of the positions afforded. The latest trend in all-terrain bicycle saddles is the "nothing" saddle, a leather cover based on a titanium rail. These saddles weigh as little as 170 grams and depend on the titanium rail for comfort. Touring and all-terrain bicycle saddles tend to be wider and more padded than their racing counterparts, although this is a personal selection. Another contribution from the all-terrain bicycle is the quick release at the seat post, which makes raising and lowering the saddle under different riding conditions much faster. A spring-loaded clip is sometimes attached to the seat post so the rider can raise and lower the saddle without dismounting. Stationary or exercise bicycles often have the widest and most padded saddles because their users tend to sit without changing position.

▶ Materials Used in Various Parts

Most bicycle parts are made of high-grade steel and aluminum alloys. The drivetrain, chainrings, the freewheel, and derailleurs make up the largest component group on the bicycle. Different grades of steel alloys, aluminum alloys, and titanium are used for these parts. Lightness, durability, and reliability are the chief concerns for designers and manufacturers.

Rims are made either of steel or aluminum. One exception is the disc wheel, which is generally made of plastics or composites. Spokes are usually zinc or stainless steel. Tire treads incorporate different grades of rubber, depending on the intent. The sidewalls of many clincher tires include nylon or Kevlar.

Brakes are usually steel alloys or aluminum alloys. Brake pads will be a rubber compound, and again there are many different compounds.

Handlebars are steel, aluminum, titanium, or composite. They are usually wrapped with cotton or plastic tape or have foam or plastic grips. Usually stems are made of steel or aluminum alloys. Saddles can be leather, plastic, or a combination of plastics, and nylon, suede, or leather.

Many bicycle components have undergone a lot of change, often a simple reworking of the design lines of a particular part. But many manufacturers are making changes by adding more aluminum or titanium for lightness, or through the use of composite fibers for strength.

▶ Summary

The bicycling industry is an ever-growing, rapidly changing industry. The simple design of 100 years ago has been worked and reworked resulting in an incredibly efficient and amazing machine. The advances in the bicycling industry, like other technological advances, are happening very quickly. People involved in research and design are working hard to create the perfect machine, whether for the world-class racer or the local commuter.

▶ References

DeLong, F. (1974). *Delong's Guide to Bicycles and Bicycling*. Radnor, PA: Chilton Book.

Hayduk, D. (1987). *Bicycle metallurgy for the cyclist*. Boulder, CO: Johnson Publishing.

Kukoda, J. (1989, July). Titanium: The miracle metal. *Bicycling*, pp. 110-114.

Stevenson, E. (1982). *The high tech bicycle*. New York: Harper & Row.

CHAPTER 13

Aerobic Exercise Equipment

Robert Schwarzkopf, PhD, and Ellen F. Kreighbaum, PhD
Montana State University, Bozeman

Rob Branson
Owenhouse Hardware, Bozeman

Aerobic exercise can be accomplished by walking, jogging, or running. The simplicity of heading out the door for a specified distance and pace appeals to many. Time of day is not a limitation, nor are partners or memberships. Exercise machines offer the same advantages plus safety, privacy, and a way to avoid inclement weather.

This chapter covers six types of aerobic fitness equipment: cross-country ski simulators, exercise bicycles, treadmills, rowing machines, jump ropes, and stepping machines. After a discussion of these standard types of machines, a section on several devices of questionable value is presented. Innovations in design are continually being made, but you can apply the general principles discussed despite specific differences in equipment.

▶ Cross-Country Ski Simulators

Using cross-country equipment has become a popular form of home exercise for a variety of reasons:

- Some manufacturers advertise their product by associating its use with the beauty and solitude enjoyed with outdoor skiing.

- Cross-country skiing uses more of the body's musculature than running and cycling, for example, and you may be able to expend more energy per workout as a result.

- Machines can be made compact for convenient storage.

- Specific training for the sport or recreational activity is possible.

Ski simulators are divided into two categories: those adjustable for arm motion resistance only and those adjustable for both arm and leg motions (Figure 13.1) with variable resistance. The advantage of the latter is that more energy can be expended by the large leg muscles than a shuffle forward and back. Also, excessive arm exercise raises both the heart rate and perceived exertion higher than leg exercise, but at the same energy cost. Therefore, machines that rely primarily on arm motion will result in early fatigue, preventing the user from attaining either the cardiovascular conditioning or the energy expenditure effects desired.

Anatomy of Cross-Country Ski Machines

Cross-country ski movement involves use of the upper and lower extremities, thus machines that simulate cross-country skiing will have sections that serve as poles and sections that function like the resistance of skis. The sophistication of the mechanisms that provide the resistance, the quality of the materials used in the machine, and whether or not the machine has an electronic workload monitor will determine the cost and the quality of the machine. Machines range from the most simple, mechanical devices manufactured with plastics,

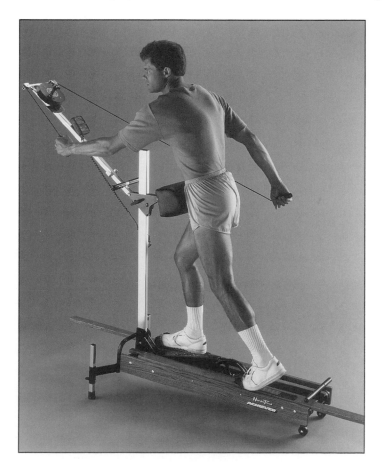

▶ **Figure 13.1** An arm and leg cross-country ski simulator.

to complex, computerized systems made of high-quality metals. The anatomy of a generic-type ski simulator is shown in Figure 13.2.

The foot plates or skates on the systems travel only forward and backward. They are attached to the resistance mechanism with a nylon, or aircraft-quality cable. The nylon strap although durable is less expensive and of lower quality than the aircraft cable, which is stronger and more durable than the nylon strap.

The resistance on the leg portion of the ski machine consists of a friction-dependent mechanism in which you tighten or loosen pressure against a belt. There is resistance against the backward motion only, or both the forward and backward motion of the legs. If the machine is designed with a cable pulled around a wheel, you cannot obtain resistance during the forward motion; resistance is provided only in the pulling or backward motion. The pulling motion is what simulates the skiing motion resistance or the extension motion. In the cable machines there is no resistance against the flexion motion, and thus the flexor muscles surrounding the hip joint in the lower extremities and the shoulder joints in the upper extremities are not stressed.

Many people use ski machines for total fitness rather than for cross-country ski practice, so they require resistance in both forward and backward motions. The machines using the friction of resistance against a belt will have resistance in both the forward and backward directions.

The resistance on the arm mechanism can be either a pressure-belt device as in the leg resistance, or friction on a cable that rolls about a wheel. Because

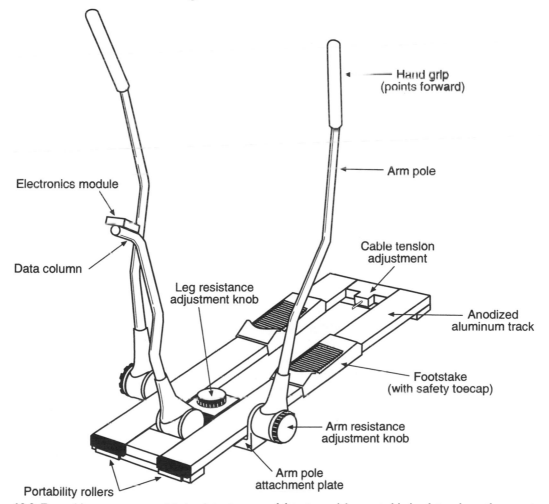

▶ Figure 13.2 From this cross-country ski simulator to more elaborate models, most ski simulators have these parts.

the cable can provide resistance only against pulling and not pushing, it can provide resistance only to the pulling or poling motion of the arms and does not provide resistance to the antagonistic muscle groups, the flexors that would push against the resistance.

There are two main types of arm devices: the handle and cable, or the handle and pole. The cable device does not provide any stability for the body. If you lean on the handheld device, no support will be available. The machines that have stiff poles, such as those used in skiing, provide a mechanism for balance if needed and are more like the poles of real cross-country skiing. Handled cable devices require some practice time to learn, because you must learn to coordinate the arms and legs, and there is no support mechanism for the upper body if balance is lost. The stiff arm poles provided by some machines will give you the feel of actual cross-country skiing, and lack of balance may be corrected through the use of the stiff poles.

Although there are no machines to the author's knowledge that have independent resistance adjustment for the right and left legs, some of the machines have independent resistance adjustment for the right and left arms. This feature is convenient for those whose arms are different in strength, or those who need to exercise one arm more than the other. Furthermore, some machines will have independent leg and arm action; others will have dependent leg and arm action. With independent upper and lower body action, you may use the machine to work the arms only, or the legs only.

Better quality machines are made of steel with copper fittings; the lesser quality machines are made of plastic or aluminum with nylon fittings. The cables are nylon in the less expensive machines; aircraft quality material is used in more expensive machines.

A final consideration is whether the stride length is adequate (determined by the length of the track), or whether it can be adjusted for a shorter excursion. For shorter people or people with short legs, it is common to overstride if there is no adjustment to shorten the stride length. Overstriding results in "getting stuck" at the end of the stride: One leg is fixed forward too far and the other is extended backward too far. The flexor and extensor muscles are not used to provide the type of force needed to get the legs back to the normal length of stride, and the entire timing of the movement is destroyed. A learning curve must be used so that you do not go beyond your normal stride length. With practice, coordinated movements will ensue. Some machines are stride-length adjustable, which reduces the need for this learning.

On those machines that have timers, typical readouts and settings use a counter to count the number of strides performed, a timer to tell you how long you have exercised, a tempo mechanism to pace yourself (as if using a metronome), and an average calorie counter. The calorie counter is based on a typical user, for example a 6-foot, 150-pound person. If you are lighter or heavier, the caloric expenditure readings will be inaccurate.

Selection of a machine should be based on your objectives and the specificity principle. If upper body strength and muscular endurance are primary as a supplement to other methods of exercise, a model with a variable pole resistance and only an unresisted sliding action for the legs, for example, would suffice. However, if total energy expenditure and cardiovascular conditioning are most important, a machine with a resistance mechanism for leg motion is necessary. The example in Figure 13.2 will provide the combination of arm, leg, and body motion most specific to the diagonal stride method of Nordic skiing; so if serious training is desired, one of this type is the wisest choice.

Most nonskiers would find most useful a form of exercise that does not rely on upper body endurance. The relatively untrained arm and shoulder muscles of the average person using a piece of home exercise equipment will be severely limited by upper body fatigue from a ski simulator, especially from one of the type seen in Figure 13.1. An alternative type of exercise machine not requiring extensive upper body muscular endurance may be the wiser choice.

Cross-Country Ski Simulators

Advantages

- The potential exists for high-energy expenditure.

- It is a good off-season conditioning method for competition or recreational skiing.

- You can listen to music, converse, or watch TV to divert attention and reduce boredom.

- Simulated skiing is a nonimpact method of exercise that minimizes orthopedic injury.

Disadvantages

- You have to practice the skill required by a specific machine, which may not be similar to actual snow skiing.

- Some machines provide only a relatively easy foot sliding motion with friction control for the arms. For optional training and conditioning, the legs should do most of the work.

- No machine at this time simulates the skating style now used in competition and that of serious recreationalists.

- The energy expenditure value given by one manufacturer (e.g., 600 calories for a 20-minute workout) is unrealistic for the average user. Unrealized expectations from this type of advertising could lead to discouragement.

- Many models have instrumentation to tell how many movement cycles have been completed and/or exercise duration. None have the capability to convert exercise effort into repeatable intensity—a major drawback for the serious exerciser.

▶ Stationary Cycles

Cycling ranks very high as a cardiovascular exercise. The absence of weight-bearing and foot-strike impact make it appealing to the general population, both old and young, to those who are overweight, and to many with lower extremity disabilities. Riding a stationary cycle also eliminates weather and traffic hazards.

There is a large variety of choices for a stationary cycle. A wind-resistance device can convert a bicycle into an indoor exerciser, or one of the many stationary resistance cycles may be used (Figure 13.3). Indoor pedaling machines range from modified regular frames with frictional resistance brakes (Figure 13.3) to programmed variation in intensity with electromagnetic resistance (Figure 13.4). Riding position may vary from a regular seat and handlebars to a near-horizontal bench seat. Some manufacturers have provided arm exercise while pedaling on an air-braked cycle.

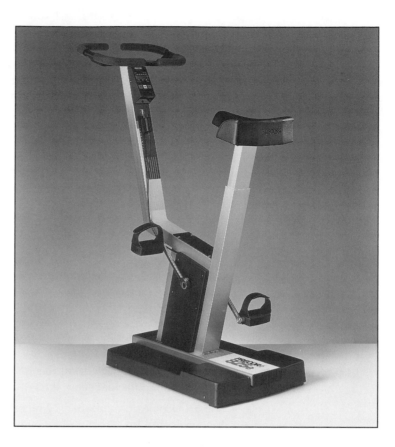

▶ **Figure 13.3** Bicycle ergometer in modified regular frame style.

▶ **Figure 13.4** Lifecycle ergometer with electromagnetic resistance.

Anatomy of the Exercise Bicycle

The resistance device on an exercise bicycle can be as simple as felt pads exerting pressure against the front wheel (like brakes on a road bicycle), or as sophisticated as an electromagnetic resistance adjustment controlled by a computer. There are exercise bicycles that have stationary handlebars, and those that have movable handles with resistance. Figure 13.5 shows the anatomy of an exercise bicycle with resistive handles.

The most basic exercise bicycle model has stationary handlebars and resistance adjusted by increasing or decreasing brake pad pressure. An alternative to the brake-pad model is one with a nylon strap on the front wheel that can be tightened or loosened to increase or decrease the resistance, respectively. Another model uses the concept of increased pedaling speed to increase the workout. This machine is based on the concept of increasing the revolutions per minute of pedaling. A more advanced model of exercise cycling incorporates arm and leg motion into the exercise. The lower end of these cycles do not have arm resistance adjustments; rather, the arm motion is dependent on the leg motion. The upper end of these machines has independent arm and leg resistances.

A basic arm-leg machine is designed with arm motion dependent on the leg motion (i.e., as you pedal, leg motion dictates arm motion or vice versa). Thus as the legs move the pedals, the arm mechanisms will move also. Other machines use independent arm and leg motions; thus the arm levers work only when the arms are applying force, and the leg mechanisms work only when the legs are applying force.

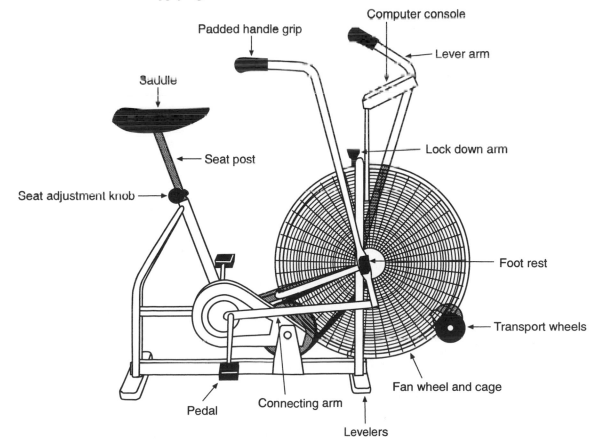

▶ **Figure 13.5** Parts of an exercise bicycle with resistive handles that work the arms.

Independent arm and leg resistance is not the only consideration; the timing of the arm and leg motions is also an important feature. With dependent arm and leg motions, their coordination and timing must be appropriate. On some machines, the timing of the arms is not synchronized with the legs. One machine has an offset pedal arm extension attached to the crank of the left side that adjusts the timing of the left and right arm leg-movements to a smooth pattern.

Timers

The timers for exercise cycles range from the purely mechanical to the electromagnetic, the former having dials and readouts for speed and distance measures. The more sophisticated machines have timers and estimate the level of work produced, revolutions per minute, and average calories burned (for the average person). The most sophisticated machines have pulse meters—the earlobe type being the most basic, and the chest-strap type being the most accurate. The most accurate machines also give the workload measurement in watts. More expensive machines have courses programmed into them. Thus, you can select a course that simulates the effort of riding up and down equally distant hills, or a course that builds upon the previous effort by simulating an uphill ride, hitting a plateau, and then riding up another hill. Eight to 10 programmed courses are available on some models.

Seats

The seats of exercise cycles must be comfortable. The wider the seat to about 8 inches, the more comfortable the seat will be. The cover may be made of leather (usually too expensive for exercise cycles); synthetic leather; or a very soft, smooth synthetic material that feels like a very fine suede (called ''emerald skin'' by one manufacturer). The padding under the seat covering is typically made of foam of variable densities with extra foam under the ischial tuberosity (bony) areas. Padding also may be gel, or a Spenco ''biosoft'' material which has a rubbery liquid feel. The amount of time one spends exercising on a bicycle will determine whether the extra expense of these new materials is cost effective.

Cycling machines marketed for home and health club use span an ever-increasing range of choices. At the low end of the spectrum are modified bicycle frames with a spoked wheel and a simple roller friction mechanism to adjust pedaling effort. Even at a low price (under $100) they are no bargain. Without a flywheel (a heavy wheel to store momentum), a smooth pedal motion is impossible, and its early retirement to a garage sale is inevitable. The opposite extreme is the computerized, electromagnetically braked cycle—some even with TV. These electronic marvels far exceed the average person's financial means and requirement for a suitable exercise machine.

The purchaser's minimum requirements should be: a weighted wheel to provide a smooth pedal action, a caliper or circumference friction brake, and a comfortable riding position (which usually cannot be adequately evaluated by a brief trial). Request a trade-in privilege on an alternative model if extended use is uncomfortable. Tall persons usually have the greatest difficulty because of insufficient adjustment range.

Stationary Cycles

Advantages

- They are relatively inexpensive (however, some cost several thousand dollars), compact, and portable.

- You can listen to music, converse, watch TV, or read to divert attention and reduce boredom.

- Cycling eliminates heel-strike forces (only about 0.6 G vs. 3 G while running).

- Some models have meters that display the amount of resistance as well as speed and time. Caloric expenditure can be estimated reasonably well from this information.

Disadvantages

- A "sore behind" can be a problem. Selecting a sex-specific anatomic saddle (broader for females with padding under the "seat bones"), adjusting the seat height properly (almost a straight leg at the lowest pedal position), and using a pressure-reducing seat cover can minimize discomfort. An alternative choice is a model with a chair-like seat.

- Many find indoor cycling boring. (However, reading, listening to music, or watching TV can make time pass more rapidly and even profitably if the distraction is entertaining or educational.)

- Cycling only works the legs. Supplemental, upper body and flexibility exercises are necessary for a balanced program. One model does add some push-pull arm exercise but does not incorporate all muscle groups or use a range of motion to replace stretching.

▶ Treadmills

Treadmills permit walking, jogging, or running indoors without traffic, dogs, snow, dust, wind, or scenery. A familiar mode of exercise with at-home convenience in a controlled environment has a lot of appeal. However, a large difference between the treadmill and other exercise machines is that they are motorized; consequently, cost, weight, and portability, among other factors should be considered. There is one type of nonmotorized treadmill that you use by pushing a movable belt backward over a series of rollers while grasping a guardrail. The change in gait pattern makes walking feel unnatural (these are not used for running) and will be less efficient. For these reasons this type of treadmill cannot be recommended and will not be discussed further.

Anatomy of a Treadmill

A quality treadmill is one of the most complicated of the exercise machines because it is among those used for a wide range of walking and running movements. A typical treadmill is shown in Figure 13.6.

The Platform and Belt

A platform may be metal, carbon fiber, synthetic, or vinyl-laminated steel. The deck upon which the belt slides should be as frictionless as possible. Some manufacturers make the deck out of a Teflon-like material with a belt made of rubber, also with a Teflon-like coating. Most treadmill belts and decks must

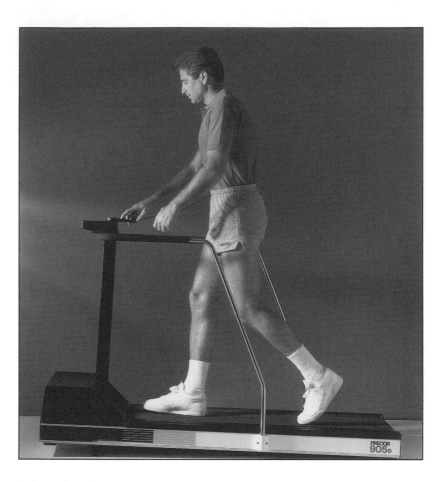

▶ **Figure 13.6** A typical treadmill.

be lubricated periodically. The particular model shown here does not have to be lubricated because of the materials used at the belt-deck interface. The platform material should be somewhat flexible to absorb the shock of landing, and rubber feet also help with shock absorption. The rear roller should have guides to keep the belt on the platform and prevent side slip. Also there should be a way to adjust the tightness of the belt to prevent slippage if the belt stretches.

The Assembly

The shroud covers the working assembly. In motorized models there should be a flywheel attached to store momentum, which makes the movement smoother. The motor drives the speed of the belt. This drive is transferred to the belt by a rubber or nylon strap attached to the motor and to a roller at the front of the belt. The best rollers are made of stainless steel with steel bearings. Motor horsepower ranges from 1/2 to 2 horsepower. Of course, the greater the horsepower potential, the better if the machine gets frequent use, if the user is heavy, or if the workout is strenuous.

Many treadmills have elevation devices. Either they crank up using a jack mechanism and gears, or they have a motor-driven elevation device. Of course, the motor-driven elevator is more convenient; you can adjust the elevation without taking a break in the exercise routine. The motor turns a shaft around which a steel cable is wound, elevating the deck. Generally, elevations range from 0 to a 16-percent grade.

The Communications System

A computerized system is the best system to set the treadmill controls and allow you to communicate with the motor assembly. The settings should include elevation, speed, distance, and calorie calculation. As with other exercise devices, the speed is calculated through the use of an electromagnetic sensor programmed to calculate speed by sensing the number of times a magnet passes by it. (The magnet is attached to a wheel that revolves as the roller turns.) Calorie calculation is done by entering your weight, along with the elevation setting and the speed setting on the machine when you begin to exercise. Once again, this calculation is an estimation only and is not entirely accurate.

Selecting a Treadmill

The suitability of a treadmill as a home exercise device should be carefully considered by an individual prior to purchase. Treadmill running may be boring without the normal distractions provided by changing scenery. To obtain optimal benefits you must purchase a model with a long belt and a large enough motor—at a large price. Motor and belt durability may prohibit extensive long and moderate-paced sessions on less expensive machines. Perhaps the treadmill's most appropriate use is for carefully controlled walking where pace and supervision are necessary.

Treadmills

Advantages

- An exercise session can be precisely controlled by regulating the speed and belt slope—a distinct advantage for rehabilitation.

- Heart rate can be monitored by an inexpensive meter or by pulse count. This feature may be a necessity for the person undergoing cardiac rehabilitation, or a nice extra for the serious trainer.

- Once adjusted to walking or running on a treadmill, your stride feels very much like normal walking or running.

- Pace for hills and intervals can be easily set to vary the training session.

Disadvantages

- Cost. Manufacturers have recently entered the home exercise market with scaled-down versions of institutional models. Although these small treadmills cost much less than the larger models, they are still several times the price of an excellent cycle, rowing machine, or ski simulator.

- Size. The home treadmill is small and light enough to be used in a room with a standard ceiling. However, the tradeoffs for small size are: little or no elevation capability to simulate hills, belt width requires attention to maintain a straight gait, and the short belt length prohibits safety while running from even an average-sized person. Standard-sized models may be too heavy for house floor supports and require a higher-than-standard ceiling.

- Noise. Laboratories that use treadmills for testing often are isolated to prevent the sound of the machine from bothering others on the same or adjacent floors. There are newer home models with smaller motors and better sound insulation; however, the durability of a smaller motor and light-duty construction may be questionable under prolonged use, or with a heavy person.

- Absence of pleasurable distraction while exercising. Treadmill noise may add either excessive background rumble to music, or cause the listener to turn up the volume to hazardous level.

▶ Rowing Machines

Properly done, rowing on a sliding seat uses the large quadriceps muscle group together with those of the back, hips, shoulder girdle, and arms. Its repetitive rhythm makes rowing a good exercise for the development of aerobic capacity. Injury to the lower back and altered respiratory action (breath holding causing a sharp increase in blood pressure) at the beginning of each stroke and its consequent reduction in venous return are unsubstantiated fears according to a study using a wide cross-section of untrained males and females (Hagerman, Lawrence, & Mansfield, 1988).

A variety of rowing machines are available. The simplest apply friction, pneumatic, or hydraulic resistance to the oars (Figure 13.7). One type of machine uses a flywheel with fan blades to provide wind resistance (Figure 13.8). Momentum is stored in the wheel spin during the recovery action by using a cycle freewheel mechanism and closely approximates actual rowing.

Anatomy of Rowing Machines

The rowing machine consists of a platform, a track upon which the seat rides, oars, some type of resistance mechanism, and usually a timer or electronic control mechanism.

The Platform and Seat Track

The platform may be constructed of plastic or metal. Metal platforms, usually made of steel or aluminum, are more stable and resist breakage. Rollers move the seat within the tracks and are usually made of tough nylon which should be constructed to glide over the tracks with little friction or sticking. In some models there is no platform per se, but rather a rail upon which the seat moves.

▶ **Figure 13.7** A simple rowing machine with mechanical resistance.

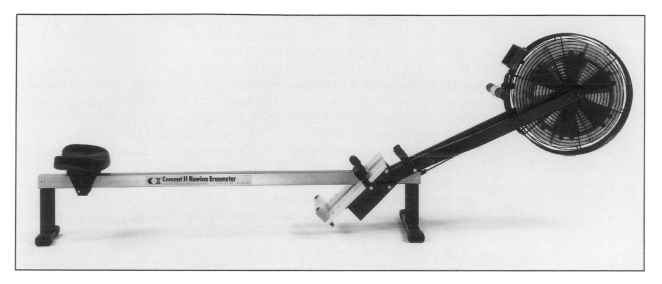

▶ **Figure 13.8** A rowing machine with wind resistance.
Reprinted by permission of Concept II, Inc.

The Oars

Oars may have a truncated form like tubes of steel, or a handlebar on the end of a cable or rope. The rigid-oar mechanism fixes the hand path during the pull. The more flexible cable mechanism allows you to vary the hand path so that different muscles may be used.

The Resistance Mechanism

Resistance mechanisms are of three types: hydraulic cylinders adjustable for each arm, an aerodynamic flywheel, or an inertia-based flywheel. Hydraulic cylinders are most susceptible to malfunction, although they are smooth and constant in their resistance. The aerodynamic flywheel is similar to the aerodynamic flywheels found on some exercise bicycles. Resistance is dependent on the speed with which the pull is made: The faster you drive the wheel, the greater the resistance. The inertial flywheel is a heavy mass that must be rotated by the use of a cable or tow rope and a handlebar. The acceleration of the mass creates the resistance. Like other inertial-based machines, the rowing machines using this mechanism have a smooth, actual rowing feel.

The Counter

Counters may range from a simple, mechanical device to count strokes to a sophisticated microprocessor-controlled timing device. Advanced counters will sum total strokes and calculate strokes per minute, or per cadence; the time of workout; the distance traveled; and an estimate of calories expended. Computerized electronic modules have programmed workouts that you can set to fabricate an imaginary competitor you can view on the screen. Once the workout starts the screen displays how you are doing relative to another boat and even send you messages about your performance; the fictitious pace boat provides visual motivation to follow your workout plan.

The Seat, Footpedals, and Handles

The seat must be comfortable and slide smoothly and easily. Most frequently seats are made of molded plastic covered by foam-padded synthetic leather.

Other padding options are gel or synthetic padding. Because rowing requires pushing the seat backward, the back portion of the seat should be raised slightly to prevent slipping off as the backward push is made.

The pedals should rotate and there should be straps of some kind to secure each foot to a pedal. The straps are usually made of ''hook and eye'' material and should be made to accommodate small and large feet. The use of straps allows you to pull the seat forward by flexing the hips and knees to provide a workout for muscle groups other than the extensors.

Handle grips are usually made of plastic, rubber, or foam. They should be comfortable and of a size that will not place undue pressure on the fingers as you pull on them. If the machine is a cable and handlebar design, the handle grips should roll about the handlebar.

For persons with orthopedic disorders that prevent jogging, sufficient walking, or even cycling, rowing may be an excellent choice. Health-related fitness can be maintained or increased with minimal stress to the foot, knee, and hip. Also, the muscular endurance developed in the back, shoulders, and arms could be supplemented with sit-ups and push-ups for a complete muscle and cardiovascular program. Machines with a flywheel are the best choice, because a smooth rowing motion is possible, very similar to the actual sport, and appropriate instrumentation for repeatable exercise is included. But the high cost of the best machines makes purchase an investment.

Rowing Machines

Advantages

- You use a larger muscle mass—more than cycling for example.

- A larger energy use per unit of time is possible than for cycling.

- The use of the hip and back extensors, shoulder horizontal adductors, and arm horizontal extensors makes rowing excellent for posture and possibly may help prevent lower back pain.

- There is no sudden impact stress (as in the foot strike of running).

- Some machines can be folded into a very compact unit for easy storage.

Disadvantages

- Untrained rowers with underdeveloped back, shoulder, and arm muscles may fatigue prematurely due to the limitation of these small muscles.

- The activity may be boring unless attention is distracted (e.g., by listening to music or watching TV).

- The lack of ground impact on the long leg bones may not provide the bone stress necessary to prevent osteoporosis. However, additional weight-bearing exercise such as normal walking could prevent osteoporotic changes.

▶ Jump Ropes

Rope jumping had a brief surge in popularity following a magazine article that presented the results of a study showing that 10 minutes of rope jumping was equivalent to 30 minutes of jogging. Shortly thereafter the flaws in that research were found and a better comparison made—that is, a slightly lower energy expenditure for jumping compared to jogging for the same heart rate. Maintaining a jumping rhythm requires a metabolic rate 8 to 10 times the resting rate, which is higher than many untrained persons could maintain for a long enough time to develop cardiovascular and body composition benefits. Even if you are well conditioned, leg strain often forces you to end jumping before you experience a general feeling of fatigue.

The ease, convenience, and minimal expense of rope jumping, however, does make it an attractive form of exercise. Injury risk and leg strain can be reduced by jumping on a resilient surface. Many will find this form of exercise a suitable way to improve adult fitness any time anywhere.

Jumping Rope

Advantages

- It is inexpensive. Even the fanciest jump ropes are sold for a nominal price.
- A minimal indoor space requirement or use anywhere outdoors makes rope jumping more convenient than walking, jogging, or running.
- The energy expenditure rate for most adults will be high enough to meet guidelines established by the American College of Sports Medicine.
- In addition to other exercise benefits, some exercise is obtained for the upper body, primarily the shoulders.

Disadvantages

- Rope jumping requires skill. Until sufficiently skilled, you may find exercise intensity too high to maintain; thus rope jumping may be a poor exercise choice for the unconditioned adult.
- Frequent, long jumping sessions, or even infrequent, short sessions if overweight, may lead to injury. (Slow, progressive conditioning, proper shoes, and a resilient floor surface can minimize risk.)
- The amount of muscle used jumping rope is less than jogging, which somewhat reduces its overall fitness value.
- Many find rope jumping both difficult and boring, limitations that prevent sufficient frequency and duration to gain significant fitness benefits.

▶ Stepping Machines

What treadmills are to running, climbers, or stepping machines, are to stair running. These devices use the leg muscles by a stair climbing action but without ascending and descending (Figure 13.9a, b). The elimination of foot strike and lengthening muscular contraction for the descent phase of stair climbing reduces injury risk and muscle soreness.

Anatomy of Stair Steppers

The design of steppers includes a heavy base for stability, foot pedals with a tread applied over the foot contact area for friction, a shroud covering the resistance assembly mechanism, handles, and in most instances an electronics module (see Figure 13.10). The base, usually made of steel, should be weighted if made of plastic. The shroud that surrounds the resistance mechanism is usually made of plastic. If there are handlebars, as in this model, they are covered with rubber or foam so that you can lean on them in a position similar

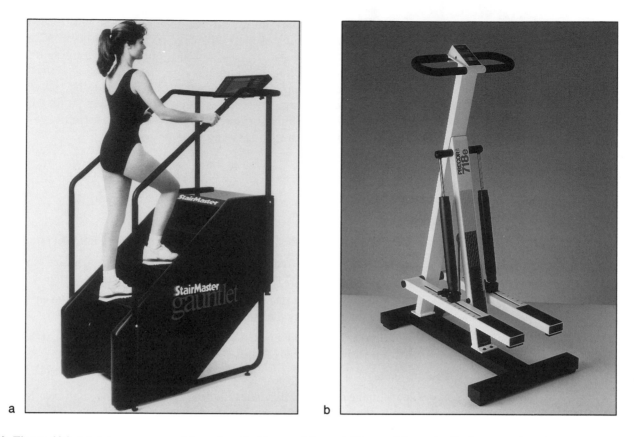

▶ **Figure 13.9** (a) A large, commercial-version climbing machine and (b) a model popular for its convenient size.

to bicycle riding. If the stepper has either front or side handrails, they will be made of aluminum, plastic, or other metal.

Resistance Mechanisms

There are three types of resistance mechanisms: the hydraulic cylinder, the flywheel, and the fan. The hydraulic cylinder is usually oil filled and may operate with one cylinder for both pedals, or one cylinder for each pedal. Separate resistance adjustment for each pedal is possible only with the two-cylinder model; however, it is difficult to adjust both pedals for equal resistance in this configuration. Hydraulic cylinders also have a tendency to leak.

The flywheel resistance mechanism is smoother than the other two types, making adjustments with gears which transfer resistance by the use of nylon straps to the flywheel. The pedal motion is controlled by a metal transfer wheel in which there is a metal coil spring. The spring is loaded by a downward push on the pedal, and upon its release returns the pedal to the "up" position. At least one model uses a chain-driven mechanism similar to an escalator rather than using nylon straps.

The fan resistance machines depend on air resistance on the fan blades to create resistance for the exerciser. The faster the exerciser moves the blades, the greater the air resistance.

Electronics Module

Most machines have devices to give you feedback about your execution of a workout program. Included in this module may be a timer, a stroke counter, a cadence calculator, and a calorie counter. Indicators will tell you the condition

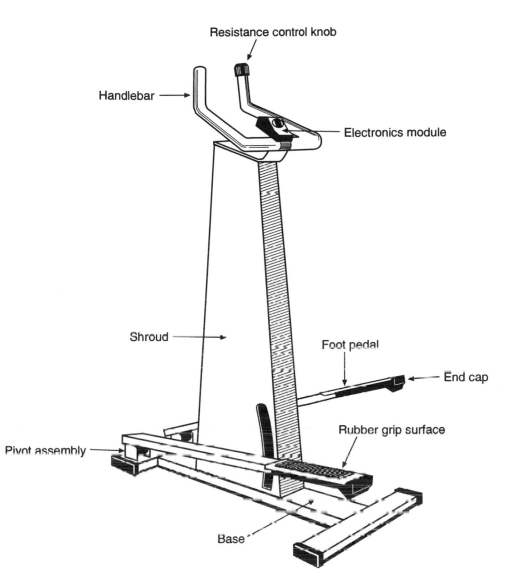

▶ **Figure 13.10** The basic stepper machine simulates the climbing of stairs and includes these parts.

of these variables as well as the resistance at which the machine is set. The caloric counter is an average, so cannot be entirely accurate for a variety of users. Some calorie counter calculations are determined by programming data for an average-sized person into the computer, and some machines offer the user a weight range selection in increments of 20 pounds.

Final Thoughts on Stepping Machines

This type of machine offers high caloric expenditure, greater use of the leg and hip muscles, little or no muscular soreness, and a relatively low purchase price for home models, making this form of exercise very popular. Many health clubs have already added more elaborate machines to their aerobic offerings. Also, serious recreational, mountain bike riders may find climbing machines excellent off-season training for the standing pedal action used on hills. Consistent use by the elderly would enable them to maintain more specific strength for this very necessary daily activity.

Stepping Machines

Advantages

- Safety is assured, because no jarring contact occurs as in running or tripping while descending stairs.

- The energy expenditure may be high, comparable to the highest for any aerobic exercise.

- These machines eliminate body-weight loaded lengthening contraction from descending stairs.

Disadvantages

- Many people become bored without diversion (such as listening to tapes or watching TV).

- No upper body or trunk exercise is gained. Climbing should be supplemented with flexibility, trunk, and upper body muscular exercises for a complete program. For example, some devices such as one for wall climbing have been introduced.

- Stepping machines may aggravate knee pain or injury.

▶ Exercise Equipment of Questionable Value

The multiplicity of products on the market and those yet to come prohibit an exhaustive critique of each. Every potential consumer must be wary of advertisements offering quick or easy results. Marketing of these products is based on consumer impulse with a probability of long-term effectiveness close to zero.

Devices to Vibrate, Melt, or Massage Away Fat

Products falling into this category are most flagrant with claims that have no merit. Rolling machines, vibrating belts and tables, or massage devices are claimed to break up, remove, or redistribute body fat. They do not have any effect on fat metabolism or distribution. This type of exercise may be hazardous to pregnant women if applied to the abdomen.

Wraps, belts, pants, or other nonporous garments worn or applied are claimed to "melt," "squeeze," or provide a magic solution for figure control. By temporarily compressing tissue or accelerating sweat loss, a brief period of weight loss and decreased measurements may be seen. But as soon as fluid movement and replacement has occurred, original weight and size returns. Aside from the quackery of the statements made, the user may be at higher risk of thermal injury, and if used during exercise they may be self-defeating. Sweat evaporation is effectively prevented over the skin area covered, which will accelerate sweating but prevent heat loss. It is the *evaporation* of sweat that carries away excess body heat. Therefore, if heat loss is sufficiently prevented, death due to heat stroke is possible. The user will also find less exercise (which *uses* calories) possible because more blood flow is used to cool the body, making exercise feel more difficult.

Saunas and Whirlpools

Heating from either source can provide temporary relaxation and relief of soreness, stiffness, and arthritis pain. However, many exaggerated and false claims have been made concerning their purported benefits. Poorly maintained equipment can result in injury due to skin diseases, water-borne bacterial disease, thermal damage, electric shock, and wounds from cracked or broken equipment. With conscientious maintenance you can safely obtain the benefits of wet or dry heat. But do not be misled into believing any fitness, weight loss, or figure control results will occur. Most of their beneficial effects also can be obtained soaking in a warm tub.

Muscle Stimulators

Electronic stimulation of muscle has been used as a therapy for many years. The involuntary contractions induced by muscle stimulators can increase muscle strength in those recovering from profound atrophy. Claims of its use for enhanced strength in normal muscles are simply incorrect. Voluntary contraction is many times more effective and also provides an element of learning for the nervous system.

Stretching, Pulling, or Pushing Devices

Springs, surgical tubing, and pneumatic, hydraulic, and friction devices have been on the market in some form for many years. Basically, the exerciser pulls or pushes with the device providing resistance. Ingenious exercises using a wide variety of major muscle groups to attain "total body exercise" reflect respectable kinesiological understanding. Aside from deterioration or breakage with use, these devices are very likely to be shelved, because there is little motivation to exert effort. With little or no knowledge of how much effort is needed or expended (feedback), incentive is lost. An inexpensive barbell set with greater durability can do as much.

Wearing or Carrying Weights

Additional weight can be carried while walking, jogging, or running to increase the activity's intensity. You can carry small dumbbells in your hands, fasten weights to your ankles, or wear a weighted vest on your trunk.

The energy expenditure of any movement task is proportional to the weight of the body or body part plus any added weight multiplied by the vertical distance used in the range of motion. However, this is only true if speed and vertical displacement are constant. For example, if hand weights are carried but arm motion is restricted, the additional energy cost would be eliminated. Advertisements claiming increased caloric expenditures of 30 to 300 percent must be considered gross exaggerations unless very heavy weights are carried. Increased energy expenditures of 5 to 10 percent have been found by several studies. Therefore an additional 5 to 15 calories may be expended in a mile walk or run.

Researchers have speculated that a change in gait pattern or increased force at foot strike may increase injury risk if you add weight on the ankle. These questions remain unresolved, although Claremont and Hall (1988) did not find a change in lower extremity kinematics with either ankle or hand weights. They did find that angular velocity and excursion of the arms were reduced when hand weights were carried, thus little additional energy was used. According to a recent issue of *Runner's World* magazine, a trunk vest may be the best device for increasing muscular endurance, cardiorespiratory endurance, and muscular power. After constantly wearing a weighted vest equal to 10 percent above their body weight for 6 weeks, runners displayed better leg muscle endurance, cardiorespiratory endurance, and leg muscle power. However, these physiological improvements did not appear until the runners went without the weighted vests for some of their training sessions. This is because muscles adapt to movements used with heavier weight (specificity of training) (Anderson, 1993).

In summary, adding weight while exercising can add to the energy expended. The added energy cost will be small for up to 1 kilogram of added load and could be more easily accomplished by a slightly faster pace or longer distance.

Rebounders or Minitrampolines

The widespread popularity of rebounders has stimulated researchers to investigate the claims made by their manufacturers. A reduction in impact stress with their use while jogging or "dancing" is an accurate claim, but those of greater exercise value per minute of exercise time are not. Comparable exercise activities include a walk-jog at 4 to 4.5 mph, bicycling at 8 mph, moderate-to-vigorous aerobic dance, and several recreational games and activities (Katch, Villanacci, & Sady, 1981). The time of recoil from a normal-height bounce makes rebounder devices unsuitable for more vigorous exercises produced by a faster bounce rate. Fitness improvements in aerobic capacity and body composition are statistically equivalent to the activity performed on or off the rebounder (Tomassoni, Blanchard, & Goldfarb, 1985).

Many users find rebounders boring because attention must be paid to landing in the proper spot to avoid the risk of injury. Consequently, distractions such as listening to music, watching TV, or even watching an exercise leader are more difficult. Safety could be increased by recessing the rebounder in the floor or by surrounding it with a padded platform. In summary, rebounders do reduce impact stress, but may produce acute lower fatigue from an unnatural bouncing movement. They do not increase caloric expenditure over the exercise performed without the bounce assist.

Parallel Turn Simulator

This new entrant into the ski-conditioning market provides a method of specific skill and muscular endurance training for the downhill skier (Figure 13.11). The specificity required for downhill turns should not be extended to overall fitness benefits. The use of small hip muscles that rapidly fatigue makes extended use for caloric expenditure or aerobic fitness unlikely. As a supplement to—not a substitute for—a more generalized fitness program, it is excellent.

▶ Summary

Many kinds of exercise equipment are on the market. You could spend less than a dollar for a ball to squeeze, or a length of surgical tubing to pull. At the opposite extreme, many thousands could be spent on a treadmill, or on a cycle ergometer with computerized attachments and even a TV screen.

Exercise is not invariably tied to a device or machine. Many authorities recommend walking as the best single form of exercise due to its many advantages: no cost (except for a pair of good shoes), anytime-anywhere convenience, low injury risk, weight-bearing stimulation to the legs for prevention of decalcification, and an effective method for using calories. Two possible liabilities for the walker are a greater time requirement (about 1 hour per day to meet most health-related recommendations), and no improvement to fitness beyond a modest level.

▶ **Figure 13.11** A parallel turn simulator.

Other home exercise alternatives such as jogging, bicycle riding, gardening, and many others offer a wide variety of activities to meet the needs of almost anyone. Exercise equipment are devices that should be viewed as meeting a need other alternatives cannot. No piece of exercise equipment can supply the motivation for use. Once its novelty has worn off, your commitment to exercise as a necessary part of your lifestyle to maintain health, vigor, and optimal appearance will determine whether or not the device will be used.

▶ References

Hagerman, F.C., Lawrence, R.A., & Mansfield, M.C. (1988). A comparison of energy expenditure during rowing and cycle ergometry. *Med. Sci. Sports Exerc.*, **20**(5), pp. 479-488.

Claremont, A.D., Hall, S.J. (1988). Effects of extremity loading upon energy expenditure and running mechanics. *Med. Sci. Sports Exerc.*, **20**(2), pp. 167-171.

Katch, V.L., Villanacci, J.F., & Sady, S.P. (1981). Energy cost of rebound-running. *Research Q. Exerc. Sport*, **52**(2), pp. 269-272.

Tomassoni, T.L., Blanchard, M.S., & Goldfarb, A.H. (1985). Effects of a rebound exercise training program on aerobic capacity and body composition. *Phys. Sports Med.*, **13**(11), pp. 110-115.

Anderson, O. (1993, November). The fast lane: vested interest. *Runners World*, p. 38.

CHAPTER 14

Resistance Training Equipment

John Garhammer, PhD
California State University at Long Beach

Paul Ward, PED
QPT Publications, Laguna Hills, California

This chapter includes an explanation of types of muscle activation, a brief exegesis of resistance classifications, some general guidelines for equipment selection, and a short discussion of computer-controlled machines.

In addition to cognitive exposure to resistance training equipment, the best method for gaining a complete understanding of the equipment is to use it. There are local, regional, and national conferences held throughout the year where visitors can try out the resistance exercise equipment that is displayed.

Additional sources of information are exercise equipment companies—most are anxious to supply brochures, catalogs, and supporting literature about their equipment. Furthermore, it is useful to visit local health clubs, which usually have an assortment of resistance equipment available for their customers. Many of the newer, progressive health clubs have a representative sampling of the "cutting edge" in resistance exercise machines that can currently be found in the marketplace.

▶ Terminology

To make informed decisions about buying or using resistance training equipment, you need to be familiar with certain terms. We'll introduce a few terms at the start and others within the chapter.

Concentric Activation

concentric—Toward the center. A muscular tension in which the muscle shortens toward its middle.

A muscle can be activated and generate tension in several ways. The most basic is the **concentric** (also called a shortening or positive) contraction, during which the muscle gets shorter. The faster the shortening, the lower the maximal possible tension will be. Concentric contractions are the most common types of muscle contraction in daily activities; all resistance equipment permits concentric contractions.

Eccentric Activation

eccentric—Off center or away from center. A muscular tension in which the muscle is lengthened while resisting the lengthening.

A muscle can also generate tension when it is forced to lengthen by some external force. This is called **eccentric** (or lengthening or negative) activation. Maximal possible tension increases with lengthening velocity to a point where the muscle's ability to generate tension rapidly falls to zero. Eccentric tension is also common in daily activities and sporting movements, such as setting a bag of groceries on the floor, or in lowering the center of gravity of the body in the final step in preparation for a long jump. Some resistance machines (such as isokinetic double positive machines) do not permit eccentric activation.

Isokinetic Activation

isokinetic—A type of exercise in which the body segment or segments are moving and the muscles involved are lengthening or shortening at a constant rate.

If an active muscle lengthens (an eccentric action) or shortens (a concentric action) at a constant speed, it is said to undergo an **isokinetic** activity. A number of machines are referred to as isokinetic, but as we discuss in the section on accommodating resistance machines, one must be careful to distinguish between constant speed of muscle lengthening or shortening and constant speed of movement of machine components. A true isokinetic activation is rare in daily activities.

Isometric Activation

isometric—A type of exercise in which the muscles are tense but no visible movement of the body segments is taking place.

A muscle generating tension while it is unable to lengthen or shorten due to external constraints is said to be activated **isometrically**, or statically. Isometric activation occurs with some regularity during work tasks and sport activities. Many simple and inexpensive techniques are available to "exercise" a muscle with this type of activation.

Isotonic Activation

dynamic activation—A term used to describe the variable tension produced in a muscle when it is moving an unchanging or fixed resistance.

The term *isotonic* is often used incorrectly in resistance training literature. Isotonic activation occurs if the tension produced in the muscle remains constant (no matter what is happening to the muscle length). This type of activation is also rare in daily activities. Exercises performed with free weights (e.g., barbells and dumbbells) and machines are often referred to as isotonic, probably because a given barbell, dumbbell, or standard machine is fixed at a constant weight. However, this only partly determines the level of tension required of muscles used to lift the weight.

Due to accelerations and changes in skeletal leverages throughout the range of motion over which muscles act, muscle tension must change continuously. Thus, the term isotonic is inappropriate to describe almost all normal movements and exercises. The term **dynamic activation** is much more accurate when describing the muscle contraction that takes place when lifting any fixed (constant) weight object. The only realistic situation in which an isotonic activation may occur is during a light-to-moderate, steady isometric activation (no acceleration or leverage change) before fatigue causes a variance in force.

Constant Resistance

constant-weight exercise— A resistance exercise in which the resistance is the same throughout the range of motion.

The use of fixed-weight objects for lifting exercises can be called **constant-weight exercise** or regular resistance exercise (e.g., when the resistance or load on a bar or machine does not change throughout the range of motion). The resistance remains fixed (constant) throughout the range of motion, but the muscular lifting effort changes as the muscular skeletal leverages change. Assuming the velocity is constant, the weight feels lighter or heavier depending upon a joint's position, even though the weight on the machine or bar remains constant. The feeling (relative effort) of heavy or light is dependent on the changing leverages and the speed of movement. The amount of weight you can lift depends on your strength at the weakest position in a given range of motion.

Barbells, dumbbells, simple, fixed-lever machines, and standard pulley machines are examples of constant resistance. These machines and devices are very effective in producing body composition changes and strength changes if appropriate training programs are followed. This type of resistance may be the best type for improving sport performance. It is still unknown which type of resistance is best for producing strength, hypertrophy, and power development (Ward, 1985; Ward & Ward, 1991).

Variable Resistance

Variable resistance exercise is possible on several types of machines. The skeletal leverage through which a muscle acts changes through the range of a joint's movement. Thus, a given muscle tension can produce a greater or lesser lifting torque depending on the position of the joint that the active muscle(s) cross(es). Manufacturers of resistance exercise machines have used several techniques for increasing or decreasing the lifting force necessary to move a constant-weight stack load. The idea is to provide the greatest resistance load in the position when the muscle has the most favorable leverage. Mechanical methods used to produce this effect are discussed in the Variable Resistance Machines section. The use of such techniques in matching resistance load to musculoskeletal capabilities has been less than totally successful (Garhammer, 1989).

Accommodating Resistance

accommodating resistance—An exercise in which the resistance maintains a constant ratio to the force being applied against it so that the speed of the resulting movement remains the same throughout the range of motion.

Accommodating resistance exercise requires specially designed machines, isokinetic being the most common. With this type of equipment the resistance experienced by the trainee increases or decreases as the force applied to the machine increases or decreases. Again, the idea is to match the resistance felt by a given trainee to his or her specific musculoskeletal capabilities at every position in the range of motion. This concept is discussed further in the Accommodating Resistance Machines section.

▶ Equipment Selection

The most important questions to consider when choosing any type of resistance equipment for use or purchase include:

- Does the equipment permit the type of muscle activation the trainee uses in normal activities, sport activities, and so on? This relates to the **specificity principle** of exercise. By far the most important types of activation are concentric and eccentric.

- Does the equipment permit the trainee to develop specific muscles through a full range of motion and in a pattern of motion that relates to the activities being trained for? This again relates to specificity of exercise. In addition, does the equipment permit the other major muscle groups of the body to be exercised? This is important to maintain or develop balanced muscle strength between agonists and antagonists at the major joints of the body (ankle, knee, hip, shoulder, etc.).

- Does the equipment provide enough resistance for the way it will be used and who will use it? Are relatively strong muscle groups of the body involved, or are the smaller, weaker muscle groups involved? Is a large, strong athlete going to train for competition, or will the equipment be used by a weaker person training for basic fitness?

- Is the equipment properly constructed for the size of person using it? Is it adjustable (seat height, back support, length of lever arm, etc.)? Is it for private or commercial use (i.e., occasional use by one person vs. almost continuous use by a large variety of people)?

- Is the equipment safe to use?

- Is the equipment uncomplicated and easy to use (user friendly)?

- Will the equipment be trouble free, or will it require constant maintenance?

- Is the equipment's value supported by unbiased and independently derived scientific evidence? Are there biomechanical and training studies to support the manufacturer's claims?

- Does the equipment follow a normal neuromuscular pattern? In other words, does it feel right when you use the equipment?

Answers to these questions can in some cases be derived from a basic knowledge of who is training and for what purpose, as well as a recognition of the types of muscle contractions. The equipment should be tried by the individual planning to use it. How does it feel? Close examination of the materials used (padding, the size or thickness of supports) and the construction methods (welding, thick or thin bolts and pins) can also help evaluate the quality and appropriateness of equipment. Additional considerations specific to a given type of equipment are given in the following paragraphs.

Finally, one must realize that these considerations are also useful in deciding whether to develop and use a home gym, or whether to join a health spa, YMCA, or other type of public exercise gym. Some additional factors related to this decision have been published elsewhere (Garhammer, 1987; Ward, 1985; Ward & Ward, 1991).

▶ Free Weights

Free weights include bars and various sized weight plates together forming barbells and dumbbells. This type of equipment (including stone and wood prototypes) have been used for centuries. Advantages of their use include the large variety of exercises possible, the balance and coordination required in many of the exercises which help transfer improved strength to work and sport activities, and low cost. Figure 14.1 illustrates free-weight equipment. Many

▶ **Figure 14.1** Free weight equipment.

books document the extensive number of exercises possible with free weights (Fahey, 1989; Garhammer, 1987; Pearl, 1982; Rasch, 1982; Schwarzenegger, 1985; Stone & O'Bryant, 1987).

There are three major levels of quality in free-weight equipment. The lowest price range includes weight plates and dumbbells that are plastic coated. The bars used with these plates are sometimes hollow, reducing the maximal weight of plates that can safely be used on the bar. This equipment is very functional for home gym use by individuals who are not at an unusually high strength level and who train primarily for physical fitness and for their improvement in recreational sports. If used frequently over many months, the weight plates and dumbbells may crack, and the inner material may begin to leak out. Thus, such equipment is generally not appropriate for a public gym.

Slightly more expensive barbell and dumbbell sets look very similar to those just described; however, the bars and plates are solid metal, making them stronger and more durable. The barbell bar will typically be 5 or 6 feet long (a plastic set is normally 5 feet or less). Adjustable sets of this type are fine for home gym use. Fixed-weight sets (plates welded on the bar) are incremented in 5 to 10 pound jumps from about 20 pounds up to about 150 pounds and are sometimes found in public gyms.

For the more serious free-weight lifter and in most public gyms and health clubs, *Olympic* bars and plates and fixed-weight incremental metal dumbbells are the rule. Olympic bars are about 7 feet long, and the plates that fit on them have 2-inch holes, as opposed to 1.125-inch holes in the common plates previously discussed. Due to the larger size of these bars, bench and squat rack supports made for them are too wide to be used with many of the shorter bar sets. Olympic bars usually weigh 45 pounds or 20 kilograms (44 pounds). They have sleeves (on which the plates rest) that revolve around the gripping bar.

This feature makes them more comfortable to use for many exercises. The highest quality bars have sleeves that revolve very smoothly, often on ball bearings.

Another point of quality on such a bar can be determined by the type of steel the bar and its sleeve are made from. The higher the *psi* (pounds per square inch) rating, the stronger the bar and less likelihood for bending. The best bars will be rated over 200 psi; less expensive bars may be rated below 100 psi. The exact type of steel will also determine whether or how readily a bar will rust. Proper lubrication and care of any Olympic bar will retard rust and reduce sleeve friction. The stiffness of a bar also depends on the exact metal composition. Bars used for weightlifting competition (snatchlift, and clean and jerk lifts) flex or give slightly without bending. Bars used in power lifting (bench press, squat, and dead lift) must support more weight and tend to be made stiffer.

Metal Olympic plates usually cost slightly more than standard metal exercise plates. Complete sets (bar plus a variety of plate sizes) usually start at about 300 total pounds. Since the mid-1970s rubber bumper plates have become more and more popular and commonplace in weight rooms. These rubber plates are less noisy and are safer than metal plates. They come in several (usually metric) weights (5, 10, 15, 20, 25, and 50 kilograms, or 10-100 pounds), but all are the same standard diameter (45 centimeters = 18 inches). These bumper plates are rather expensive.

A number of machines discussed in the next section use free-weight plates to provide resistance. Figure 14.2 illustrates their use. Thus, a standard or Olympic barbell set will also provide plates for use with such machines that accommodate the respective hole diameters of the weight plates. For years there have been arguments concerning the positive and negative aspects of free-weight versus machine exercises. Some considerations are presented in this chapter. For additional discussion on this topic see Garhammer (1987, 1989), Stone (1982), Stone and O'Bryant (1987), Starr (1976), and Ward and Ward (1991).

▶ **Figure 14.2** Free weights in use.

▶ Weight Machines

The impetus to create weight machines arose out of a desire to make weight training safe, to provide easy-to-adjust weights (training loads), to work an isolated muscle group, to eliminate the need for spotters, and to make training more diversified and effective. Simple machines like high and low pulleys have been around for a long time. In the 1950s large, bulky combination machines were introduced into the commercial health clubs in an attempt to fulfill these needs. Currently there are many equipment companies that produce a variety of weight training machines. The sales competition is fierce, and the potential for new machines is limited only by the imagination.

Basically, there are four general categories for classifying weight resistance machines: constant resistance, variable resistance, accommodating resistance, and computerized weight machines. The latter may utilize any of the other three categories mentioned and also adds a double positive or positive/negative mode (as explained following).

Equipment companies try to develop weight machines in one or more of the above categories that isolate and condition every muscle group in almost every conceivable angle. Fundamentally, the machines imitate the exercises that can be executed with either barbells or dumbbells, but may also permit movements impossible with either.

Constant Resistance Machines

Many companies develop machines that can be classified as constant resistance machines (providing constant resistance throughout the range of motion). This category includes the standard pulley devices and some lever machines such as the seated-press, bench-press, or incline-press machines where the weight attachment does not vary its position on the lever arm during movements. These machines are very basic and come in both single-station (one exercise) and multistation models (see Figure 14.3).

Variable Resistance Machines

Variable resistance machines are designed so that the resistance varies (changes) as the trainee moves through the range of motion. There is no function with these machines for controlling speed of movement. Three methods vary the resistance employed in these machines: the cam, the rolling weight stack attachment arm, and the variable lever length system.

The cam is a distinctively shaped, variable-radius pulley that changes the resistance potential of the machine, supposedly in accordance with a theoretical strength curve of the muscle, bone, and joint systems of the body (see Figure 14.4). (The strength curves for muscles, joints, and bones must be considered theoretical because there is a dearth of reliable scientific data to make a definitive statement regarding these strength curves under all conditions. However, some generalizations are acceptable.) Cams are used on all types of machines and are not restricted to any single exercise. They are found in leg curl, leg extension, arm curl, triceps press, abdominal, back extension, and lateral deltoid machines, just to mention a few examples.

The rolling weight stack attachment causes the length of the effort force lever arm to decrease which increases the required muscle torque, thus making the resistance feel greater as the person goes through the range of exercise motion (see Figure 14.5). The device is primarily used in actions involving

▶ **Figure 14.3** Constant resistance machine.

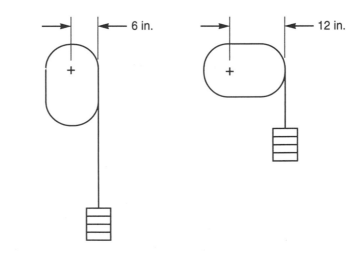

▶ **Figure 14.4** The "cam" (variable radius pulley wheel) method to provide variable resistance. As an exercise is performed, the cam rotates to provide the weight stack a longer lever arm, thus making the weight stack harder to lift.

an arm or leg pressing movement (seated press, incline or bench press, and leg press).

The variable lever length system action is somewhat like a cam without an attached variable-radius pulley. As the machine moves, the effective radius of rotation of the main lever arm changes (increases in length), in effect making the resistive torque greater as the trainee moves through the range of motion. This mechanism for varying resistance is typically seen in the seated chest press, the shoulder press, the incline press, and the seated row.

Figure 14.5 The rolling weight stack attachment method to provide variable resistance. As the handle end of the lever bar is raised the weight stack attachment point rolls along the lever bar. The lever arm length for the weight stack increases, making it harder to lift the weight.

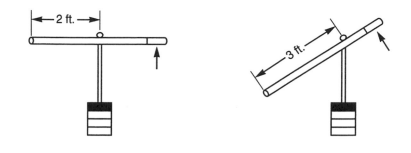

Accommodating Resistance (Isokinetic) Machines

When a machine compensates automatically for changes in applied force throughout the range of motion it is called an accommodating resistance machine. Such machines are usually air (pneumatic), hydraulic, or electromagnetic devices. They permit the application of maximum force against a balanced resistance at all points in the range of motion. Usually these devices do not permit changes in speed or movement once the motion has begun. Figure 14.6 illustrates an isokinetic machine.

In this sense they might be thought of as isokinetic in nature (that is, having the ability to vary force, but at a constant movement speed throughout the range of motion). These machines usually offer speed of movement which then remains constant during the exercise.

As already mentioned, true isokinetic contractions seldom if ever occur in normal activities. Most machines are designed to control only the speed of

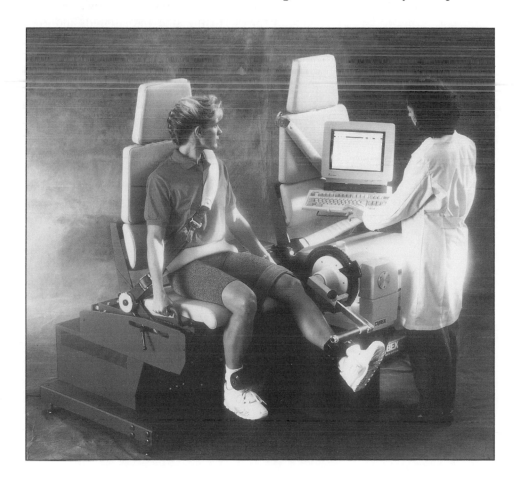

Figure 14.6 Isokinetic machine.

movement of machine components and not the speed of contraction of a muscle. For purposes of this discussion, it may be less confusing to think of isokinetic machines as those that control only the speed of movement of their components, even though the muscle's speed of activation is not controlled.

Some of these accommodating resistance machines employ in a push/pull method using agonist and antagonist muscle groups in alternating, shortening contractions (e.g., arm curl/elbow extension and shoulder press/pulldown). When using these machines *only* concentric (shortening or positive) muscle activation is possible.

On the other hand, there are accommodating resistance/isokinetic machines that permit a concentric (positive) and eccentric (negative) muscle activation of the *same* muscle group during one complete exercise cycle (see the next section on computerized machines). Free weights and variable resistance machines permit concentric and eccentric muscle activations of the same muscle group during one exercise cycle. However, the level of resistance is not controlled.

Few training studies have been published demonstrating a superiority of accommodating resistance exercise. It is hypothesized that these machines may produce good hypertrophy and strength gains, but more research has to be completed to determine the validity of this hypothesis and the benefits of training with these machines compared to other resistance training equipment.

The push/pull (double positive) machines may have a limited application for performance enhancement because they do not train the eccentric (negative) component of movement. Computer-controlled devices that allow for positive and negative components of muscle activation at varying velocities have greater potential for increasing size and strength and maximizing strength transfer to sport skills. Many machines that permit only concentric muscle activations require the user to apply force before any resistance is felt. If applied force is suddenly removed, these machines stop; thus, they are called "passive" machines. This characteristic is desirable in some rehabilitation situations. A machine that permits eccentric contractions is called an "active" machine because it actively applies force to the user.

The cost of these accommodating resistance exercise machines varies with the complexity of the construction and the method for controlling the resistance. Some of these machines are meant for use in clinical testing and rehabilitation. Their force limitations may exclude use by stronger individuals. They require more sophisticated understanding and are considerably more expensive. For a more complete discussion and an evaluation of some isokinetic machines see Hinson, Smith, and Funk (1979), Hislop and Perrine (1967), and Malone (1988).

Computer-Controlled Exercise Machines

Computers have made a significant impact on the life of the average citizen. They are used in homes, cars, at work, and in many other dimensions of life to assist in the performance of a wide variety of activities. It was a logical step to interface the computer with exercise equipment. The application of computer technology in resistive exercise equipment is in its infancy and will most assuredly escalate into more scientific and effective equipment, more diversified equipment, and more sophisticated and efficient methods of training.

Many companies have interfaced computers with resistive exercise equipment (some computer-assisted machines are Ariel, Cybex, and Life Fitness). There are many computerized testing machines used in diagnosis and rehabilitation. The focus of this discussion, however, is on those computerized exercise machines that are used for general training.

Some companies have merely taken the commonly used resistive exercise machines and replaced the weight stack with various computer-controlled resistance devices. Some adapted equipment includes changes in hydraulic devices, pneumatic devices, electromagnetic devices, and D.C. motors. To some degree the authors have impacted the development of some of the computerized equipment. Ward has been involved in various ways in the conceptualization and production of the Universal, Paramount, and Life Circuit computerized exercise machines. Garhammer has been one of the principal researchers for the Life Circuit machines as of this date.

The most sophisticated, computer-controlled equipment with the greatest application for training is that manufactured by Ariel. This is not to say that the other companies have inferior equipment, but that Ariel has the most sophisticated systems, more exercise options, and a large amount of scientific and empirical evidence to support its exercise programs. But its equipment is not simple to use, a major criticism of these devices. It is very sophisticated and requires extensive training for general use. The cost is also higher than the less sophisticated equipment.

The Ariel Computerized Exercise System, Paramount (CFS), and Universal (Fitnet) use the computer-controlled push/pull (double positive) method that only allows for concentric (positive) contraction. In contrast, the Life Circuit machines implement both concentric (positive) and eccentric (negative) muscle training when using their machines.

Although these innovative machines excite the imagination, further research and empirical observation is necessary to effectively evaluate and correctly program the various exercise options available with the machines. The application of computer-controlled resistive exercise machines will not replace the simple barbell, dumbbell, or conventional exercise machines. However, they will become part of the diverse equipment that can be used to make exercise programs different, effective, efficient, and motivational.

▶ References

Fahey, T.D. (1989). *Basic weight training*. Mountain View, CA: Mayfield.

Garhammer, J. (1987). *Sports Illustrated—strength training*. New York: Time.

Garhammer, J. (1989). Weight lifting & training. In C.L. Vaughan (Ed.), *Biomechanics of sport* (pp. 169-211). Boca Ration, FL: CRC.

Hinson, M., Smith, W.C., & Funk, S. (1979). Isokinetics: A clarification. *Research Quarterly*, **50**, 30.

Hislop, H.J., & Perrine, J.J. (1967). The isokinetic concept of exercise. *Physical Therapy*, **47**, 14.

Malone, T.R. (1988). An evaluation of isokinetic equipment. *Sport Injury Management*, **1**(1), 1-90.

Pearl, B. (1982). *Keys to the inner universe*. Pasadena, CA: Bill Pearl Enterprises.

Rasch, P.J. (1982). *Weight training*. Dubuque, IA: Brown.

Schwarzenegger, A. (1985). *Encyclopedia of modern bodybuilding*. New York: Simon and Schuster.

Starr, B. (1976). *The strongest shall survive*. Annapolis, MD: Fitness Products.

Stone, M. (1982). Considerations in gaining a strength-power effect. *National Strength & Conditioning Association Journal*, **4**(1), 22-24.

Stone, M., & O'Bryant, H. (1987). *Weight training: A scientific approach.* Minneapolis: Burgess.

Ward, P. (1985). *Health and Tennis Corporation of America information bulletin.* Los Angeles: Health and Tennis Corporation of America.

Ward, P., & Ward, B. (1992). *Encyclopedia of weight training: The use of weight training in training programs for general conditioning, sport and body building.* Laguna Hills, CA: QPT Publications.

CHAPTER 15

Watercraft

Mark A. Smith, MS

The origins of both canoes and kayaks are found in North America. American Indians pioneered the art of canoe making. Depending on where on the continent they lived, the various Indian cultures fashioned their canoes from the raw materials they had available. There is still debate raging on who exactly were the first tribes to exploit their resources to develop the ingenious design of what the Spanish originally christened *canoa*, and what we today call the canoe.

Certain western tribes fashioned their canoes from dug-out cedar logs. Cedar offers remarkable buoyancy and rot resistance, making it ideal for ocean-faring voyages. Indians toward the east used various methods for canoe fabrication. Most popular in American lore is the birchbark and cedar-ribbed canoe with tar-sealed seams.

When the white man first arrived in North America, he quickly recognized the utility of the canoe, not only as a means of basic transportation, but also as a vehicle for trade, commerce, exploration, and warfare. Admiral Samuel de Champlain (1567-1635) was dumbfounded by the ease with which the Indian canoes overtook European longboats. At his recommendation, the French adopted this craft for their North American exploits, thus setting off the love affair with the canoe, which every notable adventurer, explorer, and trapper used. Canoes have a variety of uses and designs, but today are primarily used for some sort of recreational endeavor.

Kayaks were originally fashioned from skins and wooden frames and were designed by the Aleuts (an Eskimo tribe) and Greenlanders as seagoing boats. The heritage and use of the original kayaks were all but forgotten with their introduction to Europe at the beginning of this century. Europeans modified the shape of kayaks to meet the demands of river running, which would eventually trigger the revolution in whitewater recreation. But the kayak remains an excellent seafaring craft. In fact, in recent years sea kayaking and kayak touring have experienced dramatic renewed popularity.

This chapter discusses three types of watercraft: canoes, kayaks, and rafts. All watercraft have certain attributes that set them apart from one another, as well as design characteristics that define how the watercraft is to be used. Criteria addressed for each watercraft are: anatomy, materials and construction, hull design (i.e., how the shape of the hull affects various aspects of performance), and classification by use.

▶ Canoes

Canoes have evolved for specific purposes. Materials and construction, dimensional characteristics, and hull design have evolved in response to these purposes.

Materials and Construction

Modern canoe materials range widely; however, there exist four basic construction materials: wood, aluminum, and two plastics (heat-formed and fiber-reinforced laminates) (Cichanowski, 1986). Designers consider the three primary factors of strength, weight, and cost when selecting construction materials. Depending on the overall design and the purpose of the canoe, each material has its virtues and drawbacks. Canoe manufacturers have not yet, however, developed a material suited for all conditions and budgets.

Wood

Purists champion wood as the authentic (unadulterated) material from which to create a canoe. That is probably true as wood is a natural resource, and wood canoes are classic works of art. Canoes fashioned from wood undergo a lengthy process, and the final products will cost the proud owners a sizable sum.

cedar-strip canoe—A popular, modern wooden canoe made from thin cedar strips glued together and layered over a mold.

wood-and-canvas canoes— Similar to a cedar strip canoe except they are an older design, and they have canvas over the basic wood canoe hull to reinforce and waterproof the canoe.

gunwales—The upper edge of a boat's side (pronounced gun' els).

Canadian designers first offered **cedar-strip** and **wood-and-canvas canoes** in the late 19th century; these were developed as alternatives to birchbark canoes (Davidson & Rugge, 1983). Wood-and-canvas, or rib-and-plank canoes are manufactured from white cedar ribs steamed and bent around a mold and attached to the inside **gunwales** (see Figure 15.1). White cedar planking is then nailed to the ribs. Once the hull is completed, it is covered with canvas for reinforcement and to make it waterproof (M. Garcia, personal communication, March 10, 1989).

Today's more popular wooden canoes are the cedar-strip boats, affectionately called "strippers." Basically, they are built by gluing thin strips of red cedar over a mold. When the hull is completed, it is sometimes layered with fiberglass resin or a lacquer sealer.

Aesthetics aside, wood canoes are surprisingly light weight and resilient as well as naturally buoyant. However, they can take no abuse and little punishment. Being a naturally perishable material, wood requires careful maintenance.

Aluminum

In 1945, aircraft manufacturer Leroy Grumman constructed the first aluminum canoe (Davidson & Rugge, 1983). Soon after, these metal canoes became the

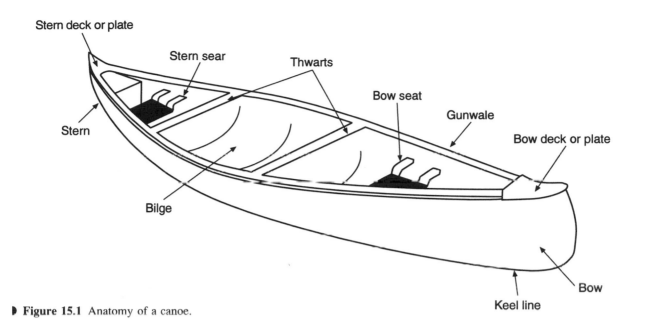

Stern deck or plate

Stern sear

Thwarts

Bow seat

Gunwale

Bow deck or plate

Stern

Bilge

Bow

Keel line

▶ **Figure 15.1** Anatomy of a canoe.

workhorse of the backcountry canoeist. Aluminum canoes are rugged, but heavy. They require almost no maintenance and are some of the cheapest canoes on the market.

The disadvantages of aluminum are: it conducts heat or cold to paddlers, it can't be formed into sleek and sophisticated hull designs (which limits its performance capabilities), it is noisy, a puncture or tear is difficult (if not too expensive) to repair, and the metallic appearance and unsophisticated hull dimensions don't offer the visual aesthetics of other construction materials.

Generally, aluminum canoes are manufactured from two dimensionally iden-

keel line—The bottom- or outermost line of the hull running from bow to stern.

bow—The front or forward end of a boat.

stern—The rear end of a boat.

tical sheets of aluminum, each stretched and formed over a male mold (M. Garcia, personal communication, March 10, 1989). The two sheets are typically riveted together at the **keel line**, and **bow** and **stern** stem plates. Some manufacturers weld the seams to eliminate the drag-producing rivets, but welded seams are weaker, thus compromising the structural integrity of the canoe. Still other manufacturers are introducing aluminum canoes with seams that are bonded together with adhesives.

Plastics

heat-formed—Any manufacturing process that uses heat to change the dimensional characteristics of a material to a desired shape.

The two prominent types of plastic hulls used in canoe manufacturing are **heat-formed** and **fiber-reinforced laminates**. Each process renders unique performance features relative to hull durability and rigidity.

Heat-Formed Plastics

fiber-reinforced laminate—A process by which sheets or particles of fibrous materials (e.g., fiberglass and Kevlar) are layered and bonded together with a resin.

Plastic canoes are noted for their extreme durability and impact resistance; but they are heavy, especially **Royalex** canoes. Durability at the expense of weight, however, isn't always the best trade-off. Another weakness of plastic hulls is their flexibility: They tend to be flimsy, which makes the canoe cumbersome to navigate. Probably the two biggest disadvantages of this construction material are its weight and price tag (Royalex is more expensive than polyethylene). Comparable in weight to aluminum but much more expensive, plastic hulls are still preferable to aluminum because they offer less water resistance (drag) and the advantages of more sophisticated hull designs and greater resiliency against impacts (M. Garcia, personal communication, March 10, 1989).

Royalex—A thermoplastic composite consisting of several layers of material sandwiched together; one layer is a foam that will form the desired shape of a hull when heated in a mold.

Royalex is a thermoplastic composite consisting of several layers of material sandwiched together. It was developed and produced by Uniroyal. The sandwich is composed of acrylonitrile butadiene styrene (ABS) and unicellular foam layered between vinyl. A "raw" Royalex sheet is formed into a canoe by placing the layers in between a male and female mold which is then heated and vacuum molded. The heating process expands the foam giving the hull its thickness, buoyancy, and strength (M. Garcia, personal communication, March 10, 1989). After the hull cools, all the accessories are then attached to the hull.

Canoes manufactured from polyethylene go through a similar process. Polyethylene, a thermoplastic polymer, begins as a pelletized resin treated to protect it against the sun's ultraviolet rays. It is also made into sheets and heated and vacuum molded into the desired hull shape.

Fiber-Reinforced Laminates

The most common fibers found in laminated hulls are Kevlar and fiberglass; oftentimes, both materials are used in one canoe. These fiber-reinforced, laminated hulls have an unrivaled combination of light weight and ruggedness. Laminated hulls derive their name from the process used to fashion the canoe (M. Garcia, personal communication, March 10, 1989). Laminated hulls are also called *lay-ups* because Kevlar and/or fiberglass sheets are layered and bonded together with a resin and cured, thus producing a laminate of multiple layers. Many manufacturers have developed their own combinations of fiber-reinforced, laminated hulls that include fibers other than fiberglass, but usually incorporate Kevlar. These manufacturer-specific materials used in hull construction are called proprietary lay-ups.

Fiberglass canoes have been in existence since the mid-1960s. Over that time, many varieties and levels of quality in canoes have been developed. With several grades of fiberglass materials available, canoe quality varies tremendously. Fiberglass materials include fine cloth, woven roving (which is a coarser fiberglass weave), mat, and chop. Chopped fiberglass is the least desirable from a performance and durability standpoint, but very inexpensive. The manufacturing of canoes made with chopped fiberglass involves a process of mixing fiberglass with resin and spraying it onto a mold. The best quality fiberglass canoes, however, are made of finely woven cloth. A cloth canoe coupled with good manufacturing techniques can produce a strong, lightweight craft with any number of hull shapes.

Distantly related to fiberglass, Kevlar is the latest and most sophisticated construction material development to be used widely in canoes. It is a gold-colored aramid (plastic-based nylon) fiber developed by DuPont in 1970 for use as a tire cord. Adopted by canoe makers for its unparalleled combination of light weight and toughness, Kevlar is the same material used in bulletproof vests. Kevlar canoes are lighter than even the lightest fiberglass canoes by 10 to 15 pounds, plus it has a higher strength:weight ratio. Of course, accompanying such advanced technological characteristics is a price to match: Kevlar canoes are typically the most expensive on the market.

Generally, laminated hulls are composed of several types of materials and fiberglass is incorporated in areas of less stress, whereas Kevlar is found at high stress points. Whatever laminated materials are used, outstandingly sleek and sophisticated hull designs can be fashioned using the laminate process.

Hull Design

The body of the canoe is called the **hull** (see Figure 15.1, p. 193). There are several factors that canoe designers consider when they establish dimensional specifications for a particular type of hull. Hull design most affects the performance of any boat; and when human rather than motorized propulsion is required you can imagine how critical hull design is. Ease of paddling, stability, tracking ability (i.e., how well the canoe can travel in a straight line), maneuverability, and seaworthiness are all important aspects of performance. No one hull design, however, can maximize all these attributes for all conditions. Designing a hull is an iterative process of compromises. Well designed canoes come in various shapes and configurations depending on their use.

Hull design characteristics can be broadly separated into either gross dimensions (the physical measurements) or shape. Dimensions include the more obvious differences in boats like the length, depth, and beam (width). Shape involves a few more subtleties; for example, rocker, waterline, cross-sectional shape, symmetry, and asymmetry, all of which will be discussed in detail.

Gross Dimensions

Gross dimensions, which define the canoe's general structure, are length, beam, and depth. Within these there are variations in size determined by the craft's design and intended use.

Length

Length is the overall distance from bow to stern. All other things being equal, the longer the boat, the faster it can travel, because it rides higher on the water, thus producing less drag. Therefore, longer canoes are propelled farther with each paddle stroke. Longer hulls also track straighter and can carry more weight. However, maneuverability is diminished and weight increases with greater canoe length. Shorter canoes turn more sharply—their greatest virtue. They also tend to be lighter and cost less (but weight and price are typically related more to construction materials). Environment and height of the canoeist are the decision factors when considering a canoe length. Generally, shorter canoes are selected by smaller people, or when maneuverability is critical (e.g., in narrow waterways or in whitewater conditions).

Beam

Sometimes called width, the **beam** of a hull has two important measurements: the molded beam and the **waterline** beam (see Figure 15.2) (Cichanowski, 1986). A less important width is the maximum beam. The molded beam width is the distance at the widest point of the canoe from gunwale to gunwale, less the portion of the gunwale that extends beyond the canoe's hull. The waterline beam is the presumed width of the canoe at the waterline loaded with paddlers. This line is usually 4 inches up from the bottom. Maximum beam is the widest beam of the boat. Beam is closely related to a canoe's cross-sectional shape, which will be discussed later.

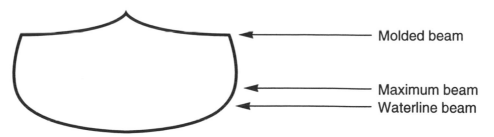

Molded beam

Maximum beam
Waterline beam

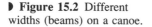

▶ **Figure 15.2** Different widths (beams) on a canoe.

Paddling is typically more comfortable with narrower beams because canoeists don't have to extend their arms as far laterally to get the paddle in the water. Also, wider beamed boats tend to plow through the water rather than efficiently slice through it. An advantage of a wider canoe is greater capacity for extended cargo-hauling trips. Compromises in beam usually come in the form of relatively lower waterline width and higher molded beam.

Depth

Depth is the last major gross dimension. It is measured in three places: the bow, the center, and the stern. Canoe designers consider depth as they design the boat for carrying capacity and seaworthiness characteristics (i.e., how well the canoe handles wind, spray, and waves). Depth has no significant effect on tracking, speed, or turning.

Freeboard is the amount of canoe that is vertically above the water and is the result of depth. While keeping the canoeist and provisions dry, freeboard can be a handicap in windy conditions. Strong winds can catch a canoe and create an unstable ride, if not a hazardous situation. The general rule on depth is that it should be high in rough-water canoes and high for carrying heavy gear; but freeboard is undesirable for calm lakes and wide, gentle river cruising.

Hull Shape

All boat designers consider every aspect of hull shape the hallmark of a boat's hydrodynamic efficiency. Radical yet dramatically improved hull shapes have recently changed the course of America's Cup yacht racing. Similar design principles are being applied to canoes, winged keels notwithstanding. A canoe will displace water weight equal to the total weight of the canoe and its contents. Given that, how does the hull designer configure the shape of the hull to minimize water resistance while optimizing speed, capacity, maneuverability, and stability for a canoeist's particular needs?

Rocker

A canoe's **rocker** is viewed in profile in Figure 15.3. The amount of curve, from bow to stern, determines maneuverability (Cichanowski, 1986). A heavy amount of rocker allows the canoe to turn on a dime, because most of the water interacting with the hull's bottom is around the boat's center. As discussed previously, turning ease depends on the length of the canoe, as well. Therefore, a shorter canoe needs much less rocker than a longer one to be equally maneuverable.

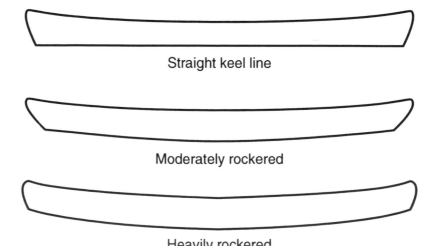

Straight keel line

Moderately rockered

Heavily rockered

▶ **Figure 15.3** Various rocker configurations.

What rockered hulls gain in maneuverability, they tend to lose in trackability. With less keel line in the water, the canoe is more difficult to keep tracking in a straight line. Rocker also tends to inhibit speed because its keel line (i.e., the shape of the hull bottom running from bow to stern) inherently isn't as streamlined as a straight keel-lined canoe.

Waterline

The "workable waterline" refers to the contour of entry and exit lines on the canoe and is largely a function of rocker. This is illustrated by entry and exit lines shown in Figure 15.4. Sharper entry and exit lines produce faster canoes and increase trackability, whereas blunted waterlines enhance maneuverability.

The distance between transition from the entry line to the exit line (Figure 15.5) renders considerable effect on speed, capacity, and stability. Swifter canoe hulls have waterlines that are sharp, opening gradually to their widest point and closing gradually. Hulls built for racing have extremely narrow waterlines that widen to their fullest point closer to the stern. These highly specialized, **asymmetrical hulls** offer maximum efficiency (i.e., minimize water resistance) and speed. Figure 15.5 illustrates symmetrical and asymmetrical hull shapes. **Symmetrical hulls** have their widest point midship, so if you were to cut the boat from gunwale to gunwale you would have two identical halves. Asymmetrical hulls widen well behind midship and essentially stretch out the entry line of the canoe, yielding a more efficient hydrodynamic hull shape. In general, canoes that demand high maneuverability are found with symmetrical hulls, whereas straight-tracking canoes often possess asymmetrical hulls. Sharp waterline and asymmetrical hulls don't have much stability and carrying capacity, however. Stability and higher capacity are achieved by widening the hull sooner and keeping it wide longer, a characteristic called "fullness" (Cichanowski, 1986).

Present manufacturing techniques and construction materials constrain the sharpness that a canoe can have. For example, aluminum and plastics are difficult materials from which to construct a sharp bow, but wood, Kevlar, and fiberglass have this potential. The intended use of a canoe often dictates the entry line. Sharp bows are designed into cruising crafts, and blunted bows are required for whitewater use to minimize, or at least distribute the impact of rocks.

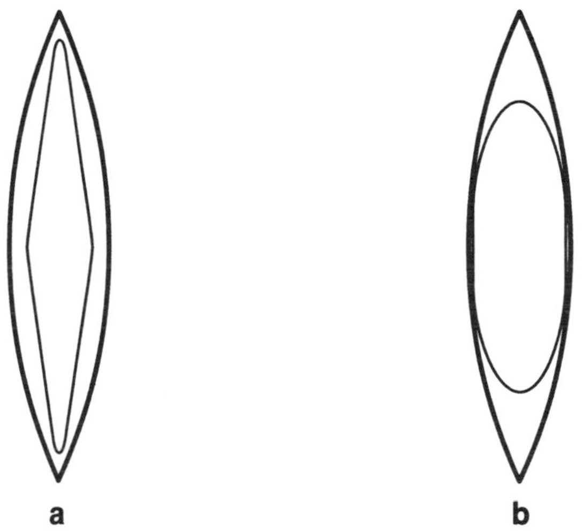

asymmetrical hull—The shape of a hull such that its widest point is aft of the boat, which makes the hull more hydrodynamically efficient and provides better tracking because the paddler does not have to push the hull through as much water. These hulls are found in racing boats.

symmetrical hull—A hull with its widest point at midship; one side is the mirror image of the other.

▶ Figure 15.4 Sharper (a) and blunted (b) waterline entry and exit lines.

a   b

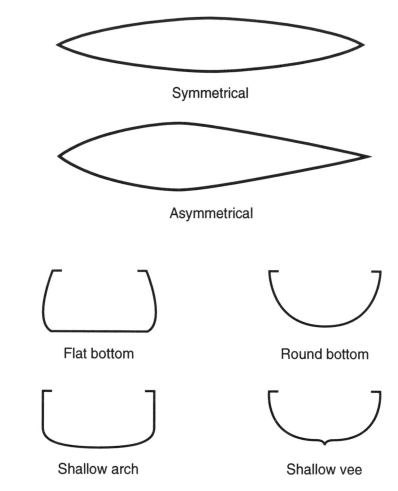

▶ **Figure 15.5** Hull symmetry.

▶ **Figure 15.6** Hull cross-sections illustrating bottom contours.

Cross-Section

A cross-sectional view of a canoe shows it cut in half from gunwale to gunwale and reveals the contours of the canoe's bottom and freeboard. These contours are the most important aspects of **stability** (Cichanowski, 1986).

stability (initial and final)—The hull characteristic that inhibits a canoe from feeling wobbly and ultimately capsizing; initial stability is relative wobbliness while the boat is flat on the water; final stability is the canoe's ultimate resistance to turning over at any given angle in the water.

critical angle—The theoretical angle at which a canoe will capsize if the angle is exceeded.

There are two types of stability, initial and final (Cichanowski, 1986). A canoe with high initial stability feels steady and secure when upright. Final stability, being the more important of the two, is a canoe's ultimate resistance to turtling or capsizing. The theoretical line along the periphery of the hull beyond which the canoe will capsize is called the **critical angle.**

Figure 15.6 illustrates the canoe's four basic bottom contours. Each type of bottom contour has different degrees of initial and final stability and a critical angle. A flat-bottom hull, found in the more traditional recreational canoes, has high initial stability and little final stability and thus can overturn rather quickly (Cichanowski, 1986). In this type of hull the canoeist has a greater sense of security relative to other bottom designs, because a flat-bottom canoe doesn't rock as much on flat water. But it is a false sense of security, because rough water can easily tip a flat-bottom canoe to its critical angle. Rounded-bottom hulls resist such critical tipping angles and so have higher final stability.

A round-bottom canoe feels wobbly on every type of water and has very little initial stability. At any angle the round-bottom hull feels unstable, because the force it applies on the water is roughly constant at every angle. Completely round-bottom canoes if they existed would have the highest final stability but that wobbly, uneasy sensation they would give to canoeists has made them unpopular. Slightly modified round hulls can be found, however. Such hulls are used by flat-water marathon racers who have expert navigating skills.

Between the extremes of the flat- and round-bottom canoes lie the expected compromises, the **shallow-arch** and the **shallow-vee hulls**. Shallow-arch hulls come in various degrees of arch, so they don't all behave the same way. Nevertheless, a shallow arch behaves similarly to a round bottom and has high final stability.

shallow-arch hull—A modified, round-bottom hull; this shape enhances initial stability yet has high final stability.

shallow-vee hull—A hull shape with the same stability characteristics as the shallow arch, but it has a slight ridge on the bottom to increase trackability.

Finally, the shallow vee is essentially a shallow arch with a ridge down the middle making the canoe very seaworthy. In fact, Mad River, the first canoe company to design a shallow-vee hull, borrowed the idea from the Vikings. Although the ridge resembles a keel, it is not a keel in the true sense (keels should be avoided in any canoe, but very small keels are found in aluminum hulls because of manufacturing limitations). However, the ridge does increase water resistance and decreases maneuverability much like a keel would, yet canoes with veed hulls track very well. Shallow-vee and shallow-arch hulls possess nearly the same stability characteristics. Both have high final stability and moderate initial stability. Note, however, that the shallower the vee, the more initial stability a canoe possesses; a deeper vee hull would lose more initial stability.

tumblehome—Freeboard that is curved inward from the waterline.

flare—When the freeboard sides of a canoe tend to go outward from the keel line.

A hull's cross-section above the waterline, that is, **tumblehome** or **flare**, can also reveal attributes of a canoe's stability (see Figure 15.7) (Cichanowski, 1986). Many canoes incorporate tumblehome, straight sides, and flare into their design. The rationale is clear once tumblehome and flare are understood. Tumblehome is freeboard that is curved inward so that the beam is narrower at the gunwale than at the hull's widest point. Flare is just the opposite, with the gunwales wider than the rest of the hull.

Totally flared hulls offer more final stability than do tumblehome hulls because when the latter rolls toward its critical angle, there is nothing to stop it from continuing to roll over. On the other hand, flare works to stop the momentum of a rolling hull and also prevents waves from splashing because this hull tends to ride over waves rather than slicing through them. The drawback of flare is that it requires the canoeist to reach farther to paddle. Tumblehome around the canoeist affords more efficient paddling because the stroking forces are closer to the paddler's body.

Canoes Classified According to Use

Canoes are designed around function. There are basically eight canoe design categories, each having tandem and solo models. (Some manufacturers break these categories down further, however.) The categories discussed here are: recreation, tripping, touring, cruising, whitewater, sport, freestyle, and competition/marathon.

Recreation

recreational canoe—A general-purpose canoe for novice canoeists.

Recreational canoes (Figure 15.8) are a general-purpose canoe. They can be used in a variety of more domesticated activities including casual cruising on a placid lake, picnicking, short camping trips, and even hunting and fishing. Not

▶ **Figure 15.7** (a) Tumblehome and (b) flare are aspects of hull design that affect how much a hull rolls in the water.

a b

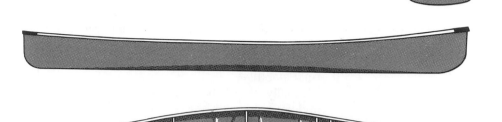

▶ **Figure 15.8** A
recreational canoe.
Reprinted by permission of
Cichanowski (1986) and
We-no-nah Canoes.

high performance by any measure, recreational canoes are built with economy in mind (Harrison et al., 1989a). Most of these hulls are unsophisticated and have rather flat bottom contours with slight rocker. As discussed earlier, flat bottoms are high on initial stability, which comforts novice canoers. These canoes are expected to take a lot of careless beating, so they are typically constructed with aluminum, although several manufacturers produce fiberglass and Royalex models. These canoes are what outfitters usually supply their customers for weekend backcountry excursions.

Touring

*touring canoe—A long-
and medium-volume canoe
used for extended trips.*

Having medium volume, **touring canoes** (Harrison et al., 1989a) are well suited for a backcountry trip up to 2 weeks. They are longer and faster than recreational canoes and can even take on lower grade whitewater rivers with gear on board. Keel lines range from straight to moderately rockered. Almost all touring hulls are symmetrical with shallow-arch bottoms. With portaging in mind, manufacturers offer fiberglass and Kevlar hulls. There seems to be no real trend in freeboard design, tumblehome or flare.

Tripping

*tripping canoe—Very wide,
deep, and long canoes
suited for rough water and
extended backcountry
expeditions.*

Wilderness **tripping canoes** feature wide, deep hulls for heavy loads with the ability to handle the roughest water on extended expeditions (refer to Figure 15.9) (Harrison et al., 1989a). Tandem trippers are usually a minimum of 18 feet long, but 16- and 17-footers are found on the market. Strong, lightweight hull design is used for tripping canoes for long portages on punishing terrain. Kevlar, along with proprietary lay-ups (i.e., some weaved combination that usually includes Kevlar) are the most popular materials for these canoes. Both asymmetrical and symmetrical hulls are used, including all but extreme rocker. A shallow-arched keel contour is the most prevalent bottom with shallow vees a distant second. For long days in the canoe, either straight or tumblehome freeboards are incorporated for comfortable paddling.

Cruising

*cruising canoe—A medium-
volume, well tracking, fast,
and lightweight canoe de-
signed for recreational
exercise.*

Cruising canoes are high-performance, medium-volume crafts that track well, are very fast, and are lightweight (see Figure 15.10) (Harrison et al., 1989a). They are designed for people who seek a good exercise vehicle with a sensation of freedom and speed. Even though cruisers are primarily for aerobic workouts, they have the capacity to carry a few days' camping cargo for weekend trips.

   Manufacturers use fiberglass, their own lay-ups, Kevlar, and wood in cruising

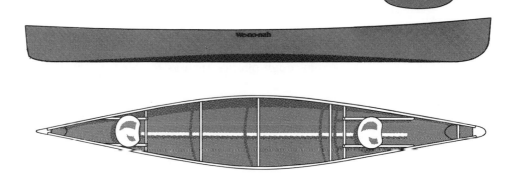

▶ **Figure 15.9** A tripping canoe.
Reprinted by permission of Cichanowski (1986) and We-no-nah Canoes.

▶ **Figure 15.10** A cruising canoe.
Reprinted by permission of Cichanowski (1986) and We-no-nah Canoes.

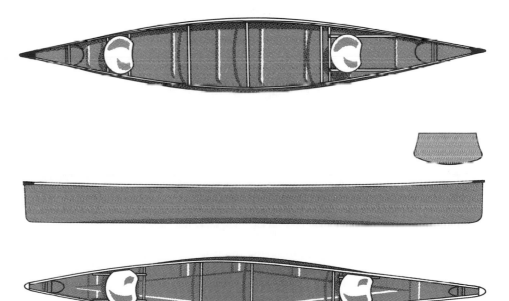

▶ **Figure 15.11** A white-water slalom racing canoe.
Reprinted by permission of Cichanowski (1986) and We-no-nah Canoes.

canoe hull construction. Fast, well-tracking canoes generally have straight keel lines, shallow-arch and asymmetrical hulls (although shallow-vee and symmetrical hulls are common). Every type of freeboard configuration exists in cruisers, with tumblehome being used most commonly.

Whitewater

whitewater craft—Either a play boat or a slalom racing canoe that has a lot of rocker for quick maneuverability in rapids.

There are two subcategories of **whitewater craft**, the whitewater play boat and the whitewater slalom racing canoe. Figure 15.11 illustrates the slalom racing design. Both types have plenty of rocker making them highly maneuverable in treacherous rapids. The slalom canoes usually have a more extreme rocker than the play boat.

With maneuverability and seaworthiness as primary concerns, these canoes tend to be short (around 15-16 feet) and slow. They also have deep hulls to keep splashing water out and full bows to ride heavy rapids. Bottom contours tend to be shallow arch, with no consistent trend in freeboard design. Whitewater canoes must withstand tremendous impacts, so manufacturers build these hulls from tough plastics such as Royalex or polyethylene.

Sport

sport canoe—A canoe designed for hunters and fishermen that can accommodate a motor and that has high initial stability and large carrying capacity.

The special needs of hunting and fishing sportsmen are the focus for designers of **sport canoes** (Harrison et al., 1989a). Rugged and stable, these canoes have square sterns that can accommodate motors. Bottom contours take some form of flatness utilizing either a shallow-vee, or flat-bottom design. Flatter bottoms facilitate high initial stability and large payloads for carrying expensive sporting equipment with confidence. Other than slight rocker and symmetrical hulls there are no apparent trends in freeboard design.

Freestyle

freestyle canoe—A personalized canoe that is paddled from a kneeling position and has excellent maneuverability.

Most **freestyle canoes** are for the solo canoeist, although several companies build tandem models. These boats have many uses for paddlers seeking a personalized leisure craft (Harrison et al., 1989a). These craft can be brilliantly personalized with neon paint and elaborate trimmings. Tandem and solo freestyle canoes alike are usually paddled from a kneeling position for quicker paddling stroke changes.

Freestyle canoes usually offer an effective compromise between directional tracking and maneuverability making them ideal for short trips or showing off sharp maneuvers on flat water. Therefore, they tend to have slight rocker and shallow-arch hulls. Either symmetrical or asymmetrical hulls can be purchased that possess flared freeboard.

Competition/Marathon

competition/marathon canoe—Any class of tandem or solo racing canoes with straight keel lines and asymmetrical hulls.

There are several types of racing class canoes for tandem and solo competitors. Whatever type, these hull designs compromise nothing to achieve flat-out speed and trackability (Harrison et al., 1989a). Thus, **competition/marathon canoes** invariably have straight keel lines and asymmetrical hulls, a combination above all others that renders a canoe highly trackable and very fast. Other commonalities of competition canoes include extreme tumblehome around the racer for efficient paddling technique, low profiles to minimize wind resistance, Kevlar construction for the best combination of rigidity, and lightweight and shallow-arch bottoms.

Flat-water marathon competition falls into two major categories, sanctioned and unsanctioned (Cichanowski, 1986). Sanctioned events are for amateurs and are under the auspices of the United States Canoe Association (USCA) and the International Canoe Federation (ICF). Unsanctioned events are professional-class competition in which rules are set by the sponsors.

The USCA and the ICF have very strict hull configuration rules and class definitions. Tandem class cruisers, for example, are defined to be 18 feet 6 inches long, at the 4-inch waterline the hull must be widened to at least 14.375 percent of the canoe's length, and the widest point must be within 1 foot fore or aft of center. These are only half of the hull specifications for this class, the aim is that every competition canoe be equal at the starting line. ICF rules allow a little more interpretation; for instance, tandem cruisers

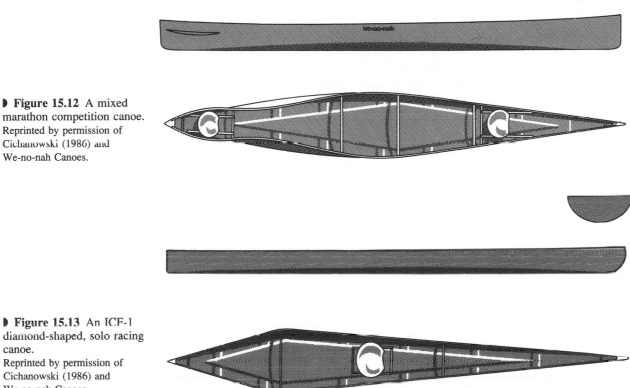

Figure 15.12 A mixed marathon competition canoe. Reprinted by permission of Cichanowski (1986) and We-no-nah Canoes.

Figure 15.13 An ICF-1 diamond-shaped, solo racing canoe. Reprinted by permission of Cichanowski (1986) and We-no-nah Canoes.

can be up to 21 feet 4 inches long. A USCA Mixed Marathon (i.e., an adult and child, or male and female team) tandem cruiser is illustrated in Figure 15.12.

Solo racing canoes sanctioned by the USCA are enforced by the same strict rules as tandem cruisers and are typically shorter. A 17-foot ICF C-1 diamond-shaped hull is shown in Figure 15.13. There are many other types of racing hull designs.

Summary

Clearly, design limitations imposed by the laws of physics prevent one single canoe from doing everything well. The safe and efficient function of a canoe is strictly dependent on the design of the hull itself. The marathon racer, whitewater rapids shooter, and the sportsman all need uniquely fashioned hull designs. As discussed in this chapter, depending on the canoe's use, construction materials, weight, length, depth, width, hull configuration (keel line, symmetry, and bottom and freeboard contours), are all important considerations to assess canoe design and function.

The future of hull design and construction promises to be a dynamic one. Optimal performance in every canoe category is the quest of every canoe designer. Over the years new manufacturing material and techniques combined with sophisticated computer-aided hull designs have sparked dramatic improvements in canoe performance. Canoes today are lighter, more durable, faster, more maneuverable, and safer than ever before. With modern technology, further improvements will continue to evolve.

▶ Kayaks

Kayaks have much in common with canoes. Like all watercraft, the same laws of physics apply to hull configuration and design, and like canoes, each type of kayak is designed with unique characteristics depending on its intended function. Kayaks are safer than canoes because the hulls are enclosed, or decked, and if rolled can be turned upright again by the paddler. This gives kayaks a much greater range of recreational possibilities. Kayaks can be divided into five general categories: *casual recreation*, *sea touring*, whitewater (which includes *play boats*, *touring*, *slalom kayaks*, and *squirt boats*), *downriver*, and *Olympic flat water racing kayaks* (Harrison et al., 1989b). The sea-touring and Olympic racing kayaks come in solo and tandem models. Figure 15.14 illustrates the anatomical parts of a touring kayak.

This section format is patterned after that for canoes, covering materials, construction, and classification of kayaks according to use. Because most of the materials, construction techniques, and hull configurations and design are similar to canoes, those corresponding to kayak sections will be brief.

Materials and Construction

Kayak manufacturers incorporate the same construction materials as canoes (refer to Materials and Construction in the Canoe section), with the addition of animal skins on wood frames (similar to the old-world Eskimo kayaks). There are no kayaks, however, made from aluminum. The most widely used materials are thermoplastics like polyethylene that are formed into kayaks using a roto-molding construction technique (M. Garcia, personal communication, March 10, 1989). Whitewater kayaks use polyethylene almost exclusively.

roto molding—A kayak hull manufacturing process where a molten plastic is injected into a mold and spun at high rpm; this process causes the plastic molecules to form a stronger bond than with blow molding.

The **roto-molding** process starts by heating polyethylene powder to a liquid state that is then blown into the kayak mold and spun or rotated at high speed. The centrifugal force of spinning the cooling plastic makes a hull that is tough and rigid because the polyethylene molecules form a cross-linked matrix. In

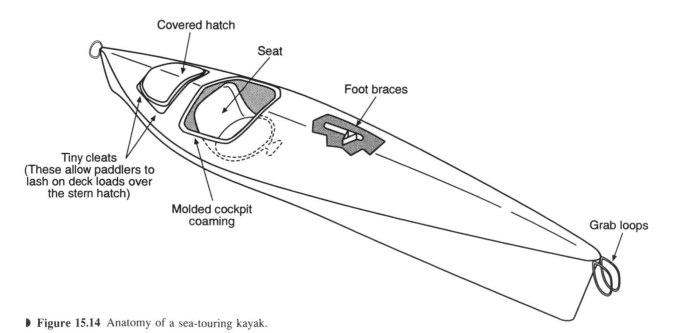

▶ **Figure 15.14** Anatomy of a sea-touring kayak.

blow molding—A manufacturing process where molten plastic is injected into a mold by air pressure.

normal **blow molding**, the plastic molecules cool in a linear fashion, which is not as strong. Whichever method is used, manufacturers usually add foam reinforcement pillars for deck rigidity, that helps to hold the kayak's shape under pressure.

Recreational and touring kayaks don't have to take the punishment whitewater kayaks are subjected to, thus lighter and less rigid laminates can be used. With construction materials like laminates (i.e., Kevlar and fiberglass) and proprietary lay-ups, the manufacturing processes of kayaks is similar to canoes.

Hull Design

Kayaks can be considered a decked canoe; therefore, dimensions like length, beam, and depth and hull shape characteristics like rocker, waterline, symmetry, and cross-section also determine performance attributes, and their relationship to intended use also holds for kayaks. That is not to say, however, that kayak hulls are designs cloned from canoes. Kayak recreationalists have different needs than canoeists do because of unique intended uses and the environment in which they will be used. Nonetheless, canoe hull design principles still hold for kayaks and will not be discussed in this section. For review of these principles refer to the Hull Design discussion of the Canoe section.

There is one major difference in hull design, however, between kayaks and canoes. Most kayaks have either airtight bulkheads or air bags to provide extra flotation. Fore and aft bulkheads, which create air chambers, are more common in touring canoes, whereas air bags are commonly found in whitewater and other kayak models. The bulkheads designed into touring kayaks also provide waterproof storage areas. O-rings seal the bulkhead hatches.

Kayaks Classified According to Use

There are five basic types of kayak with a wide variety of designs in each category. They are used for casual recreation and sea touring and whitewater, downriver, and Olympic flat-water racing. As with canoes, no single kayak design can do everything well. In this section we discuss the function and commonalities of kayak design respective to category.

Casual Recreation

Novice kayakers without convenient access to whitewater frequently opt for casual recreation kayaks (Harrison et al., 1989b). These types of kayaks in both tandem and solo models are limited by design to calm, flatwater and nontechnical rivers. Carrying capacity in **recreational kayaks** is typically high enough for weekend trips or picnics on the other side of the lake. They generally have slight rocker, symmetrical hulls, and either shallow-arch or vee bottoms. Length varies in this broad category, but most casual recreation kayaks are about 15 feet long. Plastics and fiberglass laminates are the most commonly used construction materials.

recreational kayak—A nontechnical flatwater kayak used by novice kayakers.

Sea Touring

Probably experiencing the greatest increase in popularity are **sea-touring kayaks** (Noble & Scigliano, 1987). There is a broad range of designs in this category, most of which can accommodate generous loads of gear to be carried on lakes, bays, oceans, or large rivers. Many models have **skegs** (fixed, nonmovable rudders), or movable rudders that are controlled by foot pedals to keep the boats on course in currents or crosswinds. Skegs basically offer kayaks

sea-touring kayak—A longer kayak with the capacity to carry cargo for open-water journeys; it has skegs and sometimes small sails.

skeg—A small rudder aft of a kayak that is controlled by the feet.

what keels give to canoes (which is to say not much), so that if a kayak needs a skeg, hull design should be reconsidered.

Rudders make turning and tracking easy and may prove invaluable to a fatigued paddler. But some kayakers have reservations about the rudder's utility (Noble & Scigliano, 1987), which purportedly does not give the paddler incentive to improve paddling technique, or to learn lifesaving tricks in emergency situations. Furthermore, kayaks without rudders have immovable foot braces; in contrast, rudders in kayaks also double as foot braces and don't offer the solid leverage that rigid braces do. Thus, the body's thrust while paddling is not as effective, because the reaction force of the foot against the foot brace is absent or diminished.

Another interesting feature found in some sea-touring kayaks are small sail rigs. Attached toward the bow of the kayak, sails assist in propelling the kayak over long distances. Note that without a rudder, sail-rigger kayaks would be nearly impossible to navigate. These sails are not meant to take the place of paddling, but just to supplement it.

Most touring kayaks for any purpose are made from Kevlar or fiberglass, and extend to at least 16 feet and as long as 22 feet for tandem models. Touring hulls are designed to track straight; therefore, any measure of rocker is avoided, and asymmetrical designs are incorporated. Nearly all bottom contours are shallow vees or arches, and freeboard is either straight or flared.

Whitewater

whitewater kayak—A short, maneuverable, and durable boat.

Whitewater kayaks fall into four general categories:

- Play boats,
- Touring,
- Slalom, and
- Squirt boats (Harrison et al., 1989b).

Each type has an autonomous function and a slightly different design, yet all have the durability and resilience to take on the roughest, rock-laden rivers. All whitewater kayaks have generous rocker for high maneuverability when shooting rapids or avoiding trees and rocks. It is also important to note that weight is critical in proper displacement, which is essential for effective performance in kayaking. Most kayak manufacturers have weight and height displacement charts for whitewater kayaks. With the use of these calibrated charts appropriate hull dimensions specific to an individual user can be determined.

Play Boats

play boats—The standard whitewater kayaks for shooting rapids.

As the name implies, whitewater **play boats** are built for playing in rapids. These kayaks are what the general public probably considers the standard kayak. Along with rocker, these kayaks typically have asymmetrical hulls and shallow-arch bottoms (the standard in play boats). Their sides are usually rounded to enhance maneuverability when shooting rapids or surfing waves. Freeboard is not nearly as consistent with manufacturers; however, many models have either tumblehome or flared sides. Lengths range from 10 to 13 feet, with the most common length being 11 feet. Volume also varies depending on the size and weight of the kayaker. Durability and resilience is vitally important in hull construction. Therefore, polyethylene plastic is the favorite with most kayak makers, although one company makes its kayaks exclusively from a fiberglass-Kevlar combination.

Touring

touring kayaks—High volume play boats used for extended trips.

Whitewater **touring kayaks** have more in common with play boats than they do with sea-touring kayaks. Built to withstand the rigors of whitewater, these kayaks have more volume than their play-boat brethren to accommodate the storage space required for multiday river excursions (Harrison et al., 1989b). With the extra volume the additional storage requires, they don't perform as well as play boats. Whitewater touring kayaks, like play boats, have asymmetrical hulls and enough rocker to be highly maneuverable in rapidly changing currents. Bottom contours are primarily shallow-arch, and freeboard is flared or tumblehome.

Slalom

The International Canoe Federation (ICF) also sanctions whitewater slalom kayak races, and it also determines hull specifications for slalom competition. Length, the primary criterion, is a standard 13 feet 2 inches (4 meters) (Harrison et al., 1989b). In the early days of the kayak boom, all kayaks were this standard length and were used to run rivers for recreation as well as racing. Being relatively long makes these kayaks fast, but they don't perform as well as the typically shorter play boats. In fact, today's market has many more play boats then slalom kayaks, because play boats turn faster, surf better, and roll more easily.

slalom kayaks—Competition boats designed according to required specifications for maneuvering through pyloned white-water courses.

Slalom kayaks are designed for maneuverability in carving turns in serpentine race courses and flat-out speed in straightaways. As such, they have low volume, extreme rocker, and dramatic hull contours. Most competition models are made from somewhat thinner layers of fiberglass cloth, or Kevlar-reinforced laminates.

Squirt Boats

squirt boats—Short specialty kayaks that can be plunged underwater and popped out; they are only used for acrobatic maneuvers.

An adaptation of the whitewater slalom kayak is the highly specialized, "no volume" **squirt boat** (Harrison et al., 1989b). Squirt-boat paddlers are highly proficient kayakers who seem to spend as much time above the water as on it, and they have developed their own repertoire of maneuvers to complement the dynamics of these lively kayaks—plus jargon to match. For example, squirt-boat maneuvers include cartwheels, screw-ups, splats, swipes, boofs, and mystery moves.

Only a few companies manufacture squirt boats. Those who do construct them from a variety of materials including laminates and heat-formed plastics. Squirt boat lengths generally fall between 10 to 11 feet. Other than their shorter length and more rounded curves, squirt-boats are dimensionally similar to slalom kayaks.

Downriver

downriver kayak—A 15-foot competition kayak designed for straight-course racing that has an asymmetrical hull.

Straight-ahead speed is the function of the **downriver** or wild-water **kayak** (Harrison et al., 1989b). Primarily used for straight-course racing, downriver kayaks are usually limited to 15 feet in length and a minimum of 60 centimeters beam measurement at any point, the required racing specifications. Hulls are radically asymmetrical with the widest point being well aft of the cockpit; with no rocker, this combination makes tracking effortless. These kayaks are fashioned from lightweight laminates that can produce sharply contoured bows and veed bottoms. The combination of these features renders great speed but makes the boat extremely unstable and difficult to maneuver.

Olympic Flat-Water

Olympic flat-water kayaks come in solo and tandem models, both of which are built to ICF specifications for Olympic competition (Harrison et al., 1989b). With the same purpose as downriver kayaks, the Olympic flat-water's sole function is flat-out, straight-ahead speed. This kayak, although of very low volume, sleek, and unstable like the downriver, does not have a spray skirt

Olympic flat-water racing kayak—A class of straight-line racing kayaks built and used according to strict specifications for Olympic competition; the class includes solo and tandem models, and have skegs.

around the cockpit, so the paddler's knees stick out of it. To further enhance tracking, most Olympic kayaks have a small rudder controlled by foot pedals. Rudders are included because continuous and powerful paddling strokes produce tremendous torque that otherwise would cause the kayak to drift off course with each stroke. With the rudder, paddlers can focus their energy on propulsion rather than navigation.

Solo Olympic flat-water kayaks are 17 feet long and 20 inches wide; tandems are 21 feet 4 inches long. Construction materials range from fiberglass and/or Kevlar laminates to proprietary lay-ups. For trackability, hulls are asymmetrical and have little or no rocker. Bottom contours are typically rounded or slightly veed, and freeboard is flared.

Summary

As summarized in the canoe section, effective hull design is a function of a boat's intended use. Kayak hulls follow the same design principles as canoes as they relate to function. For example, kayaks that require high maneuverability in the battery of obstacles found in whitewater rapids are designed with durable hulls and plenty of rocker. At the other end of the spectrum, sea-touring kayaks employ little rocker for tracking and high volume for extended trips.

What's new on the kayak scene? Like canoe makers, kayak manufacturers are still searching for stronger, lighter, and more resilient hull materials and better and cheaper ways to construct kayaks. Secondly, the newest craze in kayak recreation is sea touring. Sea touring doesn't require the immense skill and the "half-crazed" mentality that whitewater kayaking demands. It is a more passive endeavor, and adding sails enhances the feeling of sea and the freedom found with it. Today, sea kayakers are touring the coasts of Alaska, Baja, and the Galapagos, and some are even traveling to the shores of the Far East seeking adventure.

Lastly, the folding kayak is making a comeback after its invention by a Bavarian, Johann Klepper, in 1907 (West, 1986). In fact, several of Klepper's designs crossed the English Channel. Like Klepper's folding design, present-day folding kayaks are made for sea touring. They have either a wood or an aluminum frame, and hypalon (rubberized nylon), or waterproofed polypropylene hull materials. Most come with all the rigging, including rudder assembly, spray covers, sail rigs, and seats. They take about 30 minutes to assemble and disassemble, and many can fold up into a backpack-type unit. Such a design has great utility and portability, as it can be easily transported and assembled in the remotest of locations.

▶ Inflatables

Inflatable watercraft are typically some sort of rubberized air-filled boat used to negotiate the whitewaters of rivers like the Colorado, the Snake, and the Salmon. Commonly called "rafting," this sport is for those who seek adventure on a wild whitewater river, but who don't have the skill or the inclination to navigate such a river in a solo kayak or canoe. Rafting has grown considerably in North America because it is safe, inexpensive, and an exciting way to explore the wildlands of the continent.

Raft designs have evolved from flimsy army surplus issues to highly sophisticated inflatables that can carry a dozen people safely down the most treacherous river (assuming an experienced river guide is at the helm). Rafts use any of

paddle raft*—*A whitewater raft paddled by the complement people on board; one navigator usually controls the raft's direction from the back end of the raft.

oar raft*—*Same as a motorized raft but propelled with oars.

motorized raft*—*Any raft propelled by a motor; is most often used by professional whitewater navigators.

three types of propulsion: paddles, oars, or a motor. **Paddle rafts** are propelled with a pair of ordinary canoe-type paddles. Navigation comes from a stern paddler who pilots the boat and shouts orders to the rest of the crew. **Oar rafts** are outfitted with a set of oars and oar locks usually positioned in the center of the raft, or a single oar located at the stern. The oars are controlled by only one person. Oar rafts are used primarily to steer on wide, swiftly moving rivers—not to propel the raft forward, the river's job. Some **motors** are showing up in the bigger commercial rigs and are used because they are an effortless and efficient means to get the raft down the river in slow spots. However, they are noisy, a drawback that can ruin the pristine quality of the natural experience.

Materials for inflatables and dimensional characteristics are discussed first in this section; following are the usage categories: casual recreation, entry-level whitewater, professional whitewater, and inflatable kayaks.

Materials and Dimensional Characteristics

Hull materials of inflatables consist of a base fabric covered by some rubberized coating (Harrison et al., 1989c), frequently nylon or polyester. Coatings include hypalon (found in the more expensive rafts), neoprene, and ethylene propylene diene momomer (EPDM) (both of these are found in less expensive models), urethane, polyvinyl chloride (PVC), and vinyl. A basic guideline for quality construction couples a higher quality base fabric with a higher percentage of coating to make a more durable raft (Harrison et al., 1989c).

Coating compounds like hypalon, neoprene, and EDPM can be applied in a wide range of thicknesses and concentration to the base fabric. That is, thicker coatings in higher concentrations render better quality rafts. Fabric weight, which correlates to density and generally to strength, is referred to as *denier* in the fabric industry. Denier is the weight in grams of 9,000 meters of yarn. Specific properties such as tensile strength (breaking due to tension), and shear strength (tearing) is more a function of the type of material than its weight, however.

There are several dimensional characteristics that disclose performance ability in any class of raft. Three of the more obvious are length, width, and weight. The longer and wider the raft, the more people and gear it can accommodate. However, much like higher weight, bigger boats can be cumbersome both in and out of the water. Generally, rafts are slightly twice as long as they are wide.

Tube diameter is another important characteristic because flotation is directly dependent on it (Harrison et al., 1989c). That is, greater tube diameter offers greater flotation, plus fewer chances that water will come spilling over the sides. Single tubes are called *air chambers* (see Figure 15.15). Rafts with multiple air chambers have greater integrity and higher quality (Harrison et al., 1989c). They also offer redundancy, which means if one chamber springs a leak, the remaining ones will keep the raft afloat.

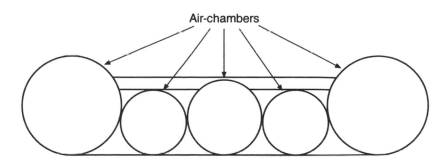

▶ **Figure 15.15** Cross-section of a raft's flotation tubes.

Lastly, self-bailing is an important raft feature on rough splashy water, especially if your attention has to be on navigation rather than bailing. Self-bailing is a function designed into the hull itself: The water that comes in is channeled back into the river.

Rafts Classified According to Use

The use of inflatables ranges from casual recreation to professional sport competition to commercial use and may be designed for one person (the inflatable kayak) up to as many as 12. Construction and design features vary in each category depending on the raft's intended use.

Casual Recreation

Casual recreation-type rafts are suited for calm lakes and gentle rivers (Harrison et al., 1989c). They can generally accommodate two to four people. These rafts are manufactured with the least durable construction techniques and materials which include polyester, vinyl, and PVC, with little or no coating compound.

Inflatable Kayaks

Inflatable kayaks, sometimes called "duckies," are the fastest growing boats on the inflatable market today (Harrison et al., 1989c). These kayaks are designed for the solo rafter, and they require very little skill to have fun. They look more like inflatable canoes than kayaks because they don't incorporate a spray skirt. Without spray skirts most inflatable kayaks require self-bailing, otherwise the water has to be dumped out by hand.

Duckies are about the same length as a hardshell, whitewater play boat (i.e., 9-1/2 feet-12 feet long). They are paddled by one or two people using kayak paddles. These crafts offer an exciting introduction to whitewater boating because they can do all that regular kayaks can do except roll. Current models come in all grades of construction quality and price.

Entry-Level Whitewater

Entry-level whitewater inflatables are used by individuals with more than novice experience in whitewater rafting (Harrison et al., 1989c). These rafts are found on rivers with navigation levels designated from intermediate to advanced. They are not durable enough for the daily use of a commercial raft, but they will perform quite well through several seasons of periodic use.

These inflatables are made of base fabrics like nylon and polyester that have thread counts corresponding to their intended use. A coating compound is found on all models; most are neoprene, hypalon, or urethane. These craft range in length from 9 to 14 feet, and they can accommodate from two to eight passengers.

Professional Whitewater

Professional whitewater rafts are designed to take on the roughest of whitewater rivers with up to 12 people (Harrison et al., 1989c). They are used privately, but most are found in the hands of commercial rafting companies. These rafts are more durable in every way compared to the preceding classes of inflatables. All manufacturers use higher denier fabrics with heavy-duty coatings, greater tube diameters, and at least 4 air chambers (some have up to 12). These rafts are 11 to 18 feet long, and widths range from 5 to 8 feet. They primarily use oar and motor propulsion.

Summary

Inflatable watercraft are aimed at the less skilled whitewater enthusiasts, and are fabricated from some sort of rubberized materials that make them forgiving to hazards of whitewater rafting. Classified according to their capacity, sophistication, and durability, raft categories range from casual recreation (which is not intended for whitewater) to entry-level whitewater and professional whitewater. Inflatable kayaks are considered among the array of inflatable watercraft. The function of these kayaks is similar to the standard kayaks, except they are intended for the less skilled.

▶ References

Cichanowski, M. (1986). Principles of canoe design. *We-no-nah Canoe Catalog*, pp. 16-19.

Davidson, J.M., & Rugge, J. (1983, March). Boats for backpackers: A guide to 1983 touring canoes. *Backpacker*, pp. 31-34.

Harrison, D.F., Parrot, B., Thomas, G.I., Vickery, J., Rice, L., Dappen, A., Huser, V., & Shepard, J.G. (1989a, December). Canoes. *Canoe*, pp. 26-56.

Harrison, D.F., Parrot, B., Thomas, G.I., Vickery, J., Rice, L., Dappen, A., Huser, V., & Shepard, J.G. (1989b, December). Kayaks. *Canoe*, pp. 57-79.

Harrison, D.F., Parrot, B., Thomas, G.I., Vickery, J., Rice, L., Dappen, A., Huser, V., & Shepard, J.G. (1989c, December). Inflatables. *Canoe*, pp. 80-83.

Noble, C., & Scigliano, E. (1987, September). The new worlds of sea kayaking. *Outside*, pp. 64-68.

West, S. (1986, May). Folding kayaks. *Outside*, p. 107.

Special thanks to Mike Cichanowski and We-no-nah Canoes for allowing use of their canoe illustrations.

Index

About the Editors

Ellen F. Kreighbaum   **Mark A. Smith**

Dr. Ellen F. Kreighbaum has been teaching a course in sports and fitness equipment design at Montana State University since 1978. The course, which she created, has been in great demand by students in health and physical education as well as in engineering and art design.

Dr. Kreighbaum is the coauthor of one of the top-selling biomechanics textbooks in the country, *Biomechanics: A Qualitative Approach for Studying Human Movement.* She has presented lectures on sports equipment design both nationally and internationally. She serves on the Board of Directors of the International Society of Biomechanics in Sports; she is alo a charter member and past president of the organization. Dr. Kreighbaum has received numerous awards, including the Wiley Award for Meritorious Research from Montana State University and the Excellence Award as an outstanding alumna of the University of Wisconsin—Lacrosse.

Dr. Kreighbaum earned her doctorate in 1973 from Washington State University. She lives in Bozeman, Montana, where she enjoys reading, horseback riding, fishing, and collecting antique sports equipment.

Mark A. Smith received his master's degree in industrial engineering from Montana State University in 1990. His education and work experience have given him insight into how things work, how they are manufactured, and how they can be used most effectively. He has conducted research on biomechanics related to exercise and rehabilitation equipment and has expertise in consumer produce ergonomics. Mark works as an independent ergonomics consultant, focusing on productivity and quality improvements in manufacturing processes, tool design, and office environments. In his leisure time he enjoys bicycling, camping, canoeing, and golf.